D0881294

A Locker Room of Her Own

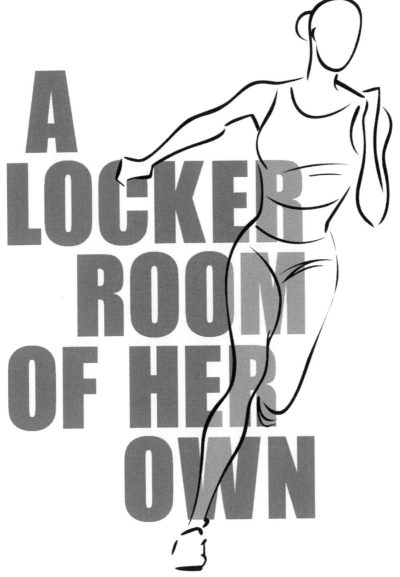

A LOCKER ROOM OF HER OWN

Celebrity, Sexuality, and Female Athletes

Edited by David C. Ogden and Joel Nathan Rosen

University Press of Mississippi / Jackson

www.upress.state.ms.us

The University Press of Mississippi is a member
of the Association of American University Presses.

First printing 2013

∞

Library of Congress Cataloging-in-Publication Data

A locker room of her own : celebrity, sexuality, and
female athletes / David C. Ogden and Joel Nathan
Rosen, editors.
    pages cm
 Includes bibliographical references and index.
 ISBN 978-1-61703-813-6 (cloth : alk. paper) —
 ISBN 978-1-61703-814-3 (ebook) 1. Women
athletes—United States—Biography. 2. Lesbian
athletes—United States—Biography. 3. Women athletes—United States—Sexual behavior. 4. Women
athletes—United States—Public opinion. 5. Public
opinion—United States. I. Ogden, David C. II. Rosen,
Joel Nathan, 1961–
 GV697.A1L62 2013
 796.0922—dc23
 [B]   2012050121

British Library Cataloging-in-Publication Data available

Contents

Foreword
A Locker Room of One's Own

—ROBERTA J. NEWMAN

INTRODUCTION

Referring specifically to the needs of potential female novelists in her land-mark essay "A Room of One's Own" (1929), Virginia Woolf observes that "a woman must have money and a room of her own if she is to write fiction; and that, as you will see, leaves the great problem of the true nature of women and the true nature of fiction unsolved."[1] Woolf's assertion that a woman writer requires space and funding to produce effectively may be applied in equal measure to the female athlete, especially the professional female athlete, the performer whose success depends not just on talent and training, but on branding, the construction of a public persona. That Penny Marshall chose to allude directly to Woolf's essay in the title of her own landmark work, *A League of Their Own* (1992), directly supports this notion.

This volume deals neither with the true nature of fiction nor the true nature of women. Rather, it approaches the very particular problem of repu-tation and the female athlete. Indeed, each of the women profiled in this vol-ume has struggled with the twinned issues of space and money in her own way. Babe Didrickson Zaharias, star of track, field, diamond, and golf course, hustler and storyteller, for example, artfully created her own brand image on her way to becoming one of the founding mothers of the Ladies Professional Golf Association (LPGA), quite literally a league of her own. So, too, in her own way, did Billie Jean King. Although she was for five years the number one ranked female tennis player in the world, she is perhaps better remembered for her participation in the 1973 "Battle of the Sexes," and the promotion thereof. Taking on and ultimately defeating fifty-five-year-old Bobby Riggs, a former Wimbledon champ and full-time self-promoter, King did more for the popularity of women's tennis—providing her with both a room and funds of her own—than all six of her own Wimbledon singles titles and her very real success on the Virginia Slims circuit had done.

What Didrikson Zaharias and King have in common, in addition to their gender and their promotional skills, is that they both participated in indi-vidual sports. Indeed, with the exception of the women of the All-American

Girls Professional Baseball League (AAGPBL), introduced to several genera-tions of young girls by Marshall's film, and WNBA star Sheryl Swoopes, this is true of each of the women in this volume; and King's match with Riggs notwithstanding, only race-car driver Danica Patrick, who used blatant sexu-ality in self-marketing, has earned both a metaphoric room and a great deal of real money of her own by competing, like Woolf's female authors, side by side with her male counterparts. In a very real sense, the leagues and locker rooms created, promoted, and occupied by most of the women in this volume are, in fact, their own, and theirs alone.

While both IndyCar and NASCAR drivers are members of teams, Patrick, by virtue of the fact that women in either circuit are few and far between, necessarily competes in what has historically been a gender segregated sport. She is alone behind the wheel, an individual woman competing alone against individual men, not alongside them. But what of the very few female athletes who were pioneers of gender desegregation in team sports? Why do the repu-tations of the very few women who "played with the big boys" not have the staying power in popular cultural memory that Billie Jean King or Danica Patrick, or the Williams sisters, or Martina Navratilova and Chris Evert have? Why is it that the disgrace of former track star Marion Jones and the fin-gernails of the late sprinter Florence Griffith Joyner, FloJo, occupy a greater piece of the popular imagination than the memory of the women who played men's team sports? A brief look at the careers of a few of those athletes may provide an answer.

CROSSING OVER

A *New York Times* obituary, published on November 10, 1996, reads, "Toni Stone, a scrappy second baseman who became a footnote to baseball his-tory in 1953 as a member of the Negro League's Indianapolis Clowns when she became the first woman to play as a regular on a big-league professional team, died on Nov. 2 at a nursing home in Alameda, Calif."[2] In fact, the first woman to play baseball in a "big league" was not a member of the Rockford Peaches or Fort Wayne Daisies. Despite increased awareness of the AAGPBL following Penny Marshall's successful elevation of the league to mythic sta-tus, it was never more than a local phenomenon, a novelty, centered in the upper Midwest, the rare exhibition games at Griffith and Yankee stadiums notwithstanding. Rather, the honor of being the first woman in the profes-sional men's game goes to Marcenia Lyle Stone, aka Toni, who played for the Indianapolis Clowns of the Negro American League in 1953 and the Kansas

City Monarchs in 1954. With an opening in the infield, owing in part to the sale of young Henry Aaron to the Milwaukee Braves, Clowns' owner Syd Pollock brought Toni Stone in to play second base and, more importantly, put rear ends in the seats, thereby staving off the inevitable demise of an institution whose time had passed.

In fact, to call the Negro American League of 1953–54 a big league is, at the very least, an exaggeration. Nevertheless, Stone is identified as the first female "big leaguer" in the reputation summary of record. Coverage during her career clearly emphasized the fact. A spot in the *Chicago Defender*, for example, touts her role as a pioneer. Aimed at attracting fans to a double-header with the rival Monarchs, it reads, "Continuing to make the headlines is the Clowns 22-year-old second baseman, Toni Stone, first girl infielder to be signed and break down the prejudice against women players in the NAL."[3] Yet, though Toni Stone was, indeed, the first woman to play Negro League ball, she was signed for one reason, and one reason alone. Her role, like that of the team's other headline attractions, King Tut, the black "clown prince of baseball," and Spec Bebop, a midget, was to increase attendance.

Though Stone was not specifically a baseball clown, her job was closer to that of the rangy comedian and his diminutive sidekick than to that of a "big leaguer." Her pseudonym itself is a key to understanding her position on the team. According to Alan Pollock, Syd's son, Marcenia changed her name to Toni based on the popularity of Toni Home Permanents.[4] Recent scholarship by Martha Ackerman, Stone's biographer, refutes Pollock's claim. Ackerman suggests that Stone, engaged in a clear act of self-reinvention, deliberately changed her own name, dropping her former nickname, "Tomboy," in favor of Toni, "a sassy, confident metamorphosis more in line with the people she met at Jack's" (the landmark San Francisco jazz club she frequented).[5]

Ultimately, it does not matter whether Pollock changed Stone's name or whether she came to him ready to be billed as "Toni," at least as far as crafting a reputation is concerned. Playing under a pseudonym and suggesting a women's hair-care product served to connect Stone to an earlier incarnation of the team, the Miami Ethiopian Clowns, who played in grass skirts and white "war paint" under stage names like Impo, Nyassas, and Kalahari, while taking on such teams as the Zulu Cannibal Giants. And just as Impo, Nyassas, and Kalahari are intended to recall African stereotypes, a name based on a women's hair-care product linked the player to a feminine stereotype. After all, women are far more interested in doing their hair than in playing second, aren't they? That she rarely appeared for more than three innings per game and that she played against stereotypes are unimportant. As Didrickson

Zaharias, King, and Patrick show, it is marketing that attracts spectators in the first place, and attract spectators she did. Stone's presence on the field, at least at the outset, helped raise the Clowns' attendance figures to levels unseen in black baseball after desegregation, while contests between all-male teams were played to empty parks.[6]

Pollock sold Stone to the Monarchs before the 1954 season, replacing her with two more women, infielder Connie Morgan and a pitcher, Mamie "Peanut" Johnson. Neither had Stone's skill. Rather, they were signed primarily for their looks, a move that says more about the role of novelty teams in keeping black baseball alive than the acceptance of women into professional men's team sports. Indeed, so desperate were the Kansas City Monarchs to draw fans that the once-premiere African-American ball club was reduced to employing the same tactics used by the Clowns, who themselves had once been a championship outfit but not necessarily beloved by all sectors of their target fan base owing to their borderline–minstrel show brand of entertainment.

And not all sectors of their target demographic were thrilled with the female presence on the diamond, either. "The opinion here is that girls should be run out of men's baseball on a softly-padded rail both for their own good and the good of the game," Doc Young, the influential sports columnist for the *Chicago Defender*, wrote.[7] He echoed the sentiment of more than a few members of the black sporting press, as well as that of some of the teammates. But the softly padded rail option was hardly necessary. The bloom was off the rose. The more female players there were in the Negro American League, the less of a novelty it was seeing a woman play. Potential fans voted a resounding "no" to women on the diamond with their pocketbooks. The experiment ended after the 1954 season. So Toni Stone and, to a lesser extent, Connie Morgan and Mamie Johnson had a locker room of their own (though technically, they had to change in their hotels, rooming houses, and/or vehicles, given the fact that Negro League venues did not exactly have sprawling clubhouses, and if they did, they were often not available to players of color of either gender), complete with metaphoric space and real money.[8]

So why aren't Stone, Morgan, and Johnson household names? In reality, even the male stars of the Negro Leagues are largely unknown to all but a small group of scholars and historically minded fans. Unless they were named Josh Gibson or Satchel Paige, or unless, like Jackie Robinson, Larry Doby, Monte Irvin, Willie Mays, and the Clowns' own Henry Aaron, they became Major League stars, Negro League players are unlikely to occupy a space in the collective popular memory. Indeed, before Ken Burns stoked interest in

African-American baseball by introducing PBS watchers to the charismatic John "Buck" O'Neill in 1994, the place of the Negro Leagues in the collective pop-cultural memory was dim, at best. As such, in the realm of reputation, Stone and her sisters are but a footnote. Had they played in organized "big league" baseball, rather than in a largely irrelevant, dying league, perhaps the story might have been different. But their signing and brief professional careers represent what amounts to a last-ditch effort of a moribund institution to stay alive. Neither the metaphoric locker room nor the real money that came with it outlasted the 1954 season.

A NOVELTY AMONG NOVELTIES

The story of the woman who broke professional basketball's gender barrier differs considerably from the Stone/Morgan/Johnson narrative. In October 1985, the Harlem Globetrotters selected Lynette Woodard, star of the University of Kansas Lady Jayhawks, holder of the record for points scored until 1998, and captain of the 1984 Olympic gold medal–winning US women's basketball squad, to "play" with the big boys.[9] "There is no sense that the Globetrotters were looking for a token female, somebody who would merely impersonate a female basketball player. The male players learned that in the past week during a training camp that saw 10 female hopefuls fighting for one job,"[10] notes George Vecsey in the *New York Times*. The very fact that Woodard's signing by the Globetrotters made the sports pages of the "paper of record," as well as those of many other major city newspapers, and was not just an afterthought, like Stone's obituary, says a great deal about the efforts of women athletes to forge locker rooms of their own. That Woodard signed with the Globetrotters more than a decade after "The Battle of the Sexes," in the age of Chris Evert and Martina Navratilova, may have had something to do with the mainstream media's respect for her as an athlete. While Woodard may have been the first woman to play high-profile men's professional basketball, the path to her acceptance was, in fact, paved by King and the others. Hailed as a groundbreaker, Woodard was named one of *Ms.* magazine's "Women of the Year," along with Lily Tomlin and Patti Davis, in 1985.[11]

Yet, despite the fact that Woodard gained a modicum of acceptance as a woman on a men's team in a way that Stone, Morgan, and Johnson did not, closer inspection suggests that her story bears some resemblance to that of the women of the Negro American League. The Harlem Globetrotters were a legitimate force in the early days of organized basketball, just as the Clowns were in black baseball in the 1940s. The Globetrotters, however, had ceased to play competitive hoops decades before Woodard joined them. Though the press was quick to note that Woodard was not hired to "clown," it is impossible to escape the fact that the Globetrotters were, and continue to be, as much travelling circus as basketball team. Nevertheless, given the fact that all professional sport is entertainment, and professional athletes regularly engage in exhibition play, it is clearly possible to identify Woodard as a highly visible woman in the man's game, even if her opponents were the Washington Generals, the team that last won a game in 1971. As Vecsey clearly notes, the Globetrotters provided their new star with her own area for changing, quite literally a locker room of her own.[12] Yet despite the rhetoric, like the women of the Negro American League, she was a novelty among novelty acts.

That Woodard made money of her own is also clear. In fact, she left the Globetrotters after two years, not because she had ceased to draw, but over a contractual dispute, which was also covered in the New York Times. Prohibited from making individual endorsement deals, the true measure of reputation and the true means of securing the funds necessary to carve out a bigger locker room of her own, Woodard opted out of her agreement with the team and her position in the men's game, as it were, choosing to compete professionally in Italy and Japan before joining the fledgling WNBA, where she was finally able to play competitive basketball in the United States. Regardless of her success with the Globetrotters, she did not open the door for women to play with the big boys in the NBA. She, like the women of the AAGPBL, was ghettoized into a league of her own.

Lynette Woodard, for her effort, was enshrined in the James Naismith Memorial Basketball Hall of Fame twice, in 2002 as part of a group of Globetrotters, and in 2004, as a player in her own right. As such, her tiny slice of the collective popular cultural memory is set in stone. Still, it is unlikely that she will ever garner the fame of Patrick, or Venus and Serena Williams, or Evert, or Navratilova, nor will she earn the same endorsement dollars, the true measure of fame and reputation.

Although the WNBA has neither the fan base nor the revenue, questionable though it may be, of its counterpart in the men's game, the strides made by the first wave of female basketball players, fronted by Woodard, the most visible of them all, opened the door for successive women in the professional game. Not least among them is Sheryl Swoopes, who made the headlines in the mainstream press not just for her skill on the hardwood, but for her openness outside the arena. Whereas Billie Jean King, victor in the Battle of the Sexes, fought to keep the closet door of her personal locker room tightly shut until forced to "come out" as bisexual when sued by a former lover for "palimony" in 1981, Swoopes is frank about her sexuality. Her reputation seemingly unaffected by her choices of partners, she has kept the faith of her fan base.

TOWARD AN ANTHOLOGY OF HER OWN

In many ways, each of the women considered in this volume might have a place in one of the two preceding volumes of this series, whether it be Babe Didrikson, Martina Navratilova, and Sheryl Swoopes in the first volume, *Reconstructing Fame*, or Marion Jones, Venus and Serena Williams, and Florence Griffith Joyner in *Fame to Infamy*. But taken together, the female athletes considered in this work frame a compelling narrative. Each, in her own way, has attempted, using various methods and with varying degrees of success, to carve out a place for herself in a world still overpopulated by men—the world of professional sports. So for the female athletes who have managed to make a living in locker rooms of their own, this collection can in its own way be identified as (and with apologies to Virginia Woolf) *An Anthology of One's Own.*

NOTES

1. Virginia Woolf, "A Room of One's Own," II, n.d., http://gutenberg.net.au/ebooks02/0200791.txt (July 8, 2011).

2. Robert McG. Thomas, Jr., "Obituary: Toni Stone, 75, First Woman To Play Big-League Baseball," *New York Times*, November 10, 1996, http://www.nytimes.com/1996/11/10/sports/toni-stone-75-first-woman-to-play-big-league-baseball.html (July 8, 2011).

3. "Expect Record Attendance at Clown-Monarch Tiff," *Chicago Defender*, June 20, 1953, 22.

4. Alan J. Pollock and James A. Riley, *Barnstorming to Heaven: Syd Pollock and His Great Black Teams* (Tuscaloosa: University of Alabama Press, 2006), 242.

5. Martha Ackerman, *Curveball: The Remarkable Story of Toni Stone, The First Woman to Play Baseball in the Negro League* (Chicago: Lawrence Hill, 2010), 59.

6. Neal Lanctot, *Negro League Baseball: The Rise and Ruin of a Black Institution* (Philadelphia: University of Pennsylvania Press, 2004), 382.

7. Doc Young, "Should Girls Play Ball; No, Says Doc," *Chicago Defender*, August 28, 1954, 11.

8. Syd Pollock claimed that he paid Stone twelve thousand dollars a season. This figure, like Pollock's rhetoric, is probably grossly inflated. Nevertheless, Stone, Morgan, and Johnson were paid relatively well for their services. See Ackerman, *Curveball: The Remarkable Story of Toni Stone*, 126.

9. "Globetrotters Hire First Woman," *San Francisco Chronicle,* October 6, 1985, 64.

10. George Vecsey, "Sports of the Times; The Newest Globetrotter," *New York Times,* October 13, 1985, A3.

11. "Women of the Year," *Jet,* January 27, 1986, p.9.

12. Vecsey, "Sports of the Times," A3.

Acknowledgments

The editors would like to thank the many people whose contributions helped make this volume a reality. First, the contributors deserve our deepest gratitude for sharing their insights and knowledge about female athletes who broke barriers for the women who would follow their paths. The essays are testaments to the contributors' extensive research and their understanding of the social and cultural milieus in which these athletes' reputations evolved. We are fortunate to have had scholars who can provide such perspectives.

Craig Gill and his staff at the University Press of Mississippi have been tremendous shepherds throughout who have believed in this project from the outset. This is our third volume with them, and their direction and encouragement to follow our instincts have been resolute and absolutely integral to our success.

We would also like to recognize some individuals whose varying contributions helped us navigate the obstacles often inherent to the writing process: Jean Hastings Ardell, Lori Boyle, and Mark S. Gutentag.

Finally, to our friends and families both, we offer up our sincerest appreciation for their unwavering support. They provide inspiration and exercise patience in accommodating our often zealous pursuit of uncovering the meaning of sport in its broader sociopolitical context.

Introduction
Engaging Contested Terrain
—DAVID C. OGDEN AND JOEL NATHAN ROSEN

A CONTEXT OF THEIR OWN

Throughout the first two volumes of our comprehensive examinations of sport and the nature of celebrity reputations,[1] we have explored what can best be called the *contested terrain* of sport. By contested terrain, we point critically to an arena in which society defines and projects what it means to occupy a specific corner of the sociocultural environment, and how the meanings heaped upon such space are then contextualized within the greater landscape.

We see this volume, which looks specifically and critically at the nature of gender within these contested sporting terrains, as a logical extension of those first two efforts. As was the case with these previous works, this collection explores the reputations of iconic and pioneering sports figures and the cultural and social forces that helped to forge their unique—if not wholly problematic—reputations. But unlike volumes one and two, this collection focuses predominantly on those obstacles specific to women, who are most typically perceived to be the quintessential interlopers in this historically male-dominated milieu. This collection also further examines the roles that any qualities ancillary to gender (i.e., race, sexual orientation, and the like) play in such discussions.

Central to this volume is our contention that women in their role as inherent outsiders in sport are placed in a unique position that veers away from many of the overlapping qualities that we have discovered relative to inequality and discord found within (and, yes, beyond) this specific world. This discussion gained momentum with us once we made the conscious decision not to include Marion Jones in the previous volume in spite of the obvious parallels to the other subjects of that work found in her narrative. To be candid, Marion Jones's story is compelling and certainly similar enough to those of the men profiled in *Fame to Infamy*. Unquestionably, when sheared clean of the particulars, it is remarkably familiar in that we have here a once-cherished athletic figure who tumbles off her celebrated perch only to incur the wrath of the very populace that put her there. As the contributors herein make clear, when placed against the backdrop of more traditional markers that suggest full access and participation in such rituals as celebrity, the *thud*, as these authors continue to make clear, is much more distinct once we discover that our heroes—especially those whose demographic profile steps outside the traditional boundaries—were never worthy of the tag in the first place. Such contradictory elements not only hasten an athlete's fall but ultimately seal the fates of subsequent yet similar celebrities who defy the profile long since established in American sporting circles from the fictional Jack Armstrong to the very real Cal Ripken, Jr. These elements also make it clear that in order to rise and remain above the din, one has to be afforded the opportunity to do so. Or to paraphrase Robert W. Reising from his engaging chapter on the reconstruction of Jim Thorpe's legacy in *Reconstructing Fame*, many celebrity athletes have the skills to be fêted by the sporting populace, but *all too few* look as if they have the right to do so.[2]

In this regard, while it is true that what befalls, say, O. J. Simpson, the model for book two's trajectory,[3] is similar to what happens to Marion Jones, the exceptionality of Jones's story takes it beyond what we were seeing in these other narratives. Indeed, when looking at this through a more gendered lens, we never could quite figure out the one glaring element of her story that separated it from the rest: namely how her demise fit within a male-dominated context in spite of its obvious parallels. Moreover, we found that the gender question itself, which we maintained then as now was at the root of most every conversation pertaining to Jones and her rise and dramatic fall, was something that would have most assuredly been buried amidst the other figures featured in that particular collection, and that was not something that we were willing to let happen to a narrative that remains such an integral and certainly compelling feature of contemporary discussions of sport in its broader context.

Of course this decision to exclude her from the previous work was met with some resistance, not the least of which came from our own ongoing debates. Much of what we said and heard had to do with the growing insistence that gender, like race, class, and any of the other markers of difference today, was finding itself in its more modern context cordoned off from the whole of these ongoing sociological debates, which stood to compartmentalize rather than provide a challenge to gender barriers found not only in sport but elsewhere. Indeed, in her foreword to this very volume, Roberta J. Newman skillfully argues that gender has become a conspicuously *ghettoized* place, which she contends situates it well outside its very context, a conclusion that we both heartily endorse.

Nevertheless, as we weighed the option of including Jones in *Fame to Infamy* up against the backdrop of our established approach to these profiles, one glaring matter continued to trouble us, and namely that she was not the first (and likely will not be the last) woman of renown to watch her career take such a dramatic nosedive in spite of her inherent outsider status. So yes, like Simpson and the many other men profiled in our previous study, Jones too would find her life altered as her reputation took on a fluidity that cast her in the role of villain. And yet, in spite of such changes, the one element of this particular narrative that held true was that while the others were perceived to be outsiders because of their position relative to the color line, they were rarely depicted as outliers in the way that female athletes have been and continue to be viewed. Thus, on the surface it made a great deal of sense to include Jones's narrative amidst the other cautionary tales that so often inform such events—especially in American life where the slightest misstep is often all it takes to bring down the most solidly built persona. The counterweight to such a decision was that her being a woman made it less likely that her public acclaim could have been anything more than an anomaly given the role that gender continues to play in sport-related deliberations writ large. And this became our greatest challenge—ferreting out gender without compartmentalizing and hence mitigating its very real place in broader discussions of inequality today.

BALANCING FEMALE ATHLETIC CELEBRITY

The fact is that whether female athletic celebrity has any relevance at all in day-to-day life remains at best ambiguous, something that each and every one of our contributors to this work addresses head-on. Nevertheless, it is this ambiguity that makes such inquiry an invaluable tool in the growing arsenal of sport-related criticism.

Certainly there are a handful of female athletes whose mark reaches beyond the confines of the more typical short arm that most women feel as they attempt to traverse the gender divide in sport, but to assess the extent to which, for example, a Billie Jean King or a Serena Williams or even a Babe Didrikson can break down such persistent barriers is a next-to-impossible task under the most opportune conditions. Ideally, female athletes who make good would be as heralded and as lauded as their male brethren, but this has rarely, if ever, been the case. At most, women have become sport's latest sideshow, similar to Negro League baseball and the sort of entertainment antics brought about by such legendary acts as the Harlem Globetrotters, the

Indianapolis Clowns, and even the House of David, whose bearded traveling *baseballers* once featured Babe Didrikson.

What separates today's female athlete from the sheer entertainment quality of their typically male predecessors, however, is that the only ones who do not seem to know that they are not spectacles or affectations or a source of public sexual relief, as exemplified in Penny Marshall's *A League of Their Own*,[4] are the women themselves. In spite of the ongoing rhetoric to the contrary, female athletes have long shown themselves to be fiercely competitive, wholly committed, and seeking fame if not fortune by the same drive to excel as exemplified by their fathers and brothers who too sweated and bled and left pieces of themselves scattered on playing fields from which they hailed. But to what end? Moreover, what does it all mean still?

In the case of Marion Jones, where she once had fame, albeit on the "B" stages of female sport, she now has infamy, which as the chapter herein concludes, could be construed as the first time she has found genuine equality before the court of public scrutiny. Where once she could be regarded as a facsimile of the great male athletes of her time, a talented one but always lurking well behind sport's real competitive male baseline, she only found true acceptance as an athlete once she fell out of favor with the fans as well as with the governing bodies that only purported to accept her as the genuine article even before the trial and subsequent conviction that effectively stopped her career in its tracks. Where once she could be written off as a mock parallel version of a Carl Lewis or a Usain Bolt, in her tragic fall she may have finally gained acceptance when, by most every measure, there could never be acceptance for one whose training was always to be underscored by the reality that under the best of conditions, a championship-caliber female athlete will always be at best a pale imitation of an actual champion, which remains sport's version of damning a segment of its best and brightest with the faintest of praise. In effect, she was living Bobby Riggs's warped made-for-TV argument that the best female athletes were the ones who were smart enough not to step on a court where the big boys tread for fear of being found out.

While race continues to dominate discussions of inequality pertaining to sport, the question of gender, precisely for the reasons outlined above, is more typically brushed into the shadows for reasons that oftentimes seem to defy the most distorted logic. The fact is that whether we choose to acknowledge it, the male-female divide remains the heretofore one piece that continues to puzzle even the most ardent champions of equality. Beyond the questions of physicality, the most basic question pertaining to women's participation in competitive sport stems from the very questions being asked as far back as Reconstruction—namely why would women even be interested in doing such things?

Still conceived of as passive and fragile, even in an age of female soldiers in combat roles, women have found that the most innocuous-seeming platitude has a way of reminding that when it comes to athletics, their place—collectively or individually—is anywhere but on the field, as demonstrated most ably in 1998 by President Clinton, whose presumed glee over the US women's soccer team's advance in that year's Women's World Cup was because the participants were not men! The competition may have been spectacular, but the commentary throughout seemed slotted along the singular notion that there could still be such surprise that women really can play games that made them worthy of the tag of athlete. But as further exemplified by many subsequent attempts to cash in on the popularity of 1998's success, women's sport as both a competitive and a financial endeavor never really moved beyond the anomaly stage that continues to underlie much if not all of the resultant commentary.

To be sure, at one point or another all those profiled in this volume have had to face down the resiliency of such a not-quite-latent misogyny. Though many have tried, women's sport has never been anything more than a side-show in the American sporting world, a cultural hub in which the line between success and failure is often found in ticket sales and television ratings. Typically the male-dominated American sport public has been unmoved by women's sports. Sports show hosts, as much a part of the American sport landscape today as the vaunted hotdogs and apple pies of yesteryear, refuse to even discuss them on their programs for fear of listener backlash from their primarily male demographic. The sad fact of the matter is that with the exception of the women's tennis and golf tours, high-profiled women's sport often runs headlong into two competitors it simply cannot beat—the men's version of the same sport with its tradition and its emphasis on speed, power, and overall athleticism, and an overwhelmingly apathetic male-dominated viewing public. And though small steps have been made to loosen the grip of the male influence, the reality of women being recognized as athletes in their own right remains the baseline for establishing equality at this particular level. So while 1972's landmark Title IX legislation may have addressed the issue of gender equity in high school and college sport, the philosophy behind the male-centric approach retains its currency all these years since. That is, female athletes in most—if not all—sports remain subjugated in terms of respect and adulation to their male counterparts.

A sample of sports media content and commentary in the United States provides ample evidence to support such a conclusion if only because such a string of gender-related dilemmas calls into question the expectations of womanhood. Competition against others runs against the grain of the traditional concept of femininity, which is thought to be marked by such "natural" behaviors as cooperation, connectedness, and caring. An important part of this volume, and a theme that runs throughout, is the struggle women face in attempting to extricate themselves from this quagmire. Or put in another way, how do elite female athletes balance existing ideals of femininity while making their mark in a world in which men set the standards? As our contributors demonstrate so vividly, the women in this volume may have used a range of means to do so, but the broader theme is that when all is said and done, it is less what means they used to make their collective and individual marks, whether sex appeal, organized protest, or merely laying waste to their opponents, and more that they had no other choice but to kick down whatever backdoors might have stood in their way, an image that even in this second decade of the twenty-first century remains oddly topical.

THE CHAPTERS

Unlike *Reconstructing Fame* and *Fame to Infamy*, there will be no straw woman whose legacy or reputational arc will serve as the barometer for this work precisely because there is no one particularly dominant narrative that underscores the enormity of female athletic participation—nor should there be. Each contributed to the legacy of elite female athletics in her own way. Babe Zaharias certainly may be considered the pioneer, or at the very least, one of the foremothers of women in sport. Her blunt, head-on approach to defending her own particular stature as an athlete certainly shocked the prudent, as did her veritably ubiquitous pubic hair quip uttered when she played with the House of David baseball team.[5] But too few of her generation showed outwardly that they were willing to take on the paternal world with such verve and gusto, let alone with such brazen sexual overtures.

To be sure, the next generation of female athletes may not have been as forthright as Zaharias, but they certainly built on her legacy that women could be exceptional athletes in their own right: Roberta Gibb and Kathrine Switzer in distance running; players in the All-American Girls Professional Baseball League; and Billie Jean King, Chris Evert, and Martina Navratilova in tennis. As they retired, others emerged and found that, in most cases, the reception within the inner sanctum of elite sports was as chilly as was that of their predecessors. Those who came later continued to struggle with being "sidebars" to the main story of men's sports. They included the Williams sisters,

Florence Griffith Joyner, Sheryl Swoopes, and, of course, Marion Jones. As of this writing, Danica Patrick is still a force in auto racing and is taking her Indy racing legacy to NASCAR.

Each approached her athletic reputation in different ways, but each faced the glaring light of public skepticism and, on occasion, downright misogyny. Each also realized the turbulence that public scrutiny of her private life could bring to her professional aspirations. The parallels between the subjects of these chapters are many, and it is those parallels and ironies that provide another framework for examining social and cultural issues at large.

One of the most obvious ironies is that the same factor that enriched the careers of some female athletes caused public consternation for others. That factor is sexuality, and as Lisa Neilson and Yvonne Sims point out in chapters 10 and 8, respectively, Patrick and Joyner used their sexuality to secure public attention while they angled to build public interest where it simply had yet to exist. Contrary to that, sexuality undermined the images of Billie Jean King, Martina Navratilova, and, to some extent, Sheryl Swoopes. Patrick's and Joyner's flaunting of their sexuality became public diversions. The homosexuality of King, Navratilova, and Swoopes became public distractions.

It is such juxtapositioning of the subjects of these chapters that provides a storyline well beyond this volume and raises questions that remain unanswered: why does the long-held image of women athletes as sports "outliers" persist? And in what ways can this image be addressed and/or corrected? Are there certain sports more conducive to changing that image (such as in Indy racing, where Danica Patrick and other women have shown that they can hold their own with male drivers)? Or are such changes destined to remain solely reliant on the ongoing cult of personality so much a part of the contemporary popular Zeitgeist?

The purpose of this volume is to raise such questions against the backdrop of the narratives of important figures in women's sport—then as now. And as editors, we think that the authors featured throughout this work have done a masterful job of capturing the essence of this ongoing debate while building a base from which those questions can be further addressed and debated.

NOTES

1. *Reconstructing Fame: Race, Sport, and Evolving Reputations,* eds. David C. Ogden and Joel Nathan Rosen (Jackson, MS: University Press of Mississippi, 2008) and *Fame to Infamy: Race, Sport, and the Fall from Grace,* eds. Ogden and Rosen (Jackson, MS: University Press of Mississippi, 2010).

2. Robert W. Reising, "Remaking an Overlooked Icon: The Reconstruction of Jim Thorpe" in *Reconstructing Fame: Race, Sport, and Evolving Reputations*, eds. David C. Ogden and Joel Nathan Rosen (Jackson, MS: University Press of Mississippi, 2008): 81–82.

3. Editors' note: Muhammad Ali's career arc served to inform the trajectory of *Reconstructing Fame*.

4. *A League of Their Own*, DVD, directed by Penny Marshall (Los Angeles, CA: Sony Pictures Home Entertainment, 1992).

5. William O. Johnson and Nancy P. Williamson, *"Whatta Gal": The Babe Didrikson Story* (Boston: Little, Brown, 1977), 130.

A Locker Room of Her Own

FOLKLORE AND FAIRY TALES
Babe Didrikson Zaharias Revealed

—MARTHA REID

INTRODUCTION

The purpose of this essay is not to rehearse a life, but rather to examine different genres of storytelling employed by a born storyteller throughout and at distinct periods of her life, specifically three types: folklore, fairy tales, and myth. The language of folklore was Babe Didrikson Zaharias's native tongue, the form she heard and mimicked in her childhood and used consciously or unconsciously to promote her early (and incredibly eclectic) athletic career between 1928 and 1938. She continued to fuse such language spontaneously and frequently until her death in 1956. Between 1938 and 1953, however, she drew heavily on fairy tale models to re-shape her image and career in terms of class, gender, and golf. Finally, from her first cancer diagnosis in 1953 until her death in 1956, her narratives took on the burden of myth, not in the sense of "mythologizing" denigrated by biographer Susan Ware,[1] but as Mircea Eliade defines myth: storytelling that "supplies models for human behavior" and "gives meaning and value to life."[2] William Johnson and Nancy Williamson characterize these three stages of Babe's life story somewhat breathlessly as "kissed by greatness," "blessed with true grit," and "ultimately . . . heroic."[3]

"The Babe Didrikson Zaharias Story," if one is expecting a single, seamless account of factual truths strung like so many pearls along a skein of days and years, does not, of course, exist. Such a simplistic account exists for no woman or man and certainly not for the richly complicated Mildred Ella Didrikson Zaharias, known as Babe. Family members, friends, competitors, contemporary fans and media, and Babe herself all had different perspectives on and perceptions of her life, some of which—certainly Babe's own version—changed over time, her lifetime and theirs. The subsequent perspectives and perceptions of biographers and other scholars have similarly shifted as the latter half of the twentieth century and beginning of the twenty-first have refocused our historical and cultural lenses, especially with regard to class and gender. The understanding that emerges from any serious study of the life of the woman whom the Associated Press named the "Greatest Female Athlete of the First Half of the Century" in 1950, while she still competed at the top of her game (golf, at the time, among all the other sports she challenged during her amazing run), and "Woman Athlete of the Twentieth Century" in 1999, forty-three years after her death, is an evolving mosaic of insight.[4] In this way of understanding her life, if there are no enduring truths, there are no important lies either, just some really good stories. And Babe loved to tell them.

She did fib about her age, of course, and about her height and weight, her winning streak of seventeen golf tournaments, typing eighty-six words per minute, and nailing a first prize at the Texas State Fair for sewing a blue dress. She claimed that she never played a round of golf before 1932, despite having played for her high school golf team in the 1920s. Early biographers William Johnson and Nancy Williamson, contrasting the supposed immutability of sports statistics with the "balderdash" of exaggerated scores, times, and distances sometimes spouted by Babe and her promoters, generously contextualize such stretches as incidental within the solid legend of actual achievement: "Yet it is the measure of her legend that many people do not doubt the truth of such fictions."[5] More recently, biographer Susan Ware complains that Babe "had a nasty habit of mythologizing her past" and that "mythologizing dogged her career."[6] Susan Cayleff's important feminist study of Babe's life suggests that her lifelong lying was honest as literature, if not as history.[7] Babe was a born storyteller, for sure, no matter whether she was born in 1911, 1913, 1914, 1915, or 1919, as she variously asserted. (It was 1911.) Babe's sister Lillie found the baptismal certificate and got it right for the tombstone, although the historical marker outside the cemetery in Beaumont, Texas, states 1914, based on Babe's autobiography.[8]

The born storyteller also became a practiced one, keenly aware of her specific audience at a particular time, of what style of narrative it required, and of what could be gained from its approval. All her life, what Babe truly wanted to gain was money, celebrity, and winning—especially winning. What she considered as her relevant audiences were her competitors, her fans and galleries, the media, and other powerful sorts. Each called for a different kind of narrative approach or mixture of styles.

The born storyteller in her was authentic and natural, and it might be said that the folk style was her default mode. While relying on exaggeration for effect, folklore remains close to what is real. The practiced storyteller that Babe became, however, orchestrated and even manipulated her material and audience with calculation that was instinctive in its own way. Her fairy tale period served a campaign of public relations and image-making that repressed, if not denied, her class, gender, and agency. It brought her life story close to what is false in order to achieve goals that were, nevertheless, genuine to her core self. Thus, her artistry was both conscious and unconscious, her modes sequential and simultaneous, and her purpose naturally calculating.

She was an intelligent or, at least, a canny artist—but not an intellectual one. Classmates and teachers reported poor grades and lack of interest in study. Her sister Lillie remembered that Babe and she were put back a grade after returning to Beaumont from an early trial run at circus school, and Ruth Scurlock, a Beaumont teacher, drily observed, "I have no doubt that Babe had the best IQ of anyone in the Didriksen family, but I don't think in her whole life she ever read a book unless it had the rules of some game in it."[9] Cayleff discovered that husband/manager George Zaharias had once squelched—because the writing was too good—a syndicated series of golf columns under Babe's byline that had been ghostwritten by golfer Betty Hicks. Cayleff asserts that Babe "consciously avoided introspection" and "was not articulate about sports, gender, or sex discrimination," yet, after extensive interviews with Babe's family and friends, concludes that "Babe and those who knew her were such eloquent storytellers."[10] Babe's as-told-to autobiography *This Life I've Led* manages to be spontaneously insightful without ever approaching self-reflection. "If I am going to tell the story of my life," she told Harry Paxton, her coauthor, "the thing for me to do is relive it."[11] Her own storytelling was purely oral. For her autobiography, she dictated memories, yarns, hype, and hopes onto tapes that Paxton translated into print. Babe was no writer, although her folk and fairy stories provided great copy for some of the best sportswriters of her half century, and the mythology of her illness and death pushed her life's celebrity into a more lasting and influential fame. The story of Babe Didrikson Zaharias, in her own words, unfolded in various narrative forms that served personal, professional, and ultimately social purposes with a success as remarkable as her athletic records of distances, times, and scores.

FOLKLORE

Mildred Ella Didriksen was born on June 26, 1911, in Port Arthur, Texas—tall tale country. Her first exposure to folklore models, however, was probably European rather than American: the seafaring yarns with which her Norwegian father entertained his seven children, of which she was the sixth. A ship's carpenter prior to emigrating, Ole Didriksen neatly appointed the family's first house in Port Arthur with built-in cabinetry throughout, like a ship's, although Babe's memory or artistry later transformed the entire house into a fantastical landlocked ship.[12] She literally learned such tale-spinning skills at her father's knee. He regaled his large brood with lively accounts of going to sea at the age of nine, sailing around Cape Horn "something like" seventeen times, being shipwrecked by storms, eating monkeys to stay alive, and saving himself and his shipmate by clinging to a mast rope for hours. "I'm not sure to this day whether he was kidding some of the time or not," Babe hedges like a master imaginer. "It could all be true."[13]

Ole quickly recast himself and his family as thoroughgoing Americans of a particular identity—Southern or, more specifically, Southwestern, white, working class, and poor (but aggressively and often hilariously proud). The favored narrative form of that time, place, and class was the tall tale of American folklore. Cayleff explains how Babe followed Ole's lead in artistically connecting thought, word, and deed: "To ensure attention, she supplemented her accomplishments, dramatic and frequent as they were, with self-aggrandizing mythmaking. Her father's penchant for storytelling, coupled with Texas's tall tale tradition, helped her create an irresistible verbal style."[14] She was surrounded by model storytellers in this style. Besides her father, there was Col. M. J. McCombs, an early basketball and track coach, who creatively touted his team, especially Babe. Later, on tour with baseball folk hero and showman Dizzy Dean, Babe excused Dean's outrageous bragging as "just his way. It was Southern Texas talk."[15] She spoke the same language. "Every grandiose Texas-twanging boast enlarged her character and inflated her legend. She had a folksy, common touch, not unlike Will Rogers. Hers was a gap-toothed country wit, ingenuous yet cutting, the kind of native wile that allowed the country boy to one-up the city slicker every time."[16] The triumphant country boy is a common character in American folklore, but Babe came from an urban, not rural, South of oil refineries and rice mills, which gave an edginess and bite to her style. Her folk were the Southern, white, industrial working class. If she spoke with a common touch, however, it was not, in her early years, with a sense of community. She spoke aggressively and defensively for herself—in order to make money, to become famous, and to win.

Kay F. Stone's discussion of the folktale in Jan Brunvand's comprehensive *American Folklore: An Encyclopedia* corrects the assumption that folktales are communal productions. "Each folktale has an author," Stone asserts, though she or he is often unnamed, and the oral origins of folktales should not obscure "the skill and sophistication of excellent narrators, the best of whom are comparable to authors of written literature."[17] That would be Babe, whose school grades were poor and whose few surviving letters are littered with grammar and spelling errors, but whose brassy ad-libs and one-liners won the hearts of golfing galleries everywhere while her barbed boasts rattled the confidence of her competition. Famed golfer and coach Harvey Penick writes that "Babe could tell the rest of the players in a tournament that she was going to beat their socks off and make them like it, because she was not only telling the truth, she was also drawing the most fans."[18] Penick's interesting books were best sellers, but the imagery Babe came up with spontaneously was usually fresher, if saltier, than Penick's "socks." Once during a baseball exhibition tour with the bearded House of David team, all males except for Babe, a woman in the stands called out to her as she relaxed on the sidelines and asked where her whiskers were. "I'm sittin' on 'em, sister, just like you are!" Babe yelled back without missing a beat.[19] Later, in her more ladylike, fairy tale period, Babe omitted that raunchy quip from her autobiography, although she had to acknowledge the oft-reported (and probably oft-repeated—not all of her one-liners were ad-libbed) "girdle" line: "It's not enough just to swing at the ball. You've got to loosen your girdle and really let the ball have it!"[20] Babe admits that "[t]he girdle crack was meant as a gag ..." but also understands that folklore exaggerations are anchored in ordinary experiences: "... and yet there was a lot of truth in it."[21]

Stone includes such one-liners within the folktale category, along with jokes, anecdotes, and longer picaresque adventure stories that are "filled with fantastic creatures, events, and objects, but their main characters are ordinary people ... who are recipients of wondrous [things]."[22] These are all present in Babe's material. Other entries in Brunvand's folklore encyclopedia are equally relevant to Babe's masterful handling of the folk tradition: boasts, the trickster figure, and namelore. The evocative nickname given to Mildred Ella in her childhood, her subsequent and ongoing tinkering with her own name, and the many sobriquets assigned to her by sportswriters are significant namelore, indeed. Susan Ware writes that Babe was "the first female athlete to be known by a singular name."[23] Typical of folk literature, her nickname is full of meaningful metaphoric association, yet based on an ordinary fact: Mildred was the baby girl of the family, and her mother, according to brother Louis, called her "Baden," American-Norwegian for "baby."[24] This makes sense for a family that called Arthur, the youngest child, "Bubba." Her mother, Hannah, Babe said, eventually but unsuccessfully tried a return to a more mature "Mildred" or "Millie."[25] Babe would have none of it. Golf pro Peggy Kirk Bell remembered that Babe hated her given name.[26] She liked, on the other hand, the fact that her family's nickname for her was the same as George Herman Ruth's, and one version of the story claimed that the neighborhood kids in Beaumont started calling her Babe because she hit home runs like Ruth.[27] In her autobiography, her caption for a photograph of herself with the baseball great reads, "the Big Babe and little one." Cayleff believes the media made the connection first.[28] If so, the little Babe ran with it. Another relevant Babe comes to mind, as well: Paul Bunyan's Babe, the blue ox. Whether that Babe derives from legitimate folklore or advertising "fakelore" of the early twentieth century is arguable. (Perhaps Stone's assertion of a singular author renders that point moot.) Still, the name's ironic connotations of physical bulk and strength are operative in all three Babes. The female Babe among the three (the ox was male) also fiddled with her last name during her folklore phase (and pointedly changed it when she married, a topic to be addressed in the section to come). The family name is spelled Didriksen, but Babe always spelled it with an "o," to emphasize her Norwegian rather than Swedish roots, she said. Norwegian practice, however, seems to lean towards the "e," according to Johnson and Williamson.[29] The truth is that Babe was thoroughly American and a poor speller. Once the mistake was made in print, whether in school or in the media, she probably would not have noticed nor cared enough to correct it.

After her track and field successes in the 1932 Olympic Games, the hyperbolic, alliterative sportswriters of the era began to christen her with catchy nicknames that sounded as if they came out of a tall tale: the Texas Tornado, Terrific Tomboy, Amazing Amazon, and World-Beating Girl Viking of Texas.[30] Babe liked those, too, but there was a darker one—Muscle Moll—that bothered her, one that she would try to change during the fairy tale phase of her life story. Despite faint demurral in her autobiography, however, she also seemed to get a kick out of being called Wonder Girl and Superwoman in the press, which reported her snagging a souvenir Olympic banner in an exaggerated account of her climbing up the side of a building to grab it.[31] Years later while ill, she accepted the gift of a palomino horse named Superman and rode him onto the eighteenth green to make the presentation of the tournament trophy that she would rather have been receiving. Yet she proudly recalls the public announcer shouting, "Here comes Superman, ridden by Superwoman!"[32] One of the stunts proposed during her barnstorming exhibition days was a race between Babe and a horse. "But I didn't do it," she observes almost wistfully of the missed opportunity for a Wonder Girl–like challenge. "I knew that wasn't really the right kind of performance for a girl to be putting on."[33]

Betty Hicks remembers Babe's colorful, often off-color quips, full of spontaneous metaphor: "[I] couldn't hit an elephant's ass with a bull fiddle today."[34] Babe was a master of the one-liner—jokes and wisecracks, both extemporaneous and rehearsed, which she used to entertain family, friends, and fans. She delivered her material in down-home character: "I'll break my neck to give the people a good show. I'll bear down on that old Texas drawl, because they seem to like it."[35] Her boasting, another short folk form, while often equally entertaining to those in her camp, especially as she often made good on her boasts, served a more serious purpose. She used it both as a psychological tool to pump herself up and as a mind-game weapon to rattle her competitors. She could, moveover, take it as well as dish it out. Trash talk, she said, "just builds me up."[36] Richard Sweterlitsch provides the following definition of the "boast" in an entry in *American Folklore*: "hyperbolic exaggeration used to impress listeners with the alleged superiority of the speaker," related to the tall tale but without narrative elements.[37] He compares it to black American taunting contests, called sounding, signifying, or "the dozens," and notes that it is a common form used in certain occupations, such as lumberjack, cowboy, oil driller, and smoke jumper.[38] He might have added "athlete" to the list. Before Muhammed Ali roped his first dope, Babe was psyching herself up and unnerving her competition with boasts about her athletic versatility, inexhaustibility, and general superiority over all comers. As a young basketball player in her very first game for the Employers Casualty Insurance team, she claims to have scored more points by herself than the defending national champion Sun Oil team members combined.[39] Like her father's sea voyages, "it could all be true." As a track and field phenomenon prior to the Olympics, she annoyed her American teammates with her tricks and embarrassed them with her boasting predictions. She scoffed at a world record holder's time— in swimming!—as something she regularly surpassed in practice. Olympic roommate Jean Shirley said that Babe had a big and intimidating mouth: "She would horn in every two minutes. If someone said they rode a kayak down from Alaska in three days, Babe would have done it better."[40] The women's professional golf tour produced, perhaps, Babe's most famous boast and also her favorite one, according to Hicks: "Hi, girls! . . . You gonna stick around to see who finishes second this week?"[41] Babe never stopped boasting even in her more secure fairy tale years, although she remembered it as an immature habit. "I talked like that in those days, and some people thought I was just popping off. But I was serious. I said it because I thought I could do it."[42] And she often could. Her pushy boasting fits all points of Sweterlitsch's definition, including "hyperbolic exaggeration," yet she delivered. She inhabited her own tall tales.

Short quips, jokes, and boasts were typical of Babe's folksy patter, but she sometimes essayed the more extended forms of anecdote and adventure story. Childhood memories of teasing a bull into chasing her to a fire truck conveniently parked nearby, Tom Sawyer–like pranks that tried her mother's patience, and hurdling neighborhood hedges to and from the store in early training for the Olympics are the first of many entertaining brief anecdotes included in her autobiography.[43]

Later in the book, one would hardly recognize the boaster who so annoyed her Olympic teammates as the ingenuous young woman who travels to training camp in "mile high" Denver expecting to see a gleaming city floating "a mile up in the air."[44] In her autobiography, she also loosely organizes longer adventure stories around significant athletic achievements that were turning points in her career, the most engaging being the account of her 1947 win in the British Women's Open Tournament. This is a wonderful tale covering several chapters about an amiable Yank winning the hearts and minds of the common Brit (and Scot) along with the championship cup. An ongoing thread running within the story, "Bundles for Babe" is a narrative gem by itself. In this account, Babe has brought the wrong clothing for Scotland's blustery links and cannot buy a warmer outfit due to postwar rationing. Hearing of her dilemma, folks from all over Great Britain send care packages to Babe, from which she selects a pair of "lucky" blue corduroy "slocks" (Scottish dialect for slacks) and—here comes the most effective element of Babe's patriotic "Bundles for Britain" variation—a World War II air raid warden's jacket. In this hands-across-the-sea getup, she wins the tournament, the first American woman to do so, and the British people love her for it. Other threads and details that make up the British Open story are equally amusing and endearing—Babe spotting the king and queen at King's Cross Station and running after them on the red carpet, the "jinx" talk, the old and older caddies. Much of Babe's autobiography consists of boring sports statistics or play-by-play commentary and revisionist image-making, but that story alone is worth the reading.

Johnson and Williamson write that the early Babe was already "producing her own myth; it lay somewhere between *You Know Me Al*, Pecos Bill and the unsinkable Molly Brown."[45] Three main types of folk characters variously appear in the Babe folklore spun by Babe and her usually cooperative press: the underdog, the giant, and the trickster. The underdog was the poor Texas girl unfairly banned by the AAU and the USGA, a plucky working-class hero, "a kid against a veteran," who perseveres and eventually prevails.[46] Famed sportswriter Grantland Rice championed this character, while his colleague Paul Gallico lampooned her viciously in a cruel *Vanity Fair* story, "Honey."[47] As a larger-than-life character in the tradition of Pecos Bill and Paul Bunyan, Babe casually remarks that she regularly hits a golf ball 250 yards. ("The folklore tops out at a 408-yard wallop."[48]) She is awarded a 15-foot, 250-pound key to the city of Denver; her piercing whistle silences an ocean liner's horn; and her gargantuan husband almost overturns the *Queen Elizabeth* when he climbs aboard.[49] (Although George Zaharias's weight did eventually approach four hundred pounds, the *Queen Elizabeth* was never really in danger.) Facing her first cancer surgery in 1953, she claims to have climbed onto the operating table unassisted.[50]

Perhaps the most interesting folk incarnation of Babe is that of the trickster. In *American Folklore*, George E. Lankford defines the trickster figure as both a reckless hustler and an impulsive transformer, one who is "as much tricked as tricker," a loner who both cons and re-creates society.[51] Babe was undeniably a hustler, beginning with a teenage scheme to extort a better salary from the Employers Casualty Insurance Company. At the 1932 Olympics, she boasted about raising her arms in victory to trick the judges at the finish line.[52] Reflecting on her supposed first round of golf in 1932, she tells how she and Grantland Rice played a trick on Paul Gallico, conning him into a race across the course to wear him out before his shot.[53] In several sports that she undertook, she practiced relentlessly, even obsessively, but often played the part of the dilettante before her unsuspecting competition. She hid injuries to keep pressure on her opponents. Yet, while promoting herself sometimes by means of questionable tactics, she also shook up the status quo consistently and helped transform professional athletics for women. She was the key figure in establishing the Ladies Professional Golf Association because she, personally, needed more competitive venues. Her effort, however, changed the world of women's golf. Some trick!

FAIRY TALES

All three character variations in the folk stories about Babe enjoyed the happy endings common to folklore. In the tradition of Babe's American West especially, the independent loner, the isolated antihero, and the innovative rule breaker are admired and ultimately rewarded. While this is true in the folk narratives about Babe, by 1935 her actual life on the road was difficult and her athletic career stalled. After an AAU ban from amateur basketball and track and field competition (for an advertising promotion later acknowledged by the AAU as not authorized by Babe, but rescinded too late to reverse her angry decision to resign), apart from a very brief foray onto the vaudeville stage, barnstorming with basketball and baseball exhibitions was about her only recourse. She began to lose the positive folk-hero image she had first established as a serious amateur athlete. When her commitment to a fresh start in amateur golf competition paid off with a classic underdog win in the 1935 Texas Women's Amateur Championship, she was snubbed by her final opponent in the tournament as a "truck driver's daughter" who did not belong at a country club playing golf.[54] Complaints were made, the AAU's earlier ruling was referenced, and the USGA barred her from subsequent amateur competition. Women's professional golf, at that time, just meant more exhibitions and more touring. Babe could still make money and might gain some additional celebrity, but she wanted to compete—and to win. She needed a new image, a new way of telling her life story, to gain acceptance back into respected competition.

Babe never entirely muzzled her folk approach to communication. It was her natural way of narrating herself, and with it she continued to win friends and influence galleries. Folklore, as a genre, offers a positive image of the working class, which was helpful to Babe's early self-promotion. It is a less effective form for middle- and upper-class consumption, however, especially if the main character is a woman. In the Depression-era world of women's competitive golf, the World-Beating Girl Viking of Texas did not have a chance. The negative image of the muscle moll and tomboy haunted her. Paul Gallico's column about her first tournament win in golf, like his earlier *Vanity Fair* story, "Honey," viciously mocked her lower-class origins, her Texas drawl, and the repulsive (to him) androgyny of her "masculine aggressiveness," "swaggering," and lack of fashion sense.[55] Babe's answer to this personal and professional bias was to recast herself as a fairy tale lady, who still had to loosen her girdle to really swing at a golf ball, but at least she was wearing one. The transformation was not easy in the living or the telling, nor was it accomplished immediately. The fairy tale genre required a Prince Charming, as well, and he was not to appear for another three years. But there was a fairy godmother and godfather immediately on the scene after Babe's 1935 championship and subsequent ban from amateur golf competition—R. L. and Bertha Bowen.[56] Well-heeled and well-placed socially, they took up Babe's cause, took her under their reinforced gossamer wings, and—in Bertha's case—took a good hard look at "the fact that she was poor and had no clothes."[57] Cinderella could not have done better. It was Bertha Bowen who talked Babe into donning her first girdle, although she soon pulled it off in frustration and discomfort and may never have worn another one, despite her famous girdle gag.[58] Bertha made other suggestions about clothes, hair, and cosmetics that softened and feminized Babe's appearance according to the taste of the time. Golfing great Gene Sarazen toured with Babe in 1935, giving exhibitions, and later commented that "[s]he learned all her golf by watching."[59] In the same way, she learned how to be a lady by watching the Bowens. Although Babe never exactly achieved the look of a Disney princess, the changes were enough to support the fairy tale narratives of romance, marriage, and gentility that Babe created in pursuit of a successful career in golf. The Bowens were certainly helpful as fairy godparents in Babe's reimagining of herself, but they were also true friends behind the storytelling scenes, and Babe was lucky to have them.

In his introduction to the *Oxford Companion to Fairy Tales*, editor Jack Zipes, drawing on the work of Jens Tismar and Vladimir Propp, points out that fairy tales are literary, that is, written constructs (rather than oral, as folktales are), while oral wonder tales seem to be an intermediary form between the two.[60] Like folktales, oral wonder tales end happily and carry over into the literary fairy tale form the theme of wish fulfillment.[61] In fairy tales, however, one must be careful about what one wishes for, and endings are not always pleasant.[62] The audience for the written fairy tale form was obviously literate and, thus, of the upper and middle classes and clergy, and a miraculous elevation in social status with an accompanying refinement of behavior is often the subject of fairy tales.[63] Fairy tales, therefore, are concerned with enhanced social status and gender appropriateness to one's class.[64] They are the perfect vehicle for breaking into the country-club world of golf.

By 1937, the year Walt Disney's film company released *Snow White and the Seven Dwarfs*, Babe's look was sufficiently different for Henry Lemore of the United Press to describe her as an awakened Sleeping Beauty.[65] The awakening, transformation, or liberation of Snow White and Beauty, along with Cinderella, Rapunzel, and a host of other fairy tale princesses and ladies, unfailingly involves the intervention of and marriage to a handsome prince, sometimes including a prince in beast's clothing. Babe's marriage to George Zaharias in 1938 was not arranged in order to tell her life story in a new, fairy tale form, but it did not hurt. From her wedding day, she was always precise in identifying herself as Babe Didrikson Zaharias. "I've always competed as Mrs. Zaharias, not Babe Didrikson. George and I are a team."[66] Eighteen years later, President Eisenhower announced the death of "Mrs. Zaharias, Babe Didrikson" at one of his press conferences.[67] After her British Open triumph in 1947, she tried unsuccessfully to lose the folksy "Babe" nickname.[68] She had to be satisfied with the media often simply calling her "Mrs. Golf."[69]

George Zaharias was, by all accounts, a good storyteller himself; and he, too, played around with his own name for effect. Born Theodore Vetoyanis, he changed his name when he competed as a professional wrestler because, according to Babe, "the promoters thought his original name wasn't catchy enough."[70] That may be code for "too ethnic." George's wrestling moniker was straight out of the folk tradition of the American West: "The Crying Greek from Cripple Creek"—referring to a small town in Colorado, although George was actually from the larger and somewhat more urban Pueblo.[71] An early ring name was "Ted Victory," before his dark good looks made him more crowd-pleasing as a villain. He also went by other names for various wrestling roles that he played on tour in the South, e.g., "The Carpetbagger," "The Southern Gentleman," and "The Weeping Behemoth." His wrestling buddies called him "Subway," for getting lost there on one memorable visit to New York.[72] It was roughhewn George, however, who provided Babe with not only the role of wife and title of "Mrs.," but also the absolute winner of a name for a fairy tale princess. He actually called her "Romance." In her autobiography, Babe recalls their wooing nostalgically.

> George took to calling me "Romance," and when I wrote a note to him I'd sign it "Romance." ... I might stop by his place and find nobody home, and slide a note under his door: "I was here, but you weren't. Romance." Then when he got back my telephone would ring, and I'd say, "Hello," and he'd say, "This is Romance."[73]

Years later, after the romance had gone out of the relationship, and Babe privately turned to young golfer Betty Dodd for significant friendship, Babe still gave the dream home she and George finally built in Tampa, Florida, a fairy tale name: Rainbow Manor. One could almost expect to find a unicorn in the driveway.

Publically, Babe kept up the fairy tale façade of the romantic marriage and soft femininity that had paved the way for her acceptance into competitive women's golf. She dedicated her 1955 autobiography, *This Life I've Led*, to her mother and father "and to my husband, George, without whom there never would have been a life to lead." Behind the façade, Babe did, in fact, owe much of her early golfing success to George's canny management of her career and to his financial backing for the three-year hiatus from paid employment that was necessary to regain her amateur status. There seems to have been sincere affection, common interest, and solid loyalty at the core of their relationship. The romantic narrative that played over the surface brings a smile at best, or, perhaps, a sneer to the cynical face of today's reader, but it worked for the mid-twentieth century. It also worked for Hollywood in *Babe*, a 1975 Susan Clark/Alex Karras film celebrating the Zaharias romance, as it had in *Pat and*

Mike, a 1952 Katherine Hepburn/Spencer Tracy film with a similar plot—a film in which Babe appeared as herself and characteristically demanded a script change that rendered her the winner of the film's climactic tournament. A 2009 survey of Tribune Company sportswriters turned up at least one—Houston Mitchell of the *Los Angeles Times*—who named Babe and George as his favorite athlete-celebrity couple of all time.[74]

In the fairy tale genre, Babe is forever planting roses whenever she and George pause in their peripatetic life together. George tends to the business of their careers, while she—when she is not playing or practicing golf—cooks, cleans, sews, decorates, and landscapes.[75] A photograph included in her autobiography pictures her laying bricks at Rainbow Manor, dressed in pearls and a cocktail dress. On the golf course, "like any other woman, I'm forever freshening up my lipstick," she deadpans when media reports accuse her of playing the trickster to unnerve her opponents with a literally cosmetic display of insouciance.[76] None of these protestations of typically feminine behavior were false—she did like to cook, clean, and sew, and she loved roses—but they were consciously staged to tell her story a different way.[77]

Some of her presentations were fabrications. Cayleff points out that Babe smoked and drank but claimed otherwise.[78] Ware questions the sincerity of Babe's desire for family life.[79] There were moments in which she reverted to the working-class folk hero. She decked an annoying jerk in a Miami country club bar in the 1950s, although she immediately appeared to regret the lapse from her image.[80] Babe never entirely suppressed the earlier and more natural folklore self, but in telling her life as a fairy tale, she pushed the tomboy antics further back in her childhood, remembered teenage boyfriends that none of her family or friends could recall, and soft-pedaled the brash Olympic triumphs and youthful participation in sports that, unlike golf, produced visible sweat.[81] Feminist scholars like Cayleff and Ware view this "makeover" as a painful denial of Babe's genuine identity. "It must have been a painful process to change her persona so dramatically and suppress key elements of her style and personality—in effect becoming someone else in order to succeed."[82]

Perhaps they are right. Friends like Peggy Kirk Bell and Betty Dodd thought that she would look much more attractive in a tailored suit than in some of the elaborate hats and dresses that she affected.[83] But Babe's persona may have been more complicated than such "either/or" judgments allow. While she was famous for her booming drives, observant fellow golfers noticed "the look of her hands—graceful, tapered fingers and a gentle light touch that was sheer magic with a golf club."[84] Perhaps the fairy tale genre suited her, too. After all, despite some irony, there was no disputing her claim to victory in 1947 in the "noble old competition [that] was known officially as 'The *Ladies* Amateur Golf Championship Tournament, Under the Management of the *Ladies* Golf Union'" of Great Britain (emphasis added).[85] Similarly, Babe was instrumental in the founding and development of the LPGA, the *Ladies* Professional Golf Association, in 1947 (more emphasis added). There was both necessity and calculation involved in naming the LPGA. When Fred Corcoran, Babe's manager when she turned professional again as a golfer, was unsuccessful in the attempt to purchase the name of the dormant Women's Professional Golf Association, it was decided that the Brits had the classier language anyway, so they called the new organization the Ladies Professional Golf Association.[86]

As the scholars of fairy tales note, however, and as Stephen Sondheim points out so astutely in the second half of his musical *Into the Woods*, ending happily ever after is more the exception than the rule for the genre. The hearty independence of the folklore Babe and the connubial bliss of her fairy tale marriage inevitably gave way to a restless loneliness that was forced, much too soon, to confront a degrading and agonizing death. In the final narrative phase of Babe's life story, yet another genre would be required, one that translated the personal tale into a shared human experience.

MYTH

In 1953, at the age of forty-one and still near the top of her game, Babe was diagnosed with colon cancer and underwent surgery that profoundly changed not only her body, but also the way in which she understood and told her life story. The crude boasts and hyperbole of her oral folklore were expressed in the language and nasal Texas twang of common folk, but they alienated many. Babe's purpose was not to make a common cause with anyone else. She was promoting herself. When she used the fairy tale genre to gain admittance to the middle-class, country club set, she was never fully accepted by that society nor entirely comfortable with the genteel role that she created for herself. There were moments when she did feel a common bond with others, usually solid working-class people. On their delayed honeymoon cruise to a working vacation in Australia in 1939, for instance, Babe and George traded their boring first-class companions for a "swell gang" of entertainers in steerage and had "a wonderful trip."[87] Initially annoyed with primitive conditions at an Outback course on that same exhibition tour, Babe soon realized that the people had come for miles to see her and were knocking themselves out to give her a sincere welcome. Touched, she remembered it as the best stop on the tour.[88]

Such moments of communal feeling, however, seem to have been rare in Babe's experience until her cancer diagnosis. Babe had previously played benefits supporting cancer charities like the Damon Runyon Foundation, but her identification with cancer patients and support of them emotionally as well as financially became a personal mission for her after 1953. A new sense of relationship to her audience is reflected in the storytelling. In *This Life I've Led*, she tells of convincing a nun in the same hospital with her, who was also suffering from colon cancer, to follow her brave example and undergo a colostomy operation. She includes in the autobiography a photograph of herself visiting children stricken with cancer.[89] Babe brought into play all the power of her competitive spirit, publicity savvy, and larger-than-life image in a new contest of mythic proportion against cancer and death. This time, moreover, she was playing a team sport in common cause with cancer survivors everywhere, sharing with them her own openness, courage, and hope.

In *Myth and Reality*, Mircea Eliade explains that myth in the nineteenth-century sense of "fiction" or "illusion" came to be understood quite differently in the twentieth century, as it had been by archaic societies, as a "true story [that is] sacred, exemplary, significant," one that "supplies models for human behavior" and "gives meaning and value to life."[90] Eliade goes on to describe myth as involving supernatural beings who undergo "ordeals," "deaths," and "resurrections," thus teaching ordinary humans how to live and die.[91] Joseph Campbell, in *The Hero with a Thousand Faces*, asserts, "It has always been the prime function of mythology . . . to supply the symbols that carry the human spirit forward."[92] Campbell's hero, like Eliade's supernatural beings, "re-emerges from the kingdom of dread . . . [and] restores the world."[93] This is the form of storytelling that Babe incorporated into her repertoire during the final years of her life. Of course, Babe's language is less grand.

> All my life I've been competing—and competing to win. I came to realize that in its way, this cancer was the toughest competition I'd faced yet. I made up my mind that I was going to lick it all the way. I not only wasn't going to let it kill me, I wasn't even going to let it put me on the shelf. I was determined to come back and win golf championships just the same as before.[94]

Her achievement—especially her winning the 1954 U.S. Women's Open Championship by twelve strokes just one year after major cancer surgery— is as amazing as any ordeal undertaken and met by the mythic heroes and sacred models described by Campbell and Eliade. Her powerful sense of herself as an important role model and symbol is equally mythic. "I lived through the cancer, and I've been living with it since. I want to say more about that later, because I believe the cancer problem should be out in the open. The more the public knows about it the better."[95] The caption in her autobiography under the photograph of her 1954 U.S. Women's Open triumph characterizes it as "one of the most satisfying victories of my life. As a beacon, it served to blink encouragement to thousands who must battle cancer."[96] In her new communal role, Babe shared—uncharacteristically, Cayleff notes—credit for the comeback success with those fellow soldiers, their supporters and hers, and her surgeon.[97]

In her final mythic story, Babe attempted to face down not only cancer, but death itself. Some of the comeback confidence after her 1953 cancer operation may be attributed to the doctors, George, and Betty Dodd withholding from her the truth that the cancer had spread and was terminal.[98] By 1955, its recurrence or persistence was undeniable. Yet in her upbeat autobiography and press releases, Babe remained committed to exemplifying courage and hope for others. The actual battle was excruciating, even grotesque.[99] Weighing about eighty pounds eleven days before her death in 1956, Babe compared herself to concentration camp victims who still "came back," Dodd later recalled.[100] Cayleff suggests that such optimism derived from Babe's "belief in her own invincibility and denial of her mortality."[101] The final words of her autobiography, dated September 1955, are "My autobiography isn't finished yet."[102] Her dying words—reported and possibly invented by George—were "I ain't gonna die, honey."[103]

But she did. Perhaps a more potent representation of the mythic genre than is provided by her denial of mortality and supposed final protestation against death can be found in a memory her sister Lillie brought away from those last days: "At the end she thought it was daylight all the time."[104] In terms of the telling of stories, surely there is some suggestion of mythical resurrection in that detail. There is something darkly reminiscent of King Arthur, also, in an anecdote told by Babe's friend Bertha Bowen about an onion she brought to Babe in the hospital as a joke, recalling the onion sandwiches that Babe loved to eat. Bowen later planted it and gathered some seeds from the resulting growth. She was never able to grow another onion from the seeds.[105] Yet the symbolic seeds, in terms of myth, are a promise, of sorts.

THE END

Besides the gravesite, there is a Babe Zaharias Museum in Beaumont, Texas, where the Babe Didrikson Zaharias Foundation and annual golf tournament are also based. The Tampa Golf Course, next to Rainbow Manor, where Babe and George lived at the end of her life, has many of her medals and trophies. The USGA Museum and Arnold Palmer Center for Golf History in Far Hills, New Jersey, has "tons of stuff" about Babe in the archives, according to Assistant Director David Normoyle, much of it collected for the fiftieth anniversary celebration of her 1954 comeback win of the U.S. Women's Open Championship.[106] Among the valuable primary and secondary sources written about Babe and cited for this essay, Susan Cayleff's biography is especially comprehensive. Another biography has been recently published.[107] Babe's story, in various forms and voices, ebbs and flows, but it goes on.

There are the statistics, of course, and they are impressive. Babe still inhabits the top tier of various media "greatest" lists. Yet numbers alone cannot explain the complexity of a life such as the one Babe lived. Even narrative tools are taxed in the attempt. Babe herself employed several of them—folklore forms, fairy tale themes, and mythic symbolism—in her own telling of the story. She was not a master storyteller, in the same way that she was not a technically perfect athlete. She was a natural. Her natural storytelling skills, like her natural golf swing, were powerful and effective. She honed both with shrewd intelligence and relentless practice. Ultimately, she used both her actions and her words for the benefit of others. If, too soon, her athletic accomplishments were cut short by the mortal nature of the human condition, Babe's stories have achieved an immortality that even her amazing body could not.

NOTES

1. Susan Ware, *Letter to the World: Seven Women Who Shaped the American Century* (Cambridge, MA: Harvard University Press, 1998), 173–175.

2. Mircea Eliade, *Myth and Reality* (New York: Harper & Row, Publishers, Inc., 1963), 2.

3. William O. Johnson and Nancy P. Williamson, *"Whatta Gal": The Babe Didrikson Story* (Boston: Little, Brown, 1977), 3.

4. Larry Schwartz, "Didrikson was a woman ahead of her time," ESPN.com, n.d., http://sports.espn.go.com/espn/classic/bio/news/story?page=Didrikson_Babe (September 16, 2012). See also Anna Kelly, "Babe Zaharias—One of the World's Greatest Female Athletes of the 20th Century," Ezine Articles, n.d., http://ezinearticles.com/?Babe -Zaharias---One-of-the-Greatest-Female-Athletes-of-the-20th-Century&id=6195655 (June 23, 2011).

5. Johnson and Williamson, *"Whatta Gal,"* 10.

6. Ware, *Letter to the World,* 173, 175.

7. Susan E. Cayleff, *Babe: The Life and Legend of Babe Didrikson Zaharias* (Urbana, IL: University of Illinois Press, 1995), 44.

8. Johnson and Williamson, *"Whatta Gal,"* 35.

9. Ibid., 45, 61.

10. Cayleff, *Babe*, xi, 249, xii.

11. Babe Didrikson Zaharias and Harry Paxton, *This Life I've Led: My Autobiography* (New York: A.S. Barnes and Company, 1955), viii.

12. Johnson and Williamson, *"Whatta Gal,"* 37; Zaharias and Paxton, *This Life I've Led*, 11.

13. Zaharias and Paxton, *This Life I've Led*, 8.

14. Cayleff, *Babe,* 81.

15. Zaharias and Paxton, *This Life I've Led*, 82.

16. Johnson and Williamson, *"Whatta Gal,"* 100.

17. Kay F. Stone, "Folktale" in *American Folklore: An Encyclopedia*, ed. Jan H. Brunvand (New York: Garland Press, 1996), 295.

18. Harvey Penick with Bud Shrake, *For All Who Love the Game: Lessons and Teachings for Women* (New York: Simon & Schuster, 1995), 171.

19. Johnson and Williamson, *"Whatta Gal,"* 130; Cayleff, *Babe*, 108.

20. Zaharias and Paxton, *This Life I've Led*, 46.

21. Ibid., 47.

22. Stone, "Folktale," 294.

23. Ware, *Letter to the World*, 169.

24. Cayleff, *Babe*, 31.

25. Zaharias and Paxton, *This Life I've Led*, 11.

26. Johnson and Williamson, *"Whatta Gal,"* 18.

27. Zaharias and Paxton, *This Life I've Led*, 11; Cayleff, *Babe*, 31.

28. Cayleff, *Babe*, 31.

29. Johnson and Williamson, *"Whatta Gal,"* 36.

30. Ibid., 99; Ware, *Letter to the World*, 169.

31. Zaharias and Paxton, *This Life I've Led*, 62.

32. Ibid., 224; Cayleff, *Babe*, 228.

33. Zaharias and Paxton, *This Life I've Led*, 5.

34. Cayleff, *Babe*, 163.

35. Zaharias and Paxton, *This Life I've Led*, 100.

36. Ibid., 166.

37. Richard Sweterlitsch, "Boast" in *American Folklore: An Encyclopedia*, ed. Jan H. Brunvand (New York: Garland Press, 1996), 95.

38. Ibid., 96.

39. Zaharias and Paxton, *This Life I've Led*, 38.

40. Johnson and Williamson, *"Whatta Gal,"* 100, 84.

41. Cayleff, *Babe*, 164.

42. Zaharias and Paxton, *This Life I've Led*, 41.

43. Ibid., 11, 21, 29.

44. Ibid., 52.

45. Johnson and Williamson, *"Whatta Gal,"* 101.

46. Zaharias and Paxton, *This Life I've Led*, 94.

47. Cayleff, *Babe*, 92–94.

48. Ibid., 160.

49. Zaharias and Paxton, *This Life I've Led*, 178–179.

50. Ibid., 211.

51. George E. Lankford, "Trickster" in *American Folklore: An Encyclopedia*, ed. Jan H. Brunvand (New York: Garland Press, 1996), 716.

52. Johnson and Williamson, *"Whatta Gal,"* 72, 105.

53. Zaharias and Paxton, *This Life I've Led*, 61.

54. Johnson and Williamson, *"Whatta Gal,"* 142.

55. Ibid., 144–145; Cayleff, *Babe,* 92–93.

56. Cayleff, *Babe,* 129.

57. Johnson and Williamson, *"Whatta Gal,"* 147.

58. Ibid., 153.

59. Ibid., 149.

60. Jack Zipes, *The Oxford Companion to Fairy Tales: The Western Fairy Tale Tradition from Medieval to Modern* (Oxford: Oxford University Press, 2000), xv–xvi.

61. Ibid., xvii.

62. Ibid., xxiv.

63. Ibid., xvi–xvii.

64. Ibid., xx.

65. Johnson and Williamson, *"Whatta Gal,"* 154; Cayleff, *Babe,* 131.

66. Zaharias and Paxton, *This Life I've Led*, 131.

67. Johnson and Williamson, *"Whatta Gal,"* 1.

68. Cayleff, *Babe,* 154.

69. Ware, *Letter to the World*, 199.

70. Zaharias and Paxton, *This Life I've Led*, 106.

71. Ibid., 105–106.

72. Johnson and Williamson, *"Whatta Gal,"* 158–162.

73. Zaharias and Paxton, *This Life I've Led*, 109.

74. "Four Corners: A Sports Debate," *Morning Call*, September 25, 2009, Sports sec.: 8.

75. Zaharias and Paxton, *This Life I've Led*, 131–132.

76. Ibid., 167.

77. Ibid., 103–104, 131–132.

78. Cayleff, *Babe,* 160.

79. Ware, *Letter to the World*, 182–183.

80. Johnson and Williamson, *"Whatta Gal,"* 21.

81. Ibid., 155–156, 175. See also Cayleff, *Babe,* 67, and Ware, *Letter to the World*, 206.

82. Ware, *Letter to the World*, 191.

83. Johnson and Williamson, *"Whatta Gal,"* 175.

84. Ibid., 191.

85. Ibid., 176.

86. Ibid., 185.

87. Zaharias and Paxton, *This Life I've Led*, 114.

88. Ibid., 117.

89. Ibid.

90. Eliade, *Myth and Reality*, 1–2.

91. Ibid., 5–6, 202.

92. Joseph Campbell, *The Hero with a Thousand Faces* (Princeton: Princeton University Press, 1968), 11.

93. Ibid., 246.

94. Zaharias and Paxton, *This Life I've Led*, 5.

95. Ibid.

96. Ibid.

97. Cayleff, *Babe*, 227; Zaharias and Paxton, *This Life I've Led*, 232.

98. Cayleff, *Babe*, 220.

99. Ibid., 237.

100. Johnson and Williamson, *"Whatta Gal,"* 19.

101. Cayleff, *Babe*, 234.

102. Zaharias and Paxton, *This Life I've Led*, 232.

103. Johnson and Williamson, *"Whatta Gal,"* 219.

104. Ibid., 216.

105. Ibid., 218.

106. David Normoyle (assistant director of the United States Golf Association) in discussion with the author, July 10, 2009.

107. Don Van Natta, *Wonder Girl: The Magnificent Sporting Life of Babe Didrikson Zaharias* (New York: Little, Brown and Company, 2011).

"TAKE ME OUT TO THE BELLEGAME"

How the AAGPBL Gained and Maintained Its Highly Respected Reputation

—KIMBERLY YOUNG

INTRODUCTION

Walking through the exhibits of the Baseball Hall of Fame, amidst Babe Ruth's uniform, Ty Cobb's bat, and Sammy Sosa's home run balls, a visitor can find another section of smaller tattered gloves, bats, and balls, adorned not with pinstripe pants, but brightly colored skirts. To the amazement of the average baseball fan, the most popular exhibit in the Baseball Hall of Fame has nothing to do with the men in baseball, but rather with the women. Surprising not only because of its deviation from the traditionally masculine conception of baseball, this exhibit's success is remarkable because the existence of the All-American Girls Professional Baseball League (AAGPBL) was virtually unknown to all but former players before the exhibit's opening in 1988.

Philip K. Wrigley, chewing gum magnate and baseball entrepreneur, founded the AAGPBL in 1943. Conceived amongst rumors that Major League Baseball (MLB) was canceling its 1943 season due to player shortages from World War II, the AAGPBL existed from 1943 to 1954. Team franchises were located primarily in the Midwest. It was originally named the All-American Girls Softball League, and the league's name and regulations changed frequently as the style of play evolved to mirror baseball instead of softball during its twelve-year existence. By 1954, the league's final year, players used official MLB-sized balls and pitching distances. The league is a historical example of a profitable and popular women's professional sporting league.

After the opening of the Baseball Hall of Fame exhibit, the league was cemented in popular consciousness with the release of Penny Marshall's blockbuster film *A League of Their Own* (1992). Nearly twenty years after the film's release, the AAGPBL remains a compelling topic of historical inquiry because of its revelations about the construction of reputation of women in sport. Unlike many other sports with female athletes who have challenged traditional conceptions of gender roles by entering athletics, and as a result have been subject to criticism and controversy, the league's reputation has remained unchallenged, in the past and present, despite its participation "in a man's world." At its inception, the league managed players' reputations through constructions of patriotism and femininity. Its players looking like girls and playing like men, the league gained acceptance from the public as an act of patriotism during World War II. With the war's conclusion, the league remained successful and respected because its reconstituted image aligned with postwar ideals of womanhood. As an "All-American" and community-driven enterprise, the AAGPBL was seen as a support, not a threat, to Cold War ideals by the public. In 1954, when the league concluded, knowledge of the league went dormant, and was forgotten for more than thirty years. While regrettable, the disappearance of the league allowed it to reconstitute itself (yet again) in the modern popular consciousness on its own terms. Memories of the league today remain popular and positive. The league is remembered outside the modern paradigms of politics, sexuality, and identity that have plagued female athletes of the last forty years with contested reputations. In present day, the AAGPBL is seen as a celebration of women's liberation and an entity that supports the values of society.

BOTH A GIRL AND AN INFIELDER: THE EARLY YEARS

In its founding years, the AAGPBL focused on constructing players' reputations by managing the public expression of players' gender through league policies, advertising, and promotion. For the AAGPBL to succeed, it had to not only offer a package of highly skilled athleticism, but also create an image of the league that was acceptable to the public. With its inception in 1943, the league's successful management of its reputation allowed it to become financially successful and accepted by the public at large. This careful management went beyond a public reception that permitted the existence of the league; the players were celebrated and promoted as role models by the public.

The AAGPBL's two main struggles for national acceptance as a legitimate sport centered on the skill level of the players and the public's accordance with the notion of *women* as athletes. While the players did not question their own femininity because they played baseball, the public did. Organizers created the league's image with the knowledge of how the public had historically received women in baseball. Regardless of the players' skill, if the public did not see "baseball" as an acceptable sport for women, the league would not be profitable.

Wrigley and his backers assembled the league in a way that brought together the seemingly contradictory concepts of femininity and athleticism. The players were highly skilled, like the players of the unconventional softball leagues, but at the same time looked like "ladies." Don Black, president of the Racine Belles, described the league's philosophy in a season-opening letter to players:

> Our league and our club have only two important things to sell the public; playing ability and femininity. While the playing ability of our teams has been steadily on the increase, we must not forget and grow lax about the all important femininity angle. It was one of the prime factors on which our league was founded and it is more than ever important that it should remain. You'd be surprised at the importance it holds with the average fan. Nobody is especially surprised or impressed if a rough, tough, mannish looking babe shows some ability in sports, but to realize that a truly feminine creature can reach the top in one branch of athletic endeavor is refreshing and pleasing. Your fans want you to look and act like ladies and still play ball like gentleman![1]

Simply stated, the players were to look like women and play like men. The creation and promotion of the league's rules of conduct, uniform design, and its mandatory introduction in etiquette through charm school were the chief tools through which the AAGPBL constructed its image in order to make the paradox of a woman baseball player acceptable to the public. The league and its participants represented an interesting gender dichotomy: the women took on the traditionally male role of an athlete but still maintained their femininity.

The women's memories of the league's construction support this conclusion. Mary Roundtree, who reached the height of her career in 1952 playing for the Fort Wayne Daisies, recounted that "they [the league] were trying to avoid any criticism of the application of masculinity. If we had all appeared to be extremely masculine, dressed in shorts or slacks, they would have said we were too masculine or would have thrown the proverbial homosexual criticism at us."[2] Faye Dancer, who played in the league from 1944 to 1950, and is most remembered as a member of the Fort Wayne Daisies, recalls the differences of the AAGPBL from leagues past: "We had a product to sell, women's baseball, and we did sell it. We were in competition with women's softball, which was well organized in the Midwest. A lot of softball women were very mannish, had men's haircuts, and dressed like men."[3]

The league's mantra was acceptability and normalcy—to negotiate old boundaries instead of forging new ones. Upon entering a contract with the AAGPBL, players not only agreed to provide labor as a baseball player, but also gave the league the right to regulate their conduct both on and off the field. The rules of conduct were not guidelines constructed to state desired expectations of player behavior, but rules players were contractually required to abide by. While the code stated that the regulations were "necessary as a means of maintaining order and organizing clubs into a working procedure,"[4] they were primarily designed as a way to package the players to a wary public. As player Betty Weaver Foss remembered, "The rules kept the girls looking like women and acting like ladies, and we were respected as ladies. Some of the new girls thought we would be a bunch of boys, or tomboys, but we weren't them type of people."[5]

The rules prohibited the girls from smoking and drinking in public, set curfews, regulated social engagements, and governed players' appearance. More specifically, the rules of conduct mandated that the girls must "ALWAYS appear in feminine attire when not actively engaged in practice or playing ball.... AT NO TIME MAY A PLAYER APPEAR IN THE STANDS IN HER UNIFORM, OR WEAR SLACKS OR SHORTS IN PUBLIC."[6] Girls were to appear at all times in clothing and makeup that emphasized femininity. Fines enforced the rules.

The league felt it was not enough to regulate players' behavior, but that it had to also create a new image of what a female athlete looked like. To this end, Wrigley wanted a uniform that emphasized femininity and adhered to public conceptions of the proper attire for women. Uniforms consisted of a one-piece skirted flared tunic, modeled after women's figure skating costumes and field hockey skirts. As players tried out the uniforms, the league shortened the skirts because they interfered with pitching and fielding the ball.[7] While these uniforms were feminine, they were not intended to be sexual, or in any way exploit the women wearing them. As Maxine Keenan, the league secretary, explained, "We do not want our uniforms to stress sex, but they should be feminine, with emphasis on the clean American sports girl."[8]

CONSTRUCTING A PALATABLE PRODUCT

The final step in the league's creation of its unique reputation was what came to be called the AAGPBL Charm School. During spring training of the first two seasons, players attended charm school at night. Charm school served a two-fold purpose. It added to the feminine persona of the league, putting players through finishing-school type activities, but it also served the concrete purpose of teaching the players public relations skills, reinforcing that effective interaction with the fans and press would be necessary for the league's survival.

In charm school, each girl was given "A Guide for All-American Girls: How to Look Better, Feel Better, and Be More Popular" that contained suggestions on beauty routines, personal hygiene, etiquette, and proper dress.[9] The guide emphasized the necessity of beauty care for the players who must "at all times [be] presentable and attractive, whether on the playing field or at leisure." The guide concluded by emphasizing that players must be "polite and considerate in your daily contacts, avoid noisy rough and raucous talk and be in all respects a truly All-American girl." In an effort to refine players' conduct and appearance, charm school modeled the standards presented by the rules of conduct.

The success of the rules of conduct, uniform design, and charm school in obtaining these purposes is debatable. All were successful as a means of transmitting femininity to the public, and players generally abided by the rules and standards of femininity the league set out for them, as witnessed by Vivian Kellogg, a member of the Fort Wayne Daisies, who kept several scrapbooks of her years in the league. Her photos show players abiding by the rules of conduct, dressed in skirts with perfectly done hair when venturing out on the town.[10] Kellogg's remembrances are supported by Kenosha Comets player Lefty Hohlmayer, who recalled, "When we went out in public, we thought about what we had learned. We wore make-up, we crossed our legs, and we acted like ladies."[11]

Many players followed the rules not to help portray the femininity of the league but because of their commitment to being baseball players and athletes. The schedule of an All-American player was grueling. Every day of the week, players had some type of baseball commitment which generally came down to practice in the morning and games at night. Games were scheduled six to seven days a week, sometimes as doubleheaders. Days off were spent traveling. Maxine Kline, a Fort Wayne Daisy, was vigilant in her pregame preparation:

If it was the day and the night off before when I knew I was gonna pitch, I'd go to bed, and I could see them girls I had to face, and every pitch. The day I pitched I didn't want to do nothin', no physical stuff, like the laundry or wash the car. I just wanted to lay around. Because I didn't weigh very much and I needed all the strength I had![12]

Players took the league very seriously, conscious of both the mental and physical preparations necessary to perform at peak ability. Chaperone Helen Hannah observed, "The thing was that they were so involved in baseball, it didn't enter most of their minds to be rambunctious or boisterous or out of line."[13] Even known prankster Pepper Paire from the Grand Rapids Chicks succinctly stated, "Baseball always came first."[14]

Players were aware of how drinking, smoking, and lack of sleep could affect their quality of play. In Racine Belle Betty Russell's diary of the 1946 season, for example, the focus of her writing was on baseball—the scores of the games, good plays made, and players on hitting streaks. She occasionally mentioned going out for "a little beer," but her accounts focused primarily on baseball.[15]

If the girls' cognizance of their roles as athletes often kept them from breaking the rules, pictures of the players from an off-season trip to California show a different side. The players wore shorts and pants with their hair pulled back in ponytails and very little makeup.[16] While this normally would be unacceptable league behavior, since it was done in the off-season, and out of the eyes of the public, the players were not fined. Still, an incongruity existed between rule enforcement depending on the public's knowledge of the infraction. The same inconsistency between standards of public and private behavior held for the girls' appearance on road trips. It was not uncommon for players to dress in slacks on the bus or in the hotel. This disparity of enforcement shows the league was not concerned so much with the players *being* ladies but rather *looking* like ladies to the public. Whether or not the girls followed these steps was not as important as the public knowing that they had been taught these rules.

The AAGPBL players, however, did not let the rules of conduct inhibit their performance as athletes. The women most typically challenged these codes when playing the game. Players' fierce competitiveness and desire to win often challenged their ability to remain reserved. The rules kept the women from becoming overly confrontational and rude on the field, but the restrictions did not prevent them from showing their competitiveness during contests. Newspapers reported players arguing with umpires over calls, much to the fans' amusement.[17] While such displays of emotion were a departure from the rules of conduct, they added entertainment value to the games and demonstrated the authenticity of the rivalries. Despite their entertainment value, players received heavy fines and suspensions for such behavior because it constituted a public infraction of the rules.

In the founding of the AAGPBL, league organizers stressed the primacy of image to its success. The rules of conduct, uniforms, and charm school were all methods of creating an image of what the league thought the public would receive as an acceptable image of a woman baseball player. Organizers repeatedly stressed that "[w]e will select the kind of players that people will want to see in action. Then we will groom them, to make sure they are acceptable."[18]

The league's construction and policies of image creation were not necessarily driven by the league's personal beliefs about gender, implicitly, but the league conformed to traditional expectations, did nothing to challenge traditional notions of gendered behavior. The league continued to perpetuate the dichotomy of gender roles with a heavy focus on the "femininity principle," allowing a woman to be an athlete only if she still appeared feminine. The league's strategy mirrors feminist historian Janet Felshin's concept of the "female apologetic." Felshin argues that women in sport can compete at the level of men, but they still must look feminine, thus reassuring both participants and others that sport participation does not interfere with being a real woman.[19]

IMAGE WAS QUEEN

Once the league was conceived, communication of its image and product was the next essential step in the AAGPBL's road to public acceptance and success. The league's advertising and promotional campaign strategy was three-prong. In each city the league entered, whether for an exhibition game or to establish a permanent team, it followed roughly the same pattern of promotion, reception, and acceptance of the players' femininity and playing ability.[20] The advertising and press purpose was foremost to inform the public that the league existed and when and where the league games would be played in partial and full page ads.[21] Some teams issued matchbooks with the printed schedules,[22] while others posted easels in hotels that displayed large glossy action shots of the players for guests seeking local entertainment.[23] In addition to newspaper and magazine advertisements, teams ran promotional gimmicks to attract fans to the stadium on certain nights. One might hear an orchestra at a pre-game show in Minneapolis,[24] enjoy Ladies Night[25] and mimes[26] in Kenosha, or see Swedish gymnastics in Peoria.[27] Cinema was also used in 1947, when the league released a short feature film called "Diamond Gals."[28]

The publicity's second task was to broadcast assurances to the public of the player's femininity. In the local media, the first article announced the league's arrival and explained the league's philosophy. The women's uniforms, the rules of conduct, and charm school were often the first issues touched upon by sportswriters. It was in these initial introduction/announcement articles, in the headlines, captions, and opening paragraphs, that women's femininity, rather than their ability, was highlighted. Instead of action shots, photos showed the players fixing their hair or touching up lipstick.[29] Writers used mostly feminine adjectives and sexual imagery, such as "Glamour League," "home town cuties," or a "sweet young thing" to describe players.[30]

Sex, undoubtedly, was a part, but not the main emphasis of this femininity. While previous women's softball and baseball leagues underwent public rebuking of their sexuality, the players in the AAGPBL were presented as acceptable and desirable examples. For example, in a 1944 issue of *Esquire*, a Vargas girl appeared dressed as an AAGPBL player, accompanied by a poem:

> The war has made some changes
> In our nation's fav'rite game.
> For 'teen age kids are making
> A bid for baseball fame.
> And though these "All-American Boys"
> Will star as sure as fate,
> We'll add an "All-American Babe"
> And overflow the gate![31]

The inclusion of an iconic AAGPBL player in *Esquire* demonstrates how the public received the idea of the woman ballplayer as an acceptable addition to American society. League publicity was successful in selling the players as women, opening the door for the public to then see them as baseball players.

The more ridiculous images and bylines of the women from the initial announcement articles are often the most reproduced and discussed scholarship relating to the league, but they are not representative of the vast majority of newspaper and magazine stories written. The final aim of the league advertising campaign was to legitimize the girls as ballplayers. After its initial femininity laden story, the press shifted its reporting away from the mention of gender while mimicking traditional sports coverage. In league flyers and programs, images of players always showed them in action shots, highlighting the players' ability as ballplayers.

Local papers also carried daily stories about league games, well beyond just the box score. The *Kenosha News* often ran stories about other teams in the league as well as the Comets. Stories focused on the home team's progress, along with league standings and features on individuals. In a feature in *American Magazine*, Dotty Kamenshek was described as "a flawless fielder" and "at one time or another during the last seven years, she has led the league in just about every department."[32] Photographs of the players showed them in action poses, running, catching, and batting like their male counterparts. This serious press coverage highlighted the women's athletic abilities instead of their appearance.

ACCEPTANCE

The public openly accepted this dichotomy. They enjoyed the players' femininity along with their skill and did not misconstrue the players as sexual objects. Sports analyst E. W. Moss best described the public reception of the league's combination of images:

> If by "sex" some kind of burlesque is inferred the opinion would not
> be further from the truth . . . there was not the slightest evidence of sex
> exploitation in any phase of club management or individual conduct—
> not even so little as a piece of lipstick. Apparently these young women
> had been instructed that they were expected to maintain the dignity
> of their sex and American standards of sportsmanship, and so, true to
> the feminine protective instincts they did . . . crowds did not indulge in
> indignities. The players did not reflect sex-consciousness. If by "sex" is
> meant the normal appeal of the feminine mode and attention then most
> certainly reaction was an important source of interest and legitimate ele-
> ment of the league's success. The subtlety of the influence was manifest
> in the vehement denials from officials and fans that sex entered in to the
> game at all . . . reception accorded the player of grace and charm with
> that of the ugly duckling of less feminine if more robust skill.[33]

Moss's description solidifies the public's reception of the woman ball player as no longer deviant. While the Bloomer Girl professional softball players had often been referred to as "burlesque," Moss saw the AAGPBL players as "maintain[ing] the dignity of their sex and American standards of sports-manship." The players are not "sexy"; they possess "grace and charm." The crowd respected the women as players, and it is clear that they valued the women for more than their attractive appearance.

The AAGPBL backed up its publicity and flashy image with a quality com-petitive product. In many cities, the price for admission to AAGPBL games was equal to that of the minor league games. As one sportswriter summed up, "These girls . . . have won themselves the acclamation, admiration and intense interest of many people who would ordinarily not cross the street to see a game of baseball."[34] Ninety-three percent of fans felt that the league's talent was excellent, competitive, and professional.[35]

The four-team league drew only 176,612 fans in 1943. Attendance increased to 259,000 with a six-team league in 1944, continued to increase in 1945 to 450,313, and a blossoming eight-team league in 1946 drew 754,000 fans.[36] The league set its peak attendance records in 1948 with close to 1,000,000 fans.[37] Newspapers told of the league's burgeoning success in more colorful terms. In a 1949 article appearing in *Collier's* magazine, one writer extolled, "Talk about crowds—why, some towns draw four times their population every season. If the New York Yankees stirred up that kind of excitement, they'd draw 32,000,000 fans, instead of 2,000,000."[38] *American Magazine* proclaimed, "Not so long ago girls' baseball rated along with checkers for spectator interest. Now there are nights when you have to stand up in the back to see what is going on at the plate."[39] The public, and the media, accepted the women as highly skilled ballplayers, in many cases equal to that of the male players.

Unlike women's softball and baseball teams from the late nineteenth century to the 1930s, for the first time the AAGPBL's unique structure initiated a brand of popular and respected women's baseball into American society. The image of the "lady ballplayer" became not only an acceptable but also a successful role for women. The media, and America in general, welcomed the girls of the AAGPBL as highly skilled and legitimate athletes. Although marketing was vital to the league's initial acceptance by the public, the league did not survive for more than a decade because of its feminine image. It survived because of the women's skills as excellent ballplayers.

ROSIE IN SPIKES

Discussion of the AAGPBL and the image of womanhood it promoted is not complete without acknowledgment of its historical context and reference to the image and phenomenon of "Rosie the Riveter." Like many of the women on the home front who were called to replace men in factories during the World War II era, women were called to the AAGPBL to replace men as the nation's athletic entertainers. Set against World War II and Rosie the Riveter, the AAGPBL's "Rosie the Infielder" gains larger historical significance as a part of the women's wartime movement into the workforce. This analysis is complicated, however, by the AAGPBL's continued existence a decade after the conclusion of the war. While the public image of Rosie the Riveter disappeared after the war's conclusion, the woman player did not because of the successful management of the league's reputation to fit with postwar value systems.

The theme of patriotism and service to the war effort permeated early aspects of the AAGPBL. In a league memorandum dated December 12, 1942, the promotional theme was stated as "patriotic service in building morale" with an emphasis on serving the country.[40] At the beginning of each game, players would run onto the field in a "V for victory" formation during the national anthem.[41] League-sponsored promotions often granted members of service organizations or the Red Cross free admission to games.[42] Games also at times doubled as recruiting drives for blood donations or for joining war service organizations.[43] League exhibitions were held on military bases as entertainment for soldiers, with postgame dances and players visiting with wounded soldiers the typical outcome.[44] Racine Belle player Sophie Kurys remembered, "When we first started playing, the war was on, of course, and it was felt that we should entertain the soldiers, which we were perfectly glad to do. So we went to the various army camps in Wisconsin and Illinois."[45]

Teams themselves bought war bonds and ran drives to support the war effort.[46] A radio program reported, "The entire Minneapolis girls Ball Club went 100% for war bonds in this 5th War Bond Drive. Every girl bought a bond."[47] Individual players, such as Dottie Green, also contributed to the patriotic flavor of the early league years. Green wrote to more than eighty servicemen and threw a party for each serviceman from her hometown.[48]

Women's war work was never viewed as a permanent phenomenon by the recruiters or society at large. It was seen as an emergency wartime solution that mandated a temporary readjustment in gender roles. It was the widespread belief that women would quietly and willingly withdraw from the labor force once the war concluded, and therefore their new roles posed no threat.[49]

The initial inspiration for the development of the AAGPBL happened within the same context. More than three thousand male baseball players joined the service or did war-related work, significantly depleting the number of minor league teams.[50] Anticipating an MLB shutdown, Wrigley drew inspiration from the entry of women into factory work, and envisioned a women's league as a temporary replacement for men's baseball.[51] When MLB decided not to suspend operations, Wrigley did not abandon the idea of a women's league and shifted his focus away from it as a temporary replacement. Wrigley envisioned the league being a permanent staple in American sports entertainment. Unlike the Rosie the Riveter situation, it was never assumed that Rosie the Infielder would retire when the war was over.

When the war ended in 1945, women were fired from their industry jobs, and women's wages decreased as production halted and soldiers returned from war needing employment. The media dropped the image of Rosie the Riveter and pushed to humble women back into a domestic role. Television, magazines, and newspapers focused on the prewar traditional conceptions of womanhood. Advice shifted from negotiating factory life to being an excellent housekeeper, mother, and wife. *Look* magazine articulated this national shift: "no longer a psychological immigrant to man's world, she works . . . less toward a big career than as a way of filling a hope chest or buying a new home freezer. She gracefully concedes the top job rungs to men."[52] Postwar marriage and birth rate numbers skyrocketed, and the public image of womanhood shifted from the powerful Rosie the Riveter to the safe and submissive June Cleaver.[53] A 1955 report done by the Commission on the Education of Women stated, "Almost without exception, women consider marriage, homemaking and child rearing as major goals and responsibilities."[54]

Media messages were also latent with cautionary and threatening warnings of what would happen to America if women did not return to traditional roles. This is especially seen in the fears of juvenile delinquency that became rampant postwar. Working and raising children were seen as incompatible roles for a woman. When the mother was at work, it was believed that the uncared-for children would turn to delinquency. The restrengthening of family ties evoked a safe fortress of regularity for America.[55] Returning women to the home as caretakers marked a return to normalcy for the United States.[56]

The accuracy of the June Cleaver image as a reflection of women's postwar lives is questionable.[57] While wages and flexibility in employment drastically declined postwar, overall women's employment figures stayed stable. Many women did not leave their jobs willingly. One housewife employed as a valve maker remarked, "Speaking for myself, I shall be sorry to leave my job . . . I have not enough to do to occupy me intelligently in the house."[58] Of importance in understanding the evolution of the reputation of the AAGPBL is not whether women's postwar lives returned to traditional ideals, but the change of the public image of what "womanhood" consisted of in a postwar world. Rosie the Riveter died, while the image of the AAGPBL player remained vital for nearly another decade. Why was Rosie the Infielder able to survive while the Riveter did not?

THE NEW LOOK OF THE ALL-AMERICAN BALLPLAYER

Upon the war's conclusion, the AAGPBL quickly shifted its image from a national symbol of patriotism to a local medium for community development.

A 1947 article in *Forbes* magazine extolled the AAGPBL's community-driven virtues. It stated that the league had "resulted in notably heightened enthusiasm among plant workers and their families, new town pride and all-around friendliness, and a sharp cut in juvenile delinquency," which created "a terrific new community spirit. It makes adults and youngsters proud to live here."[59] An advertisement in the Peoria yearbook read, "Hats off to the Red Wings, Win or Lose. All Peoria is loyal to our Redwings. We like their spirit. We cheer their sparkling plays. Their will to win deserves our admiration. For they bring to our community a spirit of teamwork. And that's good for Peoria—good for all of America too!"[60]

Similarly, the Lassies were described as being "a tempering force in the community and a binding influence between Muskegon and Muskegon Heights—two cities that in other respects are warm rivals."[61] The league was able to take the feminine baseball player, a departure from traditional roles of femininity, and recast her as a part of the growing Cold War media focus on local community.

As the postwar center of each midsized Midwestern town's identity, the AAGPBL team worked in service to the community. The AAGPBL's message of community support began with emphasizing the locally owned, organized, and nonprofit nature of the clubs. A Roman Catholic parish operated the Chicago Colleens,[62] and other local Kiwanis Clubs sponsored other teams.[63] The AAGPBL ran various promotions and sponsored events to make the teams the center of local social gatherings and entertainment. Teams sponsored parades and contests before games,[64] and fans were responsible for voting for all-star teams.[65] Fort Wayne ran a contest to create its team's mascot,[66] and Rockford issued a motor vehicle tax stamp featuring the team logo.[67] The All-Americans further strengthened ties and identity to the town by living with families.[68] In return, communities rallied around the players when they were in need. When Ruth Ricard broke her ankle one season, fans raised more than six hundred dollars to help pay for her medical expenses.[69]

Teams organized local business clinics for young boys and girls to focus on serving younger fans. Youth leagues and junior teams, such as the Racine Junior Belles, played before the All-American games and were aimed to increase youth involvement in sport.[70] The Kenosha Comets went several steps further by creating youth usherettes to help with duties around the ballpark and a special fan club called the Knot Hole Gang.[71] As the heroes, role models, and big sisters of each community, the AAGPBL was deemed the "panaceas for the ills of juvenile delinquency,"[72] saving communities from the much-feared fate of youth in postwar society.

Changes were also made in terms of the reputation of players as examples of femininity to that of "All-American" girls. James Henderson, sports editor of the *Muskegon Chronicle*, touted the players as being examples of the "average North American womanhood" because they were "rough only in the way they hit the ball, stole bases, fielded and threw."[73] The league claimed the players were "typical American girls, school teachers, physical education teachers and students, high school and college students, clerks, models, librarians, secretaries and office or factory workers in the off-season."[74]

In a 1944 radio program script entitled *Calling All Women*, three players, Helen Callaghan, Annabelle Lee, and Vivian Kellogg, were interviewed by host Darragh Aldrich. Aldrich began, "I'd like to say to our listeners that, despite backgrounds, (Irish, California, Michigan) they are All-American looking girls, fresh out of door complexions, sparkling eyes and all the vigor and enthusiasm that goes with being barely twenty." Aldrich closed by thanking the girls for "showing [listeners] that real American girls . . . can carry on as a team in the best tradition of American sportsmanship—and still be natural, attractive, feminine and likeable girls that brothers in service will be proud of when they return."[75] Rosie the Infielder was not just a war heroine; she was also an All-American Girl. The reputation of players as All-American Girls served as a compatible ideal in a postwar community-driven ideology. Communities responded well and embraced the league until the mid-1950s because the AAGPBL was able to play into the newly accepted images of womanhood instead of threatening them.

DENOUNCEMENT

The AAGPBL, in its official construction, ended in 1954. Several reasons are cited for the league's closing. Players Mary Pratt and Pat Brown believed individual clubs' financial difficulties, the rejuvenation of the minor leagues, the popularity of television, a shortage of talented players, and a shift in the availability of recreational activities were reasons for the league's ending.[76] Women's sports and league historians' arguments cite similar reasons.[77]

Surprisingly, despite the league's popularity during its operational years, once it ended, the reputation and memory of the league faded. Player Nickie Fox candidly stated, "In 1954, when the league ended, it fell off the face of the earth."[78] Players, for the most part, did not talk about their experiences once they returned home. "You see, when I quit and came home I never said anything to anybody because nobody believed that there was a girls' baseball team," Vivian Kellogg recounted. "And so rather than be embarrassed by talking of something that it seemed no one heard of, I never said anything."[79] When players did speak of their experiences, Pepper Paire remembered, conversations often followed the same pattern:

> I stopped talking about our league for a long time, because whenever people would be talking about baseball, someone would ask me how I knew so much about the game, and I'd say, "Well, I played girls' professional baseball years ago." And they'd say, "You mean softball?" I'd say, "No, I mean baseball." And they'd do a double-take and say, "You mean softball." And I'd say again, "No, I mean baseball." And after I'd say it about the fourth or fifth time, they'd say, "You mean ... *baseball*? Like *men's* baseball? Like with a hardball?" And from the look in their eyes, I could see that they still didn't believe me. You can look 'em right in the eye and say "baseball," and they'll look back and say "softball." Well, you get tired of doing that, and I can't carry my scrapbooks around my back.[80]

While the thirty-year loss of consciousness about the league stands as a great disservice to the women of the league, it also allowed for the modern preservation of the league's image. Absent from the discourse of second-wave feminism struggle for women's rights in employment, education, and reproduction, the league remained separate from controversy and conflict. A 1976 master's thesis by former player Merrie Fidler was the first piece of writing done on the league since its conclusion, and marked the first interest in reviving the league's history. Fidler's thesis, "The Development and Decline of the All-American Girls Baseball League, 1943–1954," laid out a detailed history of the league's development and organization.[81]

Short books and articles by Sue Macy, Sharon Roepke, and Jack Fincher further represent the limited interest expressed in the league during the eighties, and their analyses did not move far beyond Fidler's work.[82] In the early eighties, however, players themselves also started to recongregate, hosting reunions and exhibitions. The creation of a documentary on the league in 1987 by Kelly Candaele, brother of MLB player Casey Candaele and son of AAGPBL player Helen Callaghan, was a catalyst for the true reemergence of the league. Filmmaker Candaele states, "I was taught, in high school in the late 60s, that women were only entering forcefully into athletics for 'the first time.' This 'great advance' seemed rather quizzical to me, given my mother's experience. My friend Kim Wilson and I wanted to set history straight."[83]

IN A LEAGUE OF THEIR OWN

The documentary provided the groundwork for the opening of the 1988 Baseball Hall of Fame *Women in Baseball* exhibit, which then ultimately provided the inspiration for the release of Penny Marshall's Hollywood 1992 film, *A League of Their Own*. The blockbuster film, with a $40 million budget, was a box-office success, grossing more than $107 million in the United States in spite of the fact that the fund-raising to get the film under way was quite difficult because of what was perceived to be unsupportive content.[84] Nevertheless, forty years after its conclusion, and twenty years after the passage of Title IX, the league reentered popular consciousness.

The film's release generated a revived interest in the league, and hundreds of newspaper and magazine stories examining the AAGPBL appeared in media across the country. From this interest, a large body of interviews and records of the women's accounts of their league experiences exists. While these accounts are useful to a degree, the players have developed a collective consciousness of their experiences.[85] Outspoken player Faye Dancer commented, "Now I'm on the board of directors of the All-American Girls Baseball Association (AAGBA). They said, 'When you give people an interview, why don't you leave out the beer? People will think everybody in the league drank.'"[86] As a general rule, players will not broach topics they believe might discolor the reputation and memory of the league, such as sexuality and drinking. In one study of the league, researchers commented, "The reluctance to answer some of the questions could have stemmed from the players' fierce protectiveness of the league and their desire not to be misrepresented in any way."[87] This poses a great challenge to scholars looking to examine the diversity of player's experiences and to broach topics not yet covered by the media.

In addition to scholarly interest, popular reporting on the league continued after the release of *A League of Their Own*. The movie was essential in revisiting if not re-creating the modern reputation of the league and in reviving the postwar image of the league in many ways. Players frequently make appearances at public events both large and small, ranging from minor and major league baseball games to local historical society meetings. The 1992 All-Star Game FanFest included Lefty Hohlmayer as a featured celebrity athlete.[88] Players have been inducted into local and state halls of fame, have been the subjects of museum exhibits, and have had schools and playgrounds named after them. Players' obituaries are also frequently featured in local and national newspapers.

As a whole, the reputation of the AAGPBL player is fascinating because it is an instance of positive representation of women athletes in the national consciousness. The AAGPBL's reputation has evolved throughout many decades as a reflection of American values.

NOTES

1. Quoted in Sue Macy, *A Whole New Ball Game: The Story of the All-American Girls Professional Baseball League* (New York: Henry Holt and Company, 1993), 18.

2. Quoted in Susan E. Johnson, *When Women Played Hardball* (Seattle: Seal Press, 1994),150.

3. Faye Dancer and John B. Holway, "Confessions of an All-American Girl," *Nine* 8, no. 2 (2001): 267.

4. All-American Girls Professional Baseball League, "Rules of Conduct," All-American Girls Professional Baseball League Homepage, n.d., http://www.aagpbl.org/history/hist_rc.html (December 15, 2003).

5. Quoted in Johnson, *When Women Played Hardball*, 156.

6. AAGPBL, "Rules of Conduct." Emphasis is original.

7. John W. Bailey, *Kenosha Comets: 1943–1951* (Kenosha: Badger Press, 1997), 2.

8. Quoted in Lois Browne, *Girls of Summer: In Their Own League* (Toronto: Harper Collins, 1992), preface.

9. Ester Sherman, "A Guide for All-American Girls: How to Look Better, Feel Better, Be More Popular," National Baseball Hall of Fame Library, Cooperstown, New York, n.d.

10. *Vivian Kellogg Scrapbook*, Vol.1, National Baseball Hall of Fame Library, Cooperstown, New York, n.d.

11. Quoted in Jeff Neilsen, "Belles of the Ball Game," *Ohio State Alumni Magazine* (June/July/August 2000), 28.

12. Johnson, *When Women Played Hardball*, 134.

13. Macy, *A Whole New Ball Game*, 71.

14. Ibid., 73.

15. *Betty Russell Diary*, National Baseball Hall of Fame Library, Cooperstown, New York, 1946.

16. *Vivian Kellogg Scrapbook*, Vol. 1.

17. Eddie McKenna, "Umpire Ousts Racine Players Riotous 6 to 2 Win Over Comets," *Kenosha Evening News*, July 8, 1948 (n. p.; *Vivian Kellogg Scrapbook*, Vol.1).

18. Browne, *Girls of Summer*, preface.

19. Janet J. Felshin, "The Triple Option . . . Women in Sports," *Quest* 21 (1974): 36–40.

20. This analysis is based on general conclusions drawn from an examination of the entirety of primary sources about the league, from both national and local press coverage. This press spans all years of the league and is drawn from many different locations. The bulk of local sources came from hundreds of newspaper clippings in *Audrey Wagner Scrapbook* and *Vivian Kellogg Scrapbook*.

21. Samples in *Audrey Wagner Scrapbook*, Vol. 1.

22. Macy, *A Whole New Ball Game*, 81.

23. "Tagging All the Bases in AAGPBL," *Kenosha Evening News*, July 1, 1948 (*Audrey Wagner Scrapbook*, Vol. 1).

24. "Baseball, Maestro, Please," *Time*, July 31, 1944, 40.

25. "Revise Comets July Schedule," *Kenosha Evening News*, July 2, 1948 (*Audrey Wagner Scrapbook*, Vol. 1).

26. "Arabella Opps, A Schacht of Girls' Baseball Makes Appearance at Comets Game Here Tomorrow," *Kenosha Evening News*, June 5, 1948 (*Audrey Wagner Scrapbook*, Vol. 1).

27. "5,445 See Peoria Topple Comets," *Kenosha Evening News* (*Audrey Wagner Scrapbook*, Vol. 1, National Baseball Hall of Fame Library, Cooperstown, New York).

28. J. F. Henderson, "The Press Box," (*Audrey Wagner Scrapbook*, Vol. 1).

29. *Vivian Kellogg Scrapbook*, Vol. 1.

30. Jack Stenbuck, "Glamour Girls of Big-League Ball," *Magazine Digest,* July 1946, 70.

31. Phil Stack, "All-American Babe," *Esquire*, September 1944, *Vivian Kellogg Scrapbook*, Vol. 1.

32. "Dotty Is a Slugger," *American Magazine*, August 1950, 57.

33. E. W. Moss, "Comparative Figures for Three Competing Classes of Baseball," *Baseball Blue Book Supplement #9* (Fort Wayne: Heibbroner, Baseball Bureau, 1945), 4–5.

34. Prudie M. Bretting, "Leave It to the Girls," *1948 Muskegon Lassies Year Book*, March 25, 2004, www.aagpbl.org/articles/art_lg.html (December 15, 2003).

35. Karen H. Weiller and Catriona T. Higgs, "Fandom in the 40's: The Integrating Functions of All-American Girls Professional Baseball League," *Journal of Sport Behavior*, 20, no. 2 (1997): 211–221.

36. Norman Klein, "Baseball—Business Booster," *Forbes*, April 1, 1947, 21.

37. Quoted in Jeneane Lesko, Jean Cione, and Sue Macy, "League History," All-American Girls Professional Baseball Homepage, n.d., http://www.aagpbl.org/history/History_1.html (December 15, 2003).

38. Bill Fay, "Belles of the Ball Game," *Collier's*, August 13, 1949, 44.

39. James Gordon, "Beauty at Bat," *American Magazine*, June 1945, 24–25.

40. Sharon L. Roepke, *Diamond Gals: The Story of the All-American Girls Professional Baseball League* (Marcellus: A.A.G.P.B.L. Cards, 1986), 6.

41. *Vivian Kellogg Scrapbook*, Vol.1.

42. Macy, *A Whole New Ball Game*, 35; Lois Browne, *Girls of Summer: In Their Own League* (Toronto: Harper Collins, 1992), 47.

43. Macy, *A Whole New Ball Game*, 35.

44. "Wounded Vets Like Lassies, More to Come" *Muskegon Chronicle*, July 24, 1947, 24.

45. Quoted in Jay Feldman, "Glamour Ball," *Sports Heritage*, May/June 1987, 62.

46. Browne, *Girls of Summer*, 90.

47. 1944 transcript of Minneapolis radio broadcast, *Vivian Kellogg Scrapbook*, Vol. 1.

48. Marie Keenan, *All-American Girls Mailbag,* (AAGM), 1944–45, *Vivian Kellogg Scrapbook*, Vol. 1. The All-American Girls Mailbag was a letter sent out to players frequently during the off-season to keep them updated with league news and activities of fellow players. It was written by Marie Keenan, the league secretary.

49. Susan Hartmann, *The Homefront and Beyond: American Women in the 1940s* (Boston: Twayne Publishers, 1982), 22.

50. Bailey, *Kenosha Comets*, 1.

51. Ed Burns, "Wrigley and Rickey Buddies in Softball," *The Sporting News*, February 25, 1943.

52. Laura Berquist, "A New Look at the American Woman," *Look*, October 16, 1956, 3.

53. Ibid., 163, 189.

54. Quoted in Brett Harvey, *The Fifties: A Women's Oral History* (New York: HarperCollins Publishers, 1993), 51.

55. Elaine Taylor May, *Homeward Bound: American Families in the Cold War Era* (New York: Basic Books, 1999).

56. Maureen Honey, *Creating Rosie the Riveter: Class, Gender and Propaganda during WWII* (Amherst: University of Massachusetts Press, 1984), 7.

57. Susan Hartmann, "Women's Employment and the Domestic Ideal in the Early Cold War Years," in *Not June Cleaver: Women and Gender in Postwar America, 1945–1960*, ed. Joanne Meyerowitz (Philadelphia: Temple University Press, 1994), 84–102.

58. Quoted in Dorothy Sheridan, *Wartime Women: A Mass-Observation Anthology* (London: Phoenix Press, 2000), 217.

59. Norma Klein, "Baseball—Business Booster," *Forbes*, April 1, 1974, 21.

60. *1949 Peoria Year Book* ad from Caterpillar Inc., in Macy, *A Whole New Ball Game*, 77.

61. Bretting, "Leave It to the Girls."

62. Roepke, *Diamond Gals*, 146.

63. "Comets Rained Out, South Bend Grand Rapids Winners," *Kenosha Evening News*, May 24, 1946 (*Audrey Wagner Scrapbook*, Vol. 1)

64. "All-American Game Tonight in Lure for Baseball Fans Here" (publication not identified; article found in *Vivian Kellogg Scrapbook*, Vol. 1).

65. "Pick 'Most Valuable' Comet Wednesday at 'Eagle Club Night'" (publication not identified; article found in *Audrey Wagner Scrapbook*, Vol. 1).

66. *Vivian Kellogg Scrapbook*, Vol. 1.

67. Carl L. Biemiller, "World's Prettiest Ball Players," *Holiday Magazine*, July 1952, 50.

68. Ibid., 82.

69. Macy, *A Whole New Ball Game*, 78.

70. "Comets Teach KYF GBL Players," *Kenosha Evening News*, August 7, 1948 (*Audrey Wagner Scrapbook*).

71. Browne, *Girls of Summer*, 102; *Audrey Wagner Scrapbook*, Vol. 4.

72. Bretting, "Leave It to the Girls."

73. James F. Henderson, "A New American Sport," *1947 Muskegon Lassies Year Book*, March 25, 2004, www.aagpbl.org/articles/art_ns.html (December 15, 2003).

74. "All-American Girls' Baseball League—Its History in Brief—1943 to 1946," *1947 Fort Wayne Daisies Year Book*, March 25, 2004, www.aagpbl.org/articles/arti_bh.html (December 15, 2003).

75. 1944 transcript of Minneapolis radio broadcast, *Vivian Kellogg Scrapbook*, Vol. 1.

76. Brown, *Girls of Summer*, 148, 149, 150; Mary Pratt, *Preserving Our Legacy: A Peach of a Game*, 2004 (self-published autobiography), 126 (in National Baseball Hall of Fame and Library).

77. Susan K. Cahn, *Coming on Strong* (Seattle: Free Press, 1994), 160; Debra Shattuck, "Playing a Man's Game: Women and Baseball in the United States, 1866–1954," in *Baseball History from Outside the Lines: A Reader*, ed. John E. Dreifort (Lincoln: University of Nebraska Press, 2001), 195–215.

78. Johnson, *When Women Played Hardball*, xv.

79. Ibid., xvi.

80. Feldman, "Glamour Ball," 68.

81. Merrie Fidler, "The Development and Decline of the All-American Girls Baseball League, 1943–1954," master's thesis, University of Massachusetts, 1976.

82. Sue Macy, "War, Women and Professional Baseball," *Scholastic Search*, April 30, 1982, 8–11; Roepke, *Diamond Gals*; Jay Fincher, "The 'Belles of the Ball Game' Were a Hit with Their Fans," *Smithsonian*, July 1989, 88–97.

83. Kelly Candaele, "Mom Was in a League of Her Own," *New York Times*, June 7, 1992, S9.

84. "The Last Time the Bucs Beat .500," *Pittsburgh Tribune-Review*, June 5, 2009, http://www.pittsburghlive.com/x/pittsburghtrib/news/pittsburgh/s_632297.html (June 30, 2011).

85. While I was at the Baseball Hall of Fame Archives in Cooperstown, NY, I had a conversation with the AAGPBL specialist, Tim Wiles. When I mentioned this observation to him, he agreed, saying his experiences in talking and interviewing players have been very similar.

86. Dancer and Holway, "Confessions of an All-American Girl," 267.

87. Karen H. Weiller and Catriona T. Higgs, "The All-American Girls Professional Baseball League, 1943–54: Gender Conflict in Sport?," *Sociology of Sport Journal* 11, no. 3 (1994): 292.

88. Associated Press, "FanFest Has All a Fan Desires," *San Francisco Chronicle*, July 15, 1992, C4.

THE WOMAN WHO SHOULD BE KING

The Simplification of the Life and Career of Billie Jean King

—ELIZABETH O'CONNELL

INTRODUCTION

In her 1982 autobiography, tennis star Billie Jean King candidly expressed concern for her reputation. Written in the aftermath of the palimony suit filed against her by Marilyn Barnett, King claimed that unlike other tennis champions, including Björn Borg and Chris Evert, she had never much concerned herself with the way she would be remembered. Faced with the waning days of her professional career, however, King was worried that her name would forever be associated with a lesbian love affair and not her pioneering days as a women's tennis champion.[1]

The autobiography was part of a larger press tour King had undertaken after the palimony suit. Although she initially denied the affair, King opened up to reporters at a press conference, then later to Barbara Walters and others. Questions of sexuality had long plagued women's tennis, and she worried what impact the scandal would have on the sport she had done so much to promote.

In fact, the Barnett scandal had little lasting impact on women's tennis or Billie Jean King. King's reputation as a women's tennis trailblazer had already been well established, and the affair did not alter that. King thought revealing the affair at the end of her competitive career, when it would be difficult to change the story and people's associations, would damage the way she was remembered, but this actually played to her advantage. Although the events caused her to lose advertising revenue and be the source of debates about female sexuality in sport, they have been largely forgotten because of their chronological distance from the most memorable moments of her career. As a result, the discussion of Barnett and King's own sexuality was often absent in biographies and other writings about her.

Oddly, Billie Jean King's historical reputation would be formed around one singular event: her 1973 tennis match against Bobby Riggs. The $100,000 tennis spectacle, viewed by 48 million people, has been cited not only by sports scholars but also by those seeking to tell the story of the women's liberation movement. Additionally, biographers have treated the match as the climax of her competitive career, despite the many years of tournament and champion-ship tennis that followed. For these authors, her victory in the "Battle of the Sexes" cemented King's reputation as a defiant female athlete and "militant feminist," and the events that preceded or followed have been interpreted within the context of that one match.

As Gary Alan Fine argued in his study of controversial historical figures, a reputation is a "shared, established image . . . embedded within social rela-tions" and "connected to the forms of communication embedded within a community."[2] Because of her association with the women's movement, King was both a celebrity and political entity. As such, her reputation was con-structed by the larger media, and the spectacle of the Battle of the Sexes match—reaching far beyond the traditional tennis audience and imbued with meaning far greater than any other match she had played—became the basis of her reputation.

Yet this single event has overshadowed everything else in the King biog-raphy, and all other events have been recast in light of it. Fine demonstrated that historical reputations are built around people who seem to embody cer-tain moments, movements, and ideals, and are presented in largely uncon-troversial terms today, despite the discourse of their given time;[3] but it is necessary to complicate this historical understanding of Billie Jean King. As her reputation has been established and has evolved, it has been robbed of its complexity—that which made her so newsworthy in the first place. Billie Jean King's career, as it played out across the sports pages, challenged the public's notions of female athletes and raised questions about gender and sexuality at a time when women were redefining their roles in the larger social context. It is not surprising that she was cast as the "Joan of Arc" of women's tennis. What *is* surprising—and disappointing—is that the Joan of Arc reputation has been recast as an old-fashioned Horatio Alger story that became not so much about gender revolution as about economics. Rather than her story being seen in terms of women's liberation and gender equality (both of which remain contested), King is remembered for bringing parity to tennis's prize money.

The change in narrative also reflects the way we remember the wom-en's liberation movement. As Fine noted, history that is contested is either ignored or attempts are made to pacify the audience with a more neutral tale and analysis. Such has been the case with the women's movement: it is less understood in terms of women's independence than women's *economic* independence. In this context, the neutralized King narrative works well in affirming this collective memory. That Billie Jean King rose from humble origins to revolutionize women's tennis prize money and respectability is a convenient, applicable—if simplistic—tale.

YOU'VE COME A LONG WAY, BABY

Billie Jean King's life read differently in the sports pages during her career from that in biographies and historical accounts that followed. This is natural; newspapers lack the benefits of hindsight and the gift of foresight. Journalists were required to report the day's news, with no advanced knowledge of what the next day would bring, and, as King's career would demonstrate, even retirement announcements lacked certainty. Although there was some effort at "biography" in a typical news story—usually a paragraph to establish context—the journalists' efforts were aimed at conveying a particular story, and these descriptions often established public reputations and were later used by biographers to frame their work. For these reasons, the original sports pages are important in understanding how a reputation was created and evolved.

In the case of Billie Jean King, newspapers revealed not only the story of the woman who played in tennis's largest spectacle, but one whose life on and off the court engaged people in larger questions about gender and sexuality. By the time Bobby Riggs challenged her, King had already established herself as a dominant figure in her sport and an advocate of social change.

Because King was a pioneer in women's tennis, early sports coverage revealed traditional views of female athletes and attitudes toward femininity. Outside of the Olympics, few avenues were available for female athletes in large-scale competition, and even in those where women did compete, women were expected to maintain their femininity and not play "like men." However, Billie Jean King failed to conform to expectations, was known as a "chatterbox" on the court for constantly talking to herself, and was thought to play a "man's game" by aggressively playing the ball. These descriptions would go a long way in establishing her reputation, and were dominant throughout her career. For example, coverage of her Battle of the Sexes match with Bobby Riggs contrasted their playing styles in gendered terms (his feminine, hers masculine).[4] Additionally, Chris Evert's emergence in the early 1970s brought heavy comparisons between Evert and King, because of the young phenom's traditional femininity.

Evert's femininity was an important part of her identity and attracted attention from reporters—much to the chagrin of her competitors, who felt that her girlishness was seen in sharp contrast to them.[5] Articles about Evert routinely mentioned her grace and charm as well as her clothing and hair styles. Of this, King would later write:

> Chris has always possessed a certain self-consciousness about being a sweaty old jock, and so heightening the perception of her absolute femininity is important to her. And I sympathize with her, with all of us, in this respect. Female athletes are stereotyped by the general population, and usually as homosexuals. That is our bond. Not that we are homosexuals, but that we are stereotyped.[6]

King, who was once told she would succeed in tennis because she was "ugly," was acutely aware of the different way she was perceived by the press. "A really feminine lady player is supposed to have a certain kind of non-sweaty lady's manner, but I was the worst of both worlds," King wrote. "I not only had an aggressive net-rushing style, but I didn't look the part, the way someone stylishly long-legged like [Maria] Bueno did . . . So I was never described in ways that related to the female gender. No code words like cute or elegant were ever dragged up for Billie Jean King."[7] Indeed, King was more widely known for her thick glasses, struggles with her weight and her affinity for chocolate candy bars and ice cream than for grace and elegance on the court.

Further complicating matters, King's marriage was anything but conventional. Although the women's tournament purses were small at the start of her career, she continued playing nevertheless and financially supported her husband, Larry, as he studied law. When he completed law school, they lived apart, with Larry establishing himself in a Honolulu practice. Interestingly, some members of the press attempted to cast the marriage as traditional, if unusual. For example, in 1967, the *New York Times*' Dave Anderson wrote a tellingly titled article, "Billie Jean: Tennis Queen Who Obeys Her King," in which Larry, still a law student, was presented as a nonthreatened husband and Billie Jean as his nonthreatening wife. The text of the article was actually about Larry, his support of his wife's career, and his ambition, upon finishing law school, to organize tennis players into a union. There was nothing in the article—outside of its title—that suggested Billie Jean King was submissive to her husband.[8] Yet it was important to suggest that although she was supporting her marriage financially, this was only temporary, and the Kings' marriage was a partnership—not dominated by the female half—and likely to "normalize" upon Larry's graduation.

More frequently, Billie Jean was asked about her plans for children. She bristled at the question, often responding, "Why don't you ask Rod Laver why he isn't home?"[9] Of course, no one would think to ask Rod Laver because he was his family's breadwinner, and it was not necessary for him to put off a family in pursuit of his career. At the time, men's prize money was enough to raise a family—the same could not be said of women's tennis until Billie Jean King and several of her colleagues took a stand against "tradition," which in this case marked the beginning of the Virginia Slims tour.

THE VIRGINIA SLIMS TOUR

The Virginia Slims tour was founded in October 1970, when seven of the world's top ten players signed one-dollar contracts with *World Tennis* publisher Gloria Heldman to play in a tennis tournament in Houston sponsored by the Virginia Slims cigarette brand. The United States Lawn Tennis Association (USLTA), which had refused to sanction prize money for a women's tournament in Houston, responded by suspending the women from sanctioned non-open events and stripped them of their national rankings.

A leader in the tour's formation, Billie Jean King was no stranger to criticizing and defying USLTA practices—she regularly denounced what she called "shamateurism" (a practice of paying amateur tennis stars under the table for tournament appearances) in the days before open tennis, and was one of the first women to turn professional, signing a seventy-thousand-dollar contract with the National Tennis League in 1968.[10] Faced with USLTA demands that the women abandon the Houston tournament for a sanctioned event in Los Angeles, where the prize money ratio between men and women was twelve to one, King responded: "We're not telling the USLTA to get lost, but they didn't have a schedule for us from October through March." The women who signed with *World Tennis* were guaranteed at least five tournaments in the first step of what Heldman and the press would call "women's lob."[11]

The gamble proved worthwhile. Although it would attempt its own women's tour starring Evonne Goolagong and Chris Evert, the USLTA eventually settled with the popular Slims circuit.[12] Furthermore, the success of the women's tennis tour forced a reevaluation of female tennis stars' market value as professional athletes. Writing in February 1971, the *New York Times*' Neil Amdur commented: "Women's tennis, once known more for frilly frocks than crosscourt forehands and flat first serves, is achieving unparalleled growth, identity and unity as a professional sport." Amdur remarked that pride and unity were the outstanding characteristics of the women's tour and quoted King (whom he labeled the "Rod Laver of the women's tour"): "It's been the best thing that could have happened to us. The girls have more identity, we're finally being paid well, people are beginning to realize that we can hit a ball, and we don't puff up our attendance figures like they do on the men's circuit."[13]

Her participation and leadership in the Virginia Slims tour heightened King's status in American sports. In 1971, she became the first female athlete to earn one hundred thousand dollars in prize money, having won sixteen tournaments in the tour's first year. The following year, *Sports Illustrated* selected King as its first Sportswoman of the Year,[14] a tribute that reflected her position as one of the most celebrated and accomplished athletes in sports, as well as her reputation as a standard-bearer for female athletes. The Associated Press, covering the story, described King as having long "spoken and acted militantly for greater recognition of women in sports." The article continued, cynically, that "Mrs. King, who prefers Ms. in the best of women's liberation thinking, has been trying to change people's views for most of her tennis career . . . she tries to convince fans they can derive more enjoyment from watching women's tennis than men's."[15] This one sentence revealed much about King's reputation in the sports pages: first, her constant battle with the press to carve out an identity other than "Mrs. King"; second, her desire to demonstrate the market value of female athletes. It was this second point that would lead her to tennis's greatest spectacle, which ultimately shaped her legacy, if not her reputation.

THE BATTLE OF THE SEXES

In playing Bobby Riggs in the 1973 "Battle of the Sexes," Billie Jean King demonstrated that a female athlete could hold her own on the court against a male. That said, it was never King's stated intention. She frequently remarked that the age difference between Riggs and her (she was twenty-nine, he was fifty-five) was consequential, and that the top-ranked male tennis player could have—and probably would have—defeated the top-ranked female tennis player. For King, the match was about proving that audiences would be interested in watching women's tennis, a claim that detractors had often made about the Virginia Slims tour, and a justification tournaments used in offering smaller purses to women.

In this regard, Bobby Riggs became women's biggest tennis promoter, dressed in the guise of a male chauvinist. Interestingly, Riggs was quoted as supporting the idea of a women's tennis tour three years before the Slims tour came to fruition and six years before he began challenging its stars. In December 1967, when the Wimbledon tournament was declared an open tournament and Billie Jean King was still pondering life as a professional tennis player, Bobby Riggs said that although he had "no use for women's tennis at one time," he acknowledged the current crop of female athletes were indeed talented, noting, "I think people would pay to see them."[16] When the Virginia Slims tour proved Riggs right, he was eager to share in the profits.

Bobby Riggs was a tennis champion in the 1930s, but had made a much more profitable career as a hustler after his tournament years ended. He played matches in high heels while carrying a purse, with folding chairs in his half of the court, or while holding an umbrella in one hand at all times. He once even played a series of matches while holding dogs on a leash—initially poodles, then German shepherds, and eventually Great Danes (the last of whom were finally too much to control and play winning tennis at the same time).[17]

By the 1970s, Riggs began searching for a female tennis star to challenge in a high-stakes match. Although he had his sights set on King, she repeatedly refused, claiming that she was too busy with the tennis tour.

Initially unable to challenge King, Riggs instead took on her rival Margaret Smith Court, the Australian champion who was ranked first in 1973, and captured both the Australia and French Open titles in that year. The match, whose outcome relegated it to history as the predecessor to King's match against Riggs, aired to large audiences on Mother's Day in 1973.

Court did not take the match seriously, however, assuming that the aging hustler would not present much of a challenge. But Riggs, a relentless promoter, sensed that Court's weakness was not physical but emotional (she was not as aggressive or spirited as players such as King), and so he placed pressure on her in "carrying the banner for women all over the world" while declaring himself a "washed-up has-been with one foot in the grave."[18]

The match, later dubbed the Mother's Day Massacre, proved Riggs right. Court lost in straight sets, with the *New York Times*' Amdur commenting that "the match really ended at 3–0 in the first set. Riggs knew inside that he could not lose, and he played as if it [were] the greatest hustle of all time." In contrast, "Mrs. Court, a quiet, sincere Australian, never seemed comfortable from the time the match was announced until she curtsied after Riggs presented her with a bouquet of roses during the warmup." Organizers decided Margaret Court did not have the makeup to play such a high-stakes match within the circus-like atmosphere Riggs had created, and so there was no value in a rematch. To play Billie Jean King, however, would "rekindle some interest in this format, since Billie Jean, unlike Margaret, is at her best under pressure, talking away, even on the court."[19]

This time, King was the one to issue the challenge. She had not seen Court's match, but had heard about it while traveling home from a tournament in

Japan. "That score was just outrageous," King told reporters. "I heard that she really played awful. I felt the fans got cheated. People didn't see how well women can play." Although she insisted that the players on the Virginia Slims tour never claimed they could beat the men—only that they were as entertaining—King felt compelled to play Riggs in the aftermath of Court's defeat to demonstrate women's value to the televised audience.[20]

The match quickly became a spectacle, due to Riggs's successful lobbying of sponsors (including ABC, which televised the match), a profile on *60 Minutes*, as well as the covers of *Sports Illustrated* and *Time* magazine.[21] Scheduled in the Houston Astrodome on September 20, 1973, the "Battle of the Sexes" would be played for one hundred thousand dollars in prize money, plus another hundred thousand in ancillary rights from TV, radio, and films, making it the biggest payout in tennis history.

King was just as active as Riggs in the promotion, carefully contrasting herself with Margaret Court, and she continually challenged Riggs to make sure he was prepared for the contest. Yet the press and public seemed to think the match was Riggs's to lose. Las Vegas oddsmaker Jimmy "The Greek" Snyder favored Riggs, 8–5. Ranking tennis player and commentator Gene Scott relied on gender stereotypes, claiming that "women are brought up from the time they're six years old to read books, eat candy, and go to dancing class . . . They can't compete against men. They're not used to the competition. It's unfortunate."[22]

Even Neil Amdur, who had covered much of King's career, believed Riggs would win in three straight sets.[23] Amdur explained his prediction had nothing to do with gender but with the circumstances of the match; he believed Riggs was the superior tennis player and would rise to the occasion to defeat King, still recovering from knee problems, by breaking her concentration with his high lobs. As he mused, "Riggs will dictate the tempo and pace of this match, just as he did with that first puffy serve wide to Margaret Court's forehand . . . Billie Jean simply isn't strong enough, especially in view of her recent ailments, to sustain an attacking game, and she's not steady enough to win from the backcourt against one of the game's most underrated technicians."[24]

Amdur also believed the asphalt court would play better for Riggs, who had defeated Court on the same surface, and that King would have difficulty with the indoor lighting because, although both players wore glasses, King's game was more dependent on volleys and therefore the lighting would have a larger impact. Most importantly, however, Amdur believed that Riggs's advantage rested in the absurdity of the match and its promotion, noting, "True, Billie Jean is considered a tough competitor, a defiant symbol of

American womanhood less likely to choke in the big match than the sensitive, Australian-born Mrs. Court. But this is not the classic tennis confrontation for the purists, chauvinists or feminists to analyze—it is a good, old-fashioned hu$tle."[25]

Billie Jean King was at once one of the top-ranked female athletes in the world and an underdog in a match with a man twenty-six years her senior. Yet her straight sets victory over Bobby Riggs before the thirty thousand in paid attendance and forty-eight million watching on television was not perceived by the press as the women's victory biographers would later make it. In a disconnect with their predictions, the rhetorical flourishes of the match's reviews depicted the event as a spectacle not to be taken too seriously.

Barry Tarshis, writing about the match's commercial appeal for tennis, declared that "the real appeal of the match was the real but blatantly inflated confrontation between a self-proclaimed male chauvinist and a militant spokeswoman for women's rights; a middle-aged man against a young woman; carousing, hedonistic flippancy against quiet determination."[26] Here, Riggs's persona was seen as a good-natured construction, while King was presented as the militant feminist with something to prove. In the span of a week, King had gone from being the underdog to being the always-likely victor, the young, determined woman against the older competitor who was just there for the show. How could she not win? And why should we care?

Television reviewer John J. O'Connor found the grandeur of the event to be a nation's need for psychic relief in the midst of the Watergate scandal. O'Connor offered that the "hustle was, for the most part, good naturedly recognized as a hustle, but Mrs. King's victory left a surprising number of male chauvinist faces in deep gloom on the TV screen. In the end, the manipulated event was full of sound and pictures, signifying something about our culture, but proving nothing."[27] Although he was willing to acknowledge that King's victory was not fully anticipated, and perhaps came as a disappointment to certain members of the populace, O'Connor was unimpressed with the televised circus, critiquing as much the commentary by Howard Cosell and Rosemary Casals—whom he derided for her "sophomoric antagonism" toward Bobby Riggs that "quickly became tiresome and embarrassing"—as the match and its purported importance in American culture.[28]

Even Neil Amdur hedged in his summation of King's victory. Amdur credited King with controlling the pace of the game by forcing Riggs to play her serve-and-volley game, as well as her ability to make 64 percent of her 109 points on outright winning shots. Yet he also seemed to offer excuses for Riggs's failure, claiming: "Hustling has been Riggs's lifestyle, part of the ebullience and charm that endeared him more to millions in the twilight of his career than during his prime as one of the world's leading players. Unfortunately, the 55-year-old self-proclaimed 'sugar daddy' spent so much time selling himself and promoting the match with Mrs. King that he forgot what he had continually preached to others—never lose that winning edge."[29] This analysis presented the match more as Riggs's defeat than King's victory, and laid open the possibility that a prepared Riggs would have beaten King.

By treating the match in this manner, sportswriters and commentators were actually stripping the event of its revolutionary tone. King's victory was not so much that of a woman over a man as a *young* woman over an *older* man; an active player over a retired player; an activist over an entertainer. They did not pay attention to the side bets occurring across the country where husbands and wives wagered domestic chores instead of money. These latter details became lynchpins for accounts written by scholars and biographers who would use the match to illustrate and evaluate King's career as a whole. Stories of husbands having to do the dishes or women in an office banding together to ask for a raise were not stories of the day but proved relevant context in the aftermath for the match and established its significance.

King's insistence that the "Battle of the Sexes" was really about entertainment value and not ability, and that a high-ranking man could and probably would defeat a high-ranking woman, also downplayed the importance of the outcome. Bobby Riggs's masculinity was never in question—his age and jokester persona deflected any threats to his manliness. The match has been seen as an important gender victory that can be more attributed to its ripple effect through culture and society than its immediate impact in the locker room, where King's victory was justified and in some ways expected. Although counterfactual theories of what would have been had King lost (what would it mean for women's tennis?) were intriguing, they were not visible in the sports pages' postgame analyses in 1973.

The Battle of the Sexes match was, therefore, not as significant in creating Billie Jean King's reputation as cementing what was already there. King had established herself as a tournament champion both in the opens and on the women's tour long before Bobby Riggs challenged her—her reputation had been set by the way that she performed on the court, and she had been deemed from the start a more appropriate opponent for Riggs than soft-spoken Margaret Court. The next day, King was back to the women's tour, and sports reporters were back to covering her in much the same way they had before Riggs had turned tennis upside down. Amdur said as much when he wrote: "There can be no doubt that Mrs. King's triumph, viewed by so many, has strengthened her as the Joan of Arc of athletics, the one who raised her racquet for battle when few women challenged the broad inequalities inherent in the sports culture."[30]

SEXUALITY IN THE AFTERMATH

Although King returned to the women's tennis tour immediately after her victory over Bobby Riggs, she faced injuries that kept her from competition as she aged. In 1977, following a seven-month absence after her third knee surgery, King hoped to rejoin the women's tour through a loophole that would have allowed her to play in a Virginia Slims tournament despite missing the qualifying rounds due to injury. When tournament officials refused to grant her a spot, King entered the non–Women's Tennis Association (WTA) sanctioned Lionel Cup tournament, creating yet further controversy.

King's participation in the Lionel Cup was problematic because of Renée Richards's presence. Richards, a transgendered woman who underwent sex reassignment surgery in 1975, had been barred from United States Tennis Association (USTA)–sanctioned events to that point and King's willingness to play in the same tournament was questionable to members of the WTA. "We don't have anything settled," Chris Evert said of the WTA position on Richards's eligibility status, "and all of the women should stick together." Betty Stowe added: "I would have thought Billie Jean would be very loyal to women's tennis. I know she needs the competition, but there are other ways she could have gotten it. I think it's a sour thing she did."[31]

Although her peers questioned her choice, King was again raising questions about gender through tennis. "Maybe because I'd already had one trip into the unknown, against Riggs," King later wrote, "I wasn't so troubled by Renée." King was looking to play tennis and was not worried about Richards's gender identity or the perceived advantage being born a man might have given her. Instead, King told Lionel Cup promoter Gladys Heldman, "If the doctors say she's a woman, that's good enough for me. No, I'll go even further. If Renée thinks she's a woman in her heart and mind, then she is a woman."[32]

The rest of the tennis world was not as accepting of Renée Richards. Although she passed the required chromosomal testing, the USTA banned Richards from competing in the US Open. Richards filed suit against the USTA, the US Open Tournament, and the Women's Tennis Association, claiming her exclusion was based entirely on the Barr Body sex chromosome test. Although much of her claim's support came from the medical community (especially doctors associated with transsexuality), the judge paid particular attention to an affidavit signed by Billie Jean King and the head of the WTA who had played doubles with Richards. In support of Richards, King declared "From my observation of Dr. Richards and experience with her on the court, as well as my total knowledge of the sport of tennis, she does not enjoy physical superiority or strength so as to have an advantage over women competitors in the sport of tennis."[33]

Renée Richards was a symbol of alternative sexuality, and her presence was not only problematic to promoters, who feared the public's response, but to the players themselves, and the struggle with one's identity as a woman and an athlete. Scholars have noted sports' value in society for promoting cooperation and fairness, as well as teaching young men proper masculine values, of which physical superiority was key. In contrast, female athletes were prized for exhibiting grace and elegance, and the aggression and strength demonstrated by players like Billie Jean King and Martina Navratilova was antithetical to the "women's style." Tennis, therefore, featured an inherent gender struggle wherein men's tennis supported masculinity and its perceived characteristics and women's tennis promoted femininity and its virtues. As a consequence, many female athletes struggled with their identities as "jocks," and tried to maintain their femininity—much as Billie Jean King had noted of Chris Evert. These athletes feared being associated with "masculine impulses," and fought against rumors of same-sex pairings on their tours.[34] To be "outed" was not only devastating to one's reputation, but posed a threat to the entire profession.

OUT

Although she was strong in her defense of Richards, Billie Jean King expressed these same concerns when Marilyn Barnett, with whom she had an extramarital affair, filed a palimony suit against her in 1981. The story broke with a 154-word article by the Associated Press and a strong denial by King, who claimed the allegations were "untrue and unfounded" and said she was "shocked and disappointed" in Barnett, who was labeled a "former employee."[35] In her autobiography, King explained her decision to open up about her relationship with Barnett was due in part to her attitude towards the press, whom she believed would "chew me up and spit me out." King continued, "I'm a certified controversial character to start with . . . I represent certain images to certain people and often what I represent is disliked."[36] Believing her reputation as a women's rights activist had created enemies and knowing the scandal an extramarital same-sex affair would bring, King decided to be honest and called a press conference to explain.

Much of King's defense was dedicated to portraying Barnett as vindictive. During the press conference King—with her husband and parents by her side—referred to her former lover as "unstable" and "destructive," and refuted claims that she had ever been a confidant, claiming, "Even at the height of the affair, I never told Marilyn anything that was really important. What I liked most about her was that I could escape from everything when I was with her. That was the whole point: *not* to involve her in all that had me in turmoil."[37]

King described her affair as a way of escaping the pressures of being a tennis icon. The letters that she wrote, and that Barnett attempted to leverage in her palimony suit, were a space for King to focus herself and express her feelings; Barnett was hired as her traveling secretary in 1973 for much the same reason. Yet because 1973 was such a chaotic year, it took a toll on their one-year relationship. King argued that it might have been easier to segue from lovers to friends had circumstances been different, but Barnett became difficult and tried to create distance between King and her loved ones. According to King, she told Barnett she didn't need her as a travel companion after the Riggs match, and both their physical and romantic relationship ended. Feeling sorry for Barnett, whom she let go as a secretary in 1974, King agreed to a severance package and to allow her to stay in the Malibu home they had shared until she and Larry decided otherwise.[38] When the Kings decided to sell the house in 1981—and after the landmark Lee Marvin palimony suit[39]—Barnett filed for lifetime support and the right to stay in the home.

That Billie Jean King explained the palimony suit as an example of Barnett's vices was an important tactic of her public relations campaign. Facing scandal, King avoided the topic of her sexuality as best as she could. "I don't think it has anything to do with sexual preference," she told the *New York Times*. "I feel that basically Marilyn was a mistake. For me, it's an odd situation. I don't feel homosexual. That's not my feelings, and I don't understand why people would feel I'm any less of a person."[40] Although she was sure to tell reporters that homophobia was merely a fear of the unknown, her surprising silence in regard to her sexuality allowed the press to provide much of the commentary on the matter. King, someone who made her reputation by being outspoken and an advocate of gender difference, with her refusal to address the broader questions in this instance allowed the press to do so in her place.

King's admission opened a discussion about the image of athletes and public consumption. Her affair with Barnett had happened at the peak of her career but was not disclosed for almost ten years. Was it fair to reevaluate her or one's respect for her in light of recent events? "In recent days, many athletes, fans, and journalists have seemed anguished over the possibility of homosexuals in sports, but the fear seems as much of image as of substance," George Vecsey wrote in defense of King. "Will fans all go away if one tennis player or one football player admits homosexuality? This is the unnecessary burden sports takes upon itself, presenting all athletes as public images, as role models."[41] Vecsey and others argued that King's admission raised business—not moral—concerns. Journalists and promoters worried about the impact it would have on the tour; others focused on advertising revenue.

Advertising was a conservative trade. One of the risks involved in celebrity endorsements was that the celebrity—particularly one with a blemished reputation—might overshadow the product. Advertisers avoided controversy, and so the biggest threat Marilyn Barnett posed to Billie Jean King's career was to her endorsement revenue. Although many companies that employed King vowed to support her, others who would have signed her stayed away. For example, King estimated she lost $500,000 for an about-to-be-completed deal with a Wimbledon clothing line. Additional contracts were allowed to expire without renewal: a $400,000 contract with Murjani jeans, a $45,000 deal with Charleston Hosiery, and a $90,000 deal with a Japanese clothing company. The lawsuit may have cost King an additional $1.5 million in other celebrity-based revenue, including television commercials, corporate appearances, and coaching fees.[42]

Yet if her admission cost her financially, her silence cost her status as an activist; some of the most virulent criticism was that leveled by King's supporters, who worried that her silence on the matter was a lost opportunity to talk about sexuality. Writing for *Newsweek*, Pete Axthelm panned Billie Jean King's apologetic promotional campaign and the media's attention to her as "personal survival techniques." To him, the palimony suit offered a chance to talk about the stigmas associated with women in sports. "Contrary to the favorite catchwords of last week's tabloid headlines, lesbianism in sports is neither 'rampant' nor a 'scandal,'" he wrote, while celebrating King's democratizing of professional tennis. According to Axthelm, this influx of young women into the tennis circuit from nonelite backgrounds was changing the character of the game, and went a long way in discrediting rumors of lesbianism running rampant on the tour. That said, he was careful not to suggest that eradicating lesbianism was anyone's goal, choosing instead to discuss King's failure to adequately defend herself in what was a no-win situation.

When the round of interviews was over, the Moral Majority was presumably awash in suitable outrage. Lesbians were smarting from the fact that she had called her affair "a mistake" instead of a valid alternative; later, in response to a particularly obsequious Barbara Walters question, she tried to regroup by insisting that the affair was wrong mainly because she was married at the time. As for her heterosexual colleagues, some of whom feel unfairly "branded," their mood is somewhat less sanguine than their public show of solidarity indicated.[43]

Like others, Axthelm noted that many discussions about Billie Jean King's affair were related to advertising and sponsorship money. Because King was either silent or guarded in discussing her sexuality, the ability to discuss the presence of lesbianism in sports and remove its stigma was absent. Instead, it remained a taboo topic, one that threatened the career of a female athlete.

The *Washington Post*'s Richard Cohen offered perhaps the strongest criticism of King in the wake of the Barnett affair. He condemned her press conference and subsequent public relations campaign as "not admirable, but reprehensible," and declared that King had not only turned her back on Barnett with her attempts to smear the plaintiff, but also on "what she herself is or was, no matter how apologetically: a homosexual."

Picking up on King's categorization of the affair as a mistake, Cohen argued that King thought her "mistake" was not having an affair, but having an affair with another woman. He found her apology a calculated attempt to win back public favor by first explaining how she fell into this scandalous position (distance from her husband and loneliness), then asserting that she was no longer (if ever) a lesbian. Cohen called the apology "cheating," and characterized it as the same as activities of a fallen politician: "They refuse to pay the piper, accept responsibility for who they are and what they have done. In King's case, it means making homosexuality into an aberration—a mistake. It becomes something you do when your husband is terribly busy."[44] Although he acknowledged that King's private life probably should have remained that way, Cohen faulted the way that she handled its entrance into the public domain, writing that "she's tried to co-opt the lynch mob by leading it to the person she says she used to be and, by implication, all homosexuals."[45]

The palimony suit brought against Billie Jean King thus represented another way in which the tennis star forced people to engage questions of gender and sexuality. How do one's bedroom activities impact our understanding of that person? Should such things matter? Should we dismiss a person's achievements if we disagree with one's actions? Should contemporary revelations alter long-standing regard? In many cases, coverage of King's affair and the public's response were positive, declaring that King's admission challenged the "American public to accept a fact perhaps disturbing to many, and go on from there."[46] Others chose to focus on the role of advertising in mediating scandal; the fact that King's sponsors did not abruptly drop their contracts seemed to indicate public support for King as she fought back against Barnett's claims. Yet the criticism offered also said something about public and media expectations of Billie Jean King: the women's rights crusader did not take the opportunity to discuss or defend alternative sexuality when the story was about her. Although the public ultimately sided with her, it was not because of anything she said but because of interpretations of who she was and what she did before the scandal erupted.

Such was Billie Jean King's reputation in printed media. Throughout her career, King represented a different kind of female athlete and a woman who challenged the status quo. By 1981, her image was such that she need not even speak to cause a dialogue about gender and power in the sports world and in society. Over the preceding two decades, Billie Jean King had gone from "militant activist" to feminist icon.

TAKING TWO STEPS BACK

Although much of her career crossed gender boundaries, Billie Jean King's biographers have remembered her economic contributions to women's tennis. The biography is the means by which we codify one's historical memory, and so it is important to acknowledge and analyze the ways in which Billie Jean King's life was portrayed. In this venue Billie Jean King has been transformed from the Joan of Arc of women's tennis into a Horatio Alger heroine of the late twentieth century.

As newspapers indicated, King's career regularly defied gender stereotypes, and she was noted in the press as a "militant feminist" and spokeswoman for women in tennis. And as already noted, King's willingness to stand against tennis authorities in fighting for pay equity and Renée Richards's eligibility, to take a political stand in support of Title IX legislation and abortion rights, and to put her reputation on the line in competing against Bobby Riggs had earned her the nickname the "Joan of Arc of women's tennis," conjuring images of sacrifice along with strength and heroism. We would expect scholars to address these issues in writing for adult audiences, where no excuses can be made for "appropriateness." Disappointingly, however, scholars have largely failed to take up this challenge, relegating King to segments of women's history books or chapters about the women's movement, frequently tying her story to the equal pay component.[47] There is a surprising gap in historiography related to Billie Jean King that only Selena Roberts attempted to bridge in a book-length argument. However, Roberts's *A Necessary Spectacle* took the Battle of the Sexes as its focus, attempting to incorporate other elements of the biography (including the Barnett affair) tangentially, and did not provide much by way of analysis. One should not fault Roberts too much; as a sportswriter retelling the story of an iconic tennis match, she never had historical analysis as her intention.[48]

This historiographical gap reflects the difficulty of writing women's lives. In her study of books about women, Carolyn Heilbrun identified a tradition of explaining their lives in terms of depression, madness, and powerlessness for most of the twentieth century. According to Heilbrun, women subjects were replete with "forbidden anger" without visible recourse, which often led them to take "refuge in depression or madness." Even autobiographical writings by revolutionary women such as Eleanor Roosevelt or Emma Goldman lacked self-assertion, ambitiousness, or pride.[49] Although none of these statements were true of Billie Jean King, the timing of her accomplishments might explain the difficulty in constructing her biography—the necessary framework was not yet available.

Heilbrun argued that writing about women's lives was changing in the 1970s and 1980s, when many of King's biographies—including her autobiography—were produced. In 1970, Nancy Milford's *Zelda* contradicted previous writings on F. Scott Fitzgerald's wife by arguing that it was not she who destroyed his life but, rather, the opposite—that "he had usurped her narrative." Within the next decade, poet May Sarton's memoirs defied conventions by voicing her struggle in terms of anger. As Heilbrun declares, "[R]eading her idealized life in the hopeful eyes of those who saw her as examplar, she realized that, in ignoring her rage and pain, she had unintentionally been less than honest . . . In her next book, *Journal of a Solitude*, she deliberately set out to recount the pain of the year covered by *Plant Dreaming Deep*."[50] King's competitive career, therefore, came not only on the cusp of the women's movement, but on the cusp of new women's biographies.

The phrase "on the cusp" has particular resonance for King, who used it herself in her autobiography; as James Pipkin observed in an article about female athletes in the 1960s, the phrase reflected cultural dissonance. For Pipkin, the female athletes who came of age in the 1950s and 1960s confronted "deep tension about their identities, their sexuality, and the way society 'read' their extraordinary bodies ... the site of deep-seated cultural beliefs and values as well as a site of identity. They describe their sporting experiences using terms such as 'identity crisis,' 'schizophrenia,' and 'freak.'"[51] Taking Billie Jean King as a primary subject and writing thirty-five years after Milford's book that Heilbrun identified as "watershed," Pipkin was one of the few scholars to include a gender analysis, however short, of King's career. He focused on King's often contentious relationship with her body, which "transgress[ed] the accepted boundaries between male and female, drawing disquieting reactions from the viewing public." He further argued that King's identity, formed from her body image, was torn between a female identity ("nice, polite me") and male (the aggressive athlete on the court).[52] Pipkin's writing examined King's own, and analyzed the ambiguity expressed in her autobiography, in which she struggled with her success in defeating Riggs as well as her stardom eclipsing that of her brother, Major League Baseball relief pitcher Randy Moffitt.[53]

In explaining King's ambivalence, Pipkin presented another challenge biographers faced. King's words were available to them as a wonderful resource in constructing her story, yet she was uncertain of her identity and her impact, which remained on the cusp of writing a woman's life. Thus, where King was passive and questioning of her role in culture, she was declarative in her economic accomplishments. She identified herself as the child of a blue-collar family and was not bothered by challenging the class boundaries she found in tennis, nor later by struggling with her role in changing audiences' perceptions in that context. Most King biographies mentioned the Southern California Junior Team photograph in which a young Billie Jean was denied a spot because she was wearing shorts and not the requisite white tennis dress.[54] King's mother sewed her clothes, and the story became emblematic of her outsider status. Rather than see this story as a place where gender and class connected, however, biographers have tended to focus solely on the class elements, using it as a catalyst for King's determination to change tennis economically.

Further intersections of class and gender involved Perry Jones, the director of the Southern California Lawn Tennis Association (SCLTA) who pulled King from the photograph, and his successor Jack Kramer, who appeared frequently as antagonists in King's career. So, for example, when King qualified for her first national championship, Jones insisted she have a chaperone accompany her to Middleton, Ohio, for the tournament, but did not provide travel assistance. Indeed, unable to afford two plane tickets, King and her mother rode the train and slept upright for three nights, only to watch her peers then fly off to Philadelphia after the nationals for the next tournament, while she and her mother took the train back to Long Beach. When, in 1970, King and others broke off to form the Virginia Slims tour, it was in direct defiance of Kramer, then promoting the Pacific Southwest Tournament, which had a 12 to 1 prize ratio favoring the male winner with a $12,500 purse, the female winner with $1,500, and nothing for female competitors who failed to reach the quarterfinals. Gladys Heldman originally volunteered to negotiate with Kramer, but when he refused to increase the women's prize money, Heldman used her contacts in Houston to arrange a $5,000 tournament, then brought in Virginia Slims to cosponsor. In fact, Jones and Kramer represented such opposition to women's tennis that King alleged that Kramer and his colleagues at the USLTA opposed a sanction of the Houston tournament, but lacking legitimate grounds or precedent, they nevertheless attempted to place the blame for withholding the sanction on Jones, who was in a coma! According to King, "A telegram protesting our tournament was sent to Gladys, supposedly signed by Perry. Perry died twenty-four hours [later]." Such was the conflict between King and Kramer that when ABC hired Kramer as a commentator for the Battle of the Sexes match, King refused to play until the arrangement was nullified, claiming that his history of deriding women's tennis was such that he had no place in such a match.[55]

With King ambivalent about her role in challenging certain gender boundaries, she understandably deemed her success solely to be economic in nature, but biographers and scholars must make the connections she did not. Although the SCLTA did not provide much financial support for King, they did support more "appropriate"—in dress and comportment—young athletes, particularly the boys. Debates about prize money were often in terms of entertainment value, with opponents of parity claiming the men's game featured greater strength, agility, and endurance. By addressing King only in the context of *women's* tennis, and focusing on her financial goals and gains, biographers have failed to see the whole picture.

Additionally, many of Billie Jean King's biographies were written with a children's audience in mind. Beginning in 1974, shortly after her defeat of Bobby Riggs, early juvenile biographies were hesitant to place King within the context of the controversial women's movement. Instead, they emphasized her victory in the Battle of the Sexes, a trend that has continued in her most recent biographies; her entire career has been arced to fit that narrative. The match was the pinnacle of her playing career, and the rest of her life served to build to that climax.[56]

Juvenile biographies of Billie Jean King resembled Horatio Alger, Jr.'s series of novels in the nineteenth century that were aimed at a young, male, working-class audience. Alger created heroes out of street urchins who, through "luck, pluck, and determination," became successful, respectable members of society. The Alger hero has become synonymous with the American "rags-to-riches" myth. Interestingly—and perhaps appropriately for this context—class and gender intersected in Alger's writings as well; the books served to introduce young men to the public sphere and their role therein.[57] However, class has generally taken precedence in audiences' perception of these stories, as it has in biographies of King. By using the Alger framework, King's biographers provided a modern twist by introducing *girls* to the public sphere and their changing role therein, but saw King's victories in terms of "equal opportunity," and demonstrating that women's tennis was a viable business and career path.

Billie Jean King, according to these biographers, *had* to play Bobby Riggs. Initially hesitant—as much for what would happen if she lost as not wanting the distraction from the Virginia Slims tour—King's hands were tied when Riggs defeated Margaret Court. King was the antithesis of Court's quiet demeanor (Court was also conservative in her social views), and when the latter appeared unprepared and was routed by Riggs, King, the activist, had to step in. The Battle of the Sexes, in this interpretation, was about "defending women's honor," and making a statement about equal pay. In these narratives, King demonstrated "that women could walk and chew gum at the same time ...that women need equal opportunity."[58]

The spectacle of the match that King had originally hoped to avoid also fulfilled her "average Joe dreams," according to biographers. Having presented King as a blue-collar hero and antagonistic toward elites who organized and promoted tournaments, the authors established King as wanting to expand tennis's audience, and the circus-like atmosphere in the Battle of the Sexes reached well outside country club membership.

> The noise in the Astrodome was deafening. Fans yelled and screamed; music blared. It looked much more like a college football championship or the World Series than a tennis match. Billie Jean loved it. Tennis was finally, thoroughly, out of the country club. The "average guy" she had always wanted for a fan was there. And 40 million more "average guys" watched on television.[59]

The relentless promotion of the King/Riggs match attracted curious viewers, many of whom were not familiar with tennis. By bringing in such an audience and then displaying tremendous ability, King helped democratize the sport. In this context, she not only advanced the cause of women fighting for equal opportunity, but broke down the class distinctions that had held her back as a young player.[60]

Biographies have played an important role in juvenile literature because they conveyed social and personal expectations by celebrating (or condemning) an individual's actions and demonstrating rewards for socially accepted and valued behaviors. They, therefore, aid in scaffolding, allowing children to reach the next level of their social development.[61] Juvenile biographies focused on Billie Jean King have presented her as hard-working and determined, emphasized her years of training, and explained the professional battles she fought on and off the courts to attain recognition and equality.

Many of these books offered the story of how King began playing tennis: as a young girl, she enjoyed playing baseball and football, but one of her parents (accounts differ as to which, although most indicated it was her father) encouraged her to choose a sport that was more "feminine." Given the options of tennis, golf, or swimming, she chose tennis, and after her first lesson—a free community program on a public court—she went home and told her mother she intended to become the best tennis player in the world.[62] Although some authors went on to describe King's playing style in contrast to fellow female athletes, they usually used it as an example of her rebellious nature, helping them build to the point where she would break with the USLTA to become a professional, or form the Virginia Slims tour, or play Bobby Riggs. More often, they would place emphasis on her determination to become the best, failing to note the irony that she became a women's tennis champion, pushed into the sport by parents wanting her to be more feminine, by playing the men's game. Gender, Billie Jean King demonstrated, did not predict success. However, the Horatio Alger story line did not permit this analysis, which would have been useful in modern juvenile biographies that allowed expanded gender roles for girls, and were intended to socialize America's youth.

This class-based depiction of King's life can be explained if authors wanted to remove those topics they deemed too mature for their young audiences, which ranged from early primary school students to teens. If one were to edit out sexuality, from King's abortion and advocacy of abortion rights to her affair with Marilyn Barnett, the notable stories that would be left would be her childhood and early tennis days, her amateur career and turning professional, the Virginia Slims tour, her hundred-thousand-dollar year, and the Battle of the Sexes—all of which appear in juvenile biographies and are threaded with a discussion of class and professional determination. The problem with removing sexuality, even for the older end of this audience, is that doing so keeps it taboo. Gay, lesbian, and transgender youth struggle with their identities in a society in which heterosexual life is normalized. These teens—and in some cases children—face rejection, isolation, and physical harm. They are in need of their own literature, presenting role models and building scaffolds, just as their classmates are.

Joanne Lannin's *Billie Jean King: Tennis Trailblazer*, published in 1999, was one of the few books to address King's sexuality, presenting it honestly as an issue with which King struggled before Marilyn Barnett came into her life. Lannin wrote of King's 1995 decision to check into a Philadelphia clinic specializing in eating disorders. King, who was then fifty-two, concluded that her fear and shame about her sexuality were connected to her eating and finally admitted to her parents that she was gay and the woman with whom she had lived since divorcing Larry in 1987 was her partner. Lannin explained, "Billie Jean says that the time in which she grew up made dealing with her sexuality the hardest thing she's ever done. She feels more at peace with herself, she says, than she ever has."[63] Billie Jean King had been silent in the newspapers and defensive and cautious in her 1982 autobiography in the wake of the Marilyn Barnett affair, but in the pages of Lannin's book, her voice was finally heard. As King became more open and honest with herself, she gave interviews and explained her struggle with her sexuality. Allowed its space in *Billie Jean King: Tennis Trailblazer*, this part of her story helped to build a scaffold for young people struggling with their own identities.

Lannin's work managed to accomplish something other King juvenile biographies had not—finding a voice to express King's anger and frustration that had long been denied women in biographies, while also conveying ambition, pride, personal growth, and self-acceptance. However, the author's work was not without its challenges. The biographer's task has been to look at the whole of his subject's life and create a narrative. Naturally, some events were to be elevated and many omitted in accordance with the framework in which the author constructed the biography. With figures like Billie Jean King, however, whose life and context were both potentially controversial, the author risked alienating members of one's audience if the life story did not conform to the standards of white, middle-class, heterosexual society. Therein lay the problem: how can one conform to such standards when one's subject was a woman whose life questioned gender stereotypes, broke down class barriers, and embodied the rebellion of the sixties' and seventies' social movements?

FEMINISM AND ITS DISCONTENTS

Billie Jean King's inclusion in nonbiographical history books has demonstrated her cultural impact beyond the tennis courts. Not surprisingly, scholars have highlighted the Battle of the Sexes as demonstrating a moment of victory in the women's liberation movement. Like King's biographers, however, they have struggled with the controversial nature of the movement itself. As Beth Bailey has pointed out, the women's movement struggled to gain a foothold in America because its goal—to free women from oppression—was not universally understood. Bailey cited West Virginia senator James Randolph's denunciation of the movement as a "small band of bra-less bubbleheads." Additionally, Bailey's research produced a 1972 study from the Center for Policy Research by Columbia University's Amitai Etzioni, published in the *New York Times Magazine*, that asked participants, "Is believing that there are more important issues—Vietnam, pollution, crime, and the oppression of blacks—than who leaves what hankies where, a true sign of male pigheadedness?"[64] Questions like these and comments like those of Senator Randolph dismissed the idea that women were in need of liberation. Comparisons of women's struggles with those of other minority groups were thought laughable, and parodies of the cause were disseminated throughout popular media.[65]

Furthermore, unattractive social changes were often blamed on the women's movement. The seventies experienced an increase in both out-of-wedlock births and divorces, while polls revealed the public was growing more comfortable with the concepts of cohabitation and premarital sex. The wider availability of contraception, most notably the birth control pill, drove the sexual revolution, but its consequences were associated with women's push to be more than barefoot and pregnant.[66] The difficult reputation of the women's movement, combined with internal discord between female activists over the precise meaning of "liberation," raised problems in constructing its historical legacy.

It is therefore logical that those attempting to place Billie Jean King in the context of the women's movement—particularly those who see her impact positively—would focus on her economic impact in women's tennis rather than the more debated topics of gender and sexuality. The women's movement's greatest success came economically, particularly with advancements in higher education and professional success. Although many women did not choose to work, those who did have seen more opportunities since the 1970s. According to James Patterson, between 1970 and 1996, the percentage of Ph.D.s earned by women rose from 13 percent to 45 percent; from 4 percent of M.D.s to 41 percent; and from 5 percent of law degrees to 44 percent. Women now represent the majority of college and university undergraduates, as well.[67]

Title IX, a provision of the Education Act of 1972 that barred discrimination in federally funded education on the basis of sex, contributed enormously to these expanded opportunities. Although Title IX did not specifically include sports, the legislation has produced staggering results in that area. In 1971, girls comprised 7.6 percent of high school athletes; that number improved to 41.2 percent of participants in 2007–2008. In intercollegiate athletics, the results are less dramatic but no less significant, with female athletes rising from 15 percent in 1971 to 45 percent in 2005–2006. Reports have indicated that schools were more likely to add women's sports programs to be in compliance with federal regulations than to cut those for males, and female athletes received 45 percent of athletic scholarships in 2005–2006, allowing many young women the opportunity to obtain a college education.[68] Higher education allowed women to gain access to higher-paying jobs, a mark of liberation, and in this context Billie Jean King—who lobbied in support of Title IX and openly proclaimed her goals as a "women's lobber" to be equal purses for men and women—provided a useful popular culture example, one that allowed authors to construct a narrative of success and ignore the movement's more problematic issues and shortcomings.

Yet in constructing this narrative, the complexity and controversy had been lost. Unable to present a unified understanding of the women's movement or to engage King's full reputation as feminist icon, histories and biographies have stripped both of their importance. Women's roles and their value were put into question through the women's movement; the shortcomings of the movement have repercussions today.

How did Billie Jean King succeed in the public mindset while the movement failed, and where did these matters diverge? These are interesting questions that should be addressed by scholars. And yet, in order to bring this to fruition, it seems readily obvious that this journey's first step has to begin with a look at Billie Jean King's career as consisting of much more than one exhibition match.

NOTES

1. Billie Jean King with Frank Deford, *The Autobiography of Billie Jean King* (New York: Granada Press, 1982), 16–17.

2. Gary Fine, *Difficult Reputations: Collective Memories of the Evil, Inept, and Controversial* (Chicago: University of Chicago Press, 2001), 3.

3. Ibid., 8–9.

4. Leading up to the Battle of the Sexes, the *New York Times*' Gerald Eskenazi wrote: "Their styles were tailored to a battle. He is a master of control and of dealing 'junk'—soft serves that spin dizzily, or lobs that act erratically. Some call it a 'women's style.' Mrs. King, however, attacks the ball in a 'man's style.' Yet she is also capable of playing with 'touch'— the ability to hit delicate shots." Eskenazi, "$100,000 Tennis Match: Bobby Riggs v. Mrs. King," *New York Times*, July 12, 1973, 82.

5. King, *Autobiography*, 171–172.

6. Ibid.

7. Ibid., 119.

8. Dave Anderson, "Billie Jean: Tennis Queen Who Obeys Her King," *New York Times*, September 10, 1967, 226.

9. An example: Robert Lipsyte, "Sports of the *Times*: Billie Jean," *New York Times*, August 27, 1970, 39. The article is a positive profile of King, allowing her opportunity to address some of the controversies surrounding her as a "women's libber."

10. Thomas Rogers, "Emerson and Mrs. King Sign 2-Year Contracts to Play Pro Tennis," *New York Times*, April 2, 1968, 57.

11. Parton Keese, "Women Set Up Tennis Tour," *New York Times*, October 8, 1970, 66.

12. Neil Amdur, "USLTA Warns Women Pros," *New York Times*, January 17, 1971, S1; Amdur, "Women Revolt in Tennis," *New York Times*, February 14, 1971, S10; Amdur, "Tennis Near Peace Pact for Women," *New York Times*, April 10, 1973, 51; Amdur, "Split 'Killing' Women's Tennis," *New York Times*, April 15, 1973, 232.

13. Amdur, "Women Revolt in Tennis," S10.

14. As an aside, she had also become the first athlete to share the honor, as the magazine selected UCLA men's basketball coach John Wooden as Sportsman of the Year. Since King's achievement, however, *Sports Illustrated* has selected Sportswomen of the Year five times in thirty-eight years. Chris Evert and track and field world champion Mary Decker were selected without male counterparts in 1972 and 1983, respectively. The U.S. Women's Soccer Team was awarded collectively in 1999. Olympic gold medalists Mary Lou Retton (1984) and Bonnie Blair (1994) shared the honor with fellow Olympic gold medalists Edwin Moses and Johann Olav Koss, respectively.

15. Associated Press, "Mrs. King Sportswoman of the Year," *New York Times*, December 21, 1972, 47.

16. Charles Friedman, "Women Tennis Stars Pondering Careers as Pros," *New York Times*, December 3, 1967, 275. According to Friedman, Riggs had actually staged the first women's tennis tour around 1950, as a side attraction to the Jack Kramer–Pancho Segura card: "He had Pauline Betz, a slender redhead who had won the national crown four times, and Gorgeous Gussie Moran, who had never ranked higher than fourth, but had hit the headlines by showing up on the court in lace panties." The barnstorming tour lasted six months but was ultimately not profitable enough to continue.

17. Dave Anderson, "Sex and the Singles Tennis Match," *New York Times*, May 12, 1973, 23.

18. Ibid.

19. Neil Amdur, "Riggs at 55: Life Begins Anew, Action Never Ends," *New York Times*, May 15, 1973, 45.

20. Associated Press, "Mrs. King Challenges Riggs for $10,000," *New York Times*, May 15, 1973, 45. Billie Jean King's tennis match was not alone in kind. In addition to Court's and King's battles against Bobby Riggs, "battles of the sexes" were fought on the courts between Martina Navratilova and Jimmy Connors; Karsten Braasch took on both Venus and Serena Williams in separate matches; and Yannick Noah played Justine Henin in 2003. In all but King's match, the male athlete won, usually handily. What set the King/Riggs event apart was its unique ending and tremendous promotion, combined with tennis's popularity in the early 1970s and the social changes and other battles of the sexes playing out concurrently.

21. Curry Kirkpatrick, "Mother's Day Ms. Match," *Sports Illustrated*, May 21, 1973, 35–37; "How Bobby Runs and Talks, Talks, Talks," *Time*, September 10, 1973, www.time.com/time/magazine/article/0,9171,90784301,00.html (August 21, 2010).

22. Eskenazi, "$100,000 Tennis Match: Bobby Riggs vs. Mrs. King."

23. Neil Amdur, "Riggs Will Win in Three Sets," *New York Times*, September 16, 1973, 221. Men's tennis matches were best-of-five sets; women's tennis played best of three. Male players and tennis promoters often justified the unequal tennis purses on the grounds that the men played more and were therefore more entertaining (tied into this were also ideas of strength and endurance, necessary for the longer matches). To prove women's entertainment value, King agreed to a best-of-five match. Riggs had defeated Court in a best of three.

24. Ibid.

25. Ibid.

26. Barry Tarshis, "A Lot Preceded the Ms.-Match," *New York Times*, September 23, 1973, 215.

27. John J. O'Connor, "TV Review," *New York Times*, September 21, 1973, 83.

28. Ibid.

29. Neil Amdur, "'She Played, Too Well,' Says Riggs of Mrs. King," *New York Times*, September 22, 1973, 21.

30. Ibid.

31. Neil Amdur, "Rebuff to Mrs. King Causes a Split in Women's Tennis," *New York Times*, March 23, 1977, 31.

32. King, *Autobiography*, 127–128.

33. Neil Amdur, "Dr. Richards Gets Support of Mrs. King," *New York Times*, August 11, 1977, 76. See also: "People in Sports: USTA to Review Tests on Dr. Richards," *New York Times*, April 9, 1977, 31; Amdur, "US Open Won't Recognize Test Taken by Dr. Richards," *New York Times*, April 13, 1977, 44; Amdur, "Dr. Richards Plans to Sue to Enter Open," *New York Times*, August 2, 1977, 46; Amdur, "Renee Richards Ruled Eligible for US Open," *New York Times*, August 17, 1977, 40.

34. Janice Kaplan, "Women Athletes and Their Fears about Femininity," *New York Times*, June 5, 1977, S2.

35. Associated Press, "Around the Nation: Mrs. King to Seek Eviction of Woman in Sex Dispute," *New York Times*, May 1, 1981, A12.

36. King, *Autobiography*, 13–14.

37. Ibid., 29–30.

38. Ibid., 29–41.

39. In 1971, Academy Award-winning actor Lee Marvin was sued by his former live-in girlfriend, Michelle Marvin (Triola), who claimed financial compensation under California's alimony and community property laws, despite the couple never marrying. Although the court made some distinctions between nonmarital relationships and the marital contract, Marvin was ordered to pay $104,000 to his estranged partner, and the case was seen as a watershed for cohabiting, nonmarried couples. See *Marvin v. Marvin*, 18 Cal. 3d 660 (1976).

40. Neil Amdur, "Mrs. King Offers to Quit as WTA Head, So Not to Hurt Players," *New York Times*, May 3, 1981, 5.

41. George Vecsey, "Sports of the *Times*: The Athlete as Idol—and Human Frailty," *New York Times*, May 15, 1981, A24.

42. Rudy Maxa, "Dark Side of Publicity: Billie Jean's Big Losses," *Washington Post*, July 4, 1982, 2; N.R. Kleinfeld, "When a Celebrity Becomes Notorious," *New York Times*, May 18, 1981, D1; Richard Cohen, "Billie Jean King Pays for America's Fantasy," *Washington Post*, May 7, 1981, C1.

43. Pete Axthelm, "The Case of Billie Jean King," *Newsweek*, May 18, 1981, 133.

44. Richard Cohen, "Billie Jean Apologizes—But Not Really," *Washington Post*, May 26, 1981, C1.

45. Ibid.

46. Dorothy R. Chmela, "Letters: That Touch of Class," *New York Times*, May 16, 1981, 22.

47. See: Beth Bailey, "She Can Bring Home the Bacon," in *America in the Seventies*, ed. Beth Bailey and David Farber (Lawrence: University Press of Kansas, 2004), 107–128; Edward D. Berkowitz, *Something Happened: A Political and Cultural Overview of the Seventies* (New York: Columbia University Press, 2006), 133–157; Bonnie Eisenberg and Mary Ruthsdotter, "Billie Jean King," in *Herstory: Women Who Changed the World*, ed. Ruth Asby and Deborah Gore Orhn (New York: Viking Press, 1991), 152–159, 280; Francene Sabin, *Women Who Win* (New York: Random House, 1981); Janet Woolum, *Outstanding Women Athletes: Who They Are and How They Influenced Sports in America* (Phoenix: Oryx Press, 1992).

48. Selena Roberts, *A Necessary Spectacle: Billie Jean King, Bobby Riggs, and the Tennis Match that Leveled the Game* (New York: Crown Publishers, 2005).

49. Carolyn G. Heilbrun, *Writing a Woman's Life* (New York: W.W. Norton and Company, 1988), 15, 22–23.

50. Ibid., 12–13. The works Heilbrun cites are: Nancy Milford, *Zelda: A Biography* (New York: Harper and Row, 1970); May Sarton, *Plant Dreaming Deep* (New York: W. W. Norton and Company, 1968) and *Journal of a Solitude* (New York: W. W. Norton and Company, 1973).

51. James Pipkin, "Life on the Cusp: Lynda Huey and Billie Jean King," in *Impossible to Hold: Women and Culture in the 1960s*, ed. Avital H. Bloch and Lauri Umansky (New York: New York University Press, 2005), 47.

52. Ibid., 57–58.

53. Ibid., 61; King, *Autobiography*, 136. Interestingly, in detailing King's anxiety prior to her match against Riggs, many biographers have told a story of a clubhouse attendant pointing out the Astrodome locker her brother Randy used as a visiting pitcher for the San Francisco Giants. Standing in front of it, King was said to feel comforted.

54. A version of this story is found in most writings by and about King, particularly those aimed at young audiences. For example, see Leila Gemme, *King of the Court: Billie Jean King* (Milwaukee, WI: Raintree Editions, 1976), 18–19, 24–26.

55. Billie Jean King with Cynthia Starr, *We Have Come a Long Way: The Story of Women's Tennis* (New York: McGraw-Hill Book Company, 1988), 113, 123–125.

56. Some examples: Marshal and Sue Burchard, *Sports Hero: Billie Jean King* (New York: G.P. Putnam's Sons, 1975); Carol Bauer Church, *Billie Jean King: Queen of the Courts* (Minneapolis, MN: Greenhaven Press, 1976); John M. Franco, *American Women Contributors to American Life* (Westchester, IL: Benefic Press, 1976); Leila B. Gemme, *King of the Court: Billie Jean King* (Milwaukee, WI: Raintree Editions, 1976); James and Lynn Hahn, *King!: The Sports Career of Billie Jean King* (Mankato, MN: Crestwood House, 1981); Samuel Kostman, *Twentieth Century Women of Achievement* (New York: Richards Rosen Press, Inc., 1976); Joanne Lannin, *Billie Jean King: Tennis Trailblazer* (Minneapolis, MN: Lerner Publications Company, 1999); Joanne and James Mattern, *Breaking Barriers: Athletes Who Led the Way* (Logan, IA: Perfection Learning Corporation, 2002); James T. Olsen, *Billie Jean King: The Lady of the Court* (Mankato, MN: Creative Education, 1974); Ken Rappaport, *Ladies First: Women Athletes Who Made a Difference* (Atlanta: Peachtree Publishers, 2005).

57. See Glenn Hendler, "Pandering in the Public Sphere: Masculinity and the Market in Horatio Alger," *American Quarterly* 48, no. 3 (September 1996): 415–438; Richard Bowerman, "Horatio Alger, Jr.; Or, Adrift in the Myth of Rags to Riches," *Journal of American Culture* 2, no. 1 (March 1979): 83–112; Gary Scharnhorst, "Had Their Mothers Only Known: Horatio Alger, Jr., Rewrites Cooper, Melville, and Twain," *Journal of American Culture* 5, no. 2, (June 1982), 91–95.

58. Lannin, *Billie Jean King: Tennis Trailblazer*,71–75. See also: Mattern, *Breaking Barriers*,19–21; Gemme, *King of the Court*, 36–38; Rappaport, *Ladies First*, 64–66.

59. Gemme, *King of the Court*, 37.

60. See also: Lannin, *Billie Jean King: Tennis Trailblazer*, 90–91; Olsen, *Billie Jean King: The Lady of the Court*, 28–29; Church, *Billie Jean King: Queen of the Courts*, 11–12, 46–56.

61. W. Bernard Lukenbill, *Biography in the Lives of Youth: Culture, Society, and Information* (Westport, CT: Libraries Unlimited, 2006), 2–5, 51–56.

62. A sampling of biographies including this tennis origin story include: Kostman, *Twentieth Century Women of Achievement*, 170–172; Woolum, *Outstanding Women Athletes*, 128–129; Sabin, *Women Who Win*, 6–9; Burchard, *Sports Hero: Billie Jean King*, 8–13; Hahn, *King! The Sports Career of Billie Jean King*, 13–15; Gemme, *King of the Court*, 16; Hollander, *American Women in Sports*, 37; Lannin, *Billie Jean King: Tennis Trailblazer*, 11–12; Olsen, *Billie Jean King: The Lady of the Court*, 5–7; Church, *Billie Jean King: Queen of the Courts*, 4–6.

63. Lannin, *Billie Jean King*, 117. Other references to sexuality, 55–57, 103–107.

64. Bailey, "She Can Bring Home the Bacon," 111.

65. Ibid., 111–113.

66. Ibid., 116–117; James Patterson, *Restless Giant: The United States from Watergate to Bush v. Gore* (New York: Oxford University Press, 2005), 46–50.

67. Ibid., 54–55.

68. *Play Fair: A Title IX Playbook for Victory* (East Meadow, NY: Women's Sports Foundation, 2009), 4; Deborah J. Anderson and John J. Cheslock, "Institutional Strategies to Achieve Gender Equity in Intercollegiate Athletes: Does Title IX Harm Male Athletes?," *American Economic Review* 94, no. 2 (May 2004), 307–311.

VENUS AND SERENA WILLIAMS
Traversing the Barriers of the Country Club World

—EARL SMITH AND ANGELA J. HATTERY

INTRODUCTION

In a 2009 interview, Richard Williams, father of tennis champions Venus and Serena, was exceedingly candid when asked what his daughters mean to the world of women's professional tennis:

Q: So now, after all the titles and the millions earned, have Venus and Serena exceeded your expectations?

A: Venus reached my expectations when she went to Morningside High School in Inglewood, Calif. She made A's in mathematics, in trigonometry, and set a record that stood for a long time. I pushed education. I wanted them to understand that you can be the greatest athlete in the world, but without the greatest knowledge in the world, you're going to lose all your money anyway.

Q: There's been a lot of talk—a lot of complaining, in fact—about grunting during matches these days. Were Venus and Serena grunters from way back?

A: I don't know.

Q: You don't remember?

A: No, I do not. But I don't think there's anything wrong with it. To be honest, I think there's something wrong with tennis.

Q: What do you mean by that?

A: In 1884 tennis came to America, and it has been the same, nothing has changed. They want you to sit there and be quiet. Turn your neck this way, turn it that way, and get a crick in it. Somewhere along the line you have to say, "Let's have some fun out here." Who wants to come out here, buy a ticket, and sit still? It doesn't make sense. Until Venus came along, tennis was dead. Venus brought tennis to life. When Serena came along and added more life, tennis became a very popular sport all over again. Until then, tennis had died and went to hell. I think they need to change tennis because it's dead.[1]

Indeed, more than forty years after tennis great Althea Gibson became the first African-American female to win at Wimbledon in 1957—arguably the "Cadillac" of competition on the professional tennis tour—Venus Williams won this coveted event in 2000. In the eleven years beginning with Venus's win in 2000, either Venus or her younger sister, Serena, has won the Wimbledon women's single title nine of the eleven years that the tournament was run.[2] This feat alone should be enough to seal their legacy in the Tennis Hall of Fame, but it is not going to be that easy.

In this chapter we explore the careers, lives, and challenges of two of the most successful female tennis players ever, athletes who just happen to be African Americans in the country club world of professional tennis. By exploring to some extent their biographies, and in particular the circumstances in which they were raised, as well as their journeys to dominance, this chapter will examine the ways in which their reputations were forged, altered, and ultimately sustained.

Throughout, we argue that their pathways to dominance in one of the last bastions of whiteness in sport, namely tennis, were paved by their father, Richard. He understood the need to develop their tennis skills as well as strength of character so that they were well prepared not only to win tennis matches but also to weather the virulent racism that would characterize their entire careers. Additionally, we consider the ways in which pioneers such as Althea Gibson and Billie Jean King, among others, were integral figures in the opening of the doors of opportunity through which Venus and Serena weren't content to merely walk but rather run.

STRAIGHT OUTTA COMPTON

Venus and Serena Williams, the daughters of Richard and Oracene Price Williams (now divorced), were born in Lynwood, California, but would soon move to the city of Compton, California, where they lived and learned from their father how to play the game of tennis.³ Much has been made of the tough living conditions in Compton—the California city made famous by the rap group Niggaz Wit Attitude (NWA).⁴

Edmondson reports the fact that Richard Williams would often take his young daughters to the outdoor public tennis courts of Compton, outfitted with out-of-date steel nets, and let them play while gunfire could be heard all around them.⁵ Added to this lore was that Williams was said to have believed that it would be advantageous to them later on in life to know that it was not just tennis that they needed for long-term survival but also an education, and he exposed his daughters to the circumstances that persist in impoverished neighborhoods, i.e., inadequate facilities, gang activity, and violence, as a means to instill the desire to find a way out of Compton.⁶

A 2004 CNN online profile of the Williams family details these experiences:

> Fairly or unfairly, the sisters' hometown of Compton, California, located 18 miles south of Los Angeles, is often associated with drugs, gangs and violence—not tennis, widely considered a wealthy, white sport. But it was on the city's courts that Venus, born in June 1980, and Serena, born 15 months later, got their start.
>
> Their father, who learned tennis largely from books and videos, began hitting balls to the girls at a court near their house before they started grammar school. "Those tennis courts were rotten, tore up, no nets, then they did put nets up and they were steel and they'd go boom, and you'd say another gun was shooting . . . it was terrible," Richard Williams said.
>
> He also tried to teach his daughters toughness—so they would remain strong in the face of racial slurs, cheating and the like—and instilled in them the drive to someday rule the tennis world.
>
> "It was almost like, 'Breakfast, lunch and dinner, and we'll be number one and two in the world,'" says Rick Macci, one of the sisters' former coaches. "This was . . . arrogant, cocky, as a matter of fact: This is going to happen, there's no doubt."
>
> The practice soon paid off and, by 1990, Venus was the top-ranked female player under 12 in Southern California.
>
> The story of these two black, inner-city phenoms captivated agents, tennis manufacturers and the media. By year's end, 10-year-old Venus had been on the front page of *The New York Times* and the pages of *Sports Illustrated*. Richard engineered the hype machine.⁷

The essence of the above is that the unconventional training methods, far removed from how most (read: *white*) youngsters get introduced to the sport of tennis, have stuck with the Williams sisters through the years. These sorts of depictions run similarly to those that seek to chronicle the training methods of an interloping parent of sort—those of Earl Woods, whose training regimen of his son Tiger Woods has stuck as part of the Woods's narrative if not mystique.[8]

Again, similar to the Woods story, a narrative that features the father as the sole "protector," a coalescence of both sport and life coach, ignores the fact that the Williams daughters also trained with professional coaches early in their careers as teenagers in Florida. During his daughters' teenage years, as part of his family's *escape* from Compton, Williams sought better opportunities and moved to West Palm Beach, Florida. It was there that the sisters trained with acknowledged tennis pro Richard Macci.[9] So it is not entirely true, either for the Williams sisters or for Woods, that their dominant fathers ruined or otherwise stagnated their careers by not allowing their *country club sport* talented children to be trained by professional coaches.

All of this adds to the story line for Venus and Serena Williams who have proven over time that they can play in the elite ranks of competitive professional tennis where early training is the lynchpin for future success, though the persistence of comments in the literature and from the public about their lack of professional training speaks volumes to some lingering racialized animus.

COUNTRY CLUB SPORTS IN AMERICA

Tennis remains one of the elite "country club" sports in America. It has its beginnings as one of America's primary elite "leisure class" activities that seemed to celebrate its inaccessibility to the more common elements of the country.[10] As with golf, swimming, and equestrian sports, the dearth of working-class participants, let alone participants of color, is quite palpable, so that it remains both a "white" refuge and a point of contention in the sporting terrain.

What is important to note about country club sports like tennis is that it is at both the individual level and the structural level that race, class, and gender segregation occur.[11] Sports in American life, according to noted social theorist Thorstein Veblen, began as a way for the wealthy, who had very little work to do, to occupy their time and feel productive. As such, participating in sports was a symbol of one's status above the working orders, and this became integrated into the nation's cultural armory with regards to the socialization schemes implemented especially as young boys grew into the future leaders.[12]

For example, long before the rise of the more contemporary "athletic industrial complex," as we have deemed it, and which today controls college athletics, universities such as Harvard and Yale encouraged the best and brightest young men to participate in sports. Of note here are the ubiquitous photographs of President John F. Kennedy that almost always show him running on the beach and/or throwing a football. There's also the matter of President George H. Bush who, we are often reminded, played baseball at Yale, while Senator John Kerry played football there decades later. All of this reminds and reinforces that sports are a stepping stone to leadership, and as such, leaders, who until more recently had typically been white, male, and of means, were encouraged, if not expected, to embrace the sporting culture or face the consequences. Toward this, then, the notion of sports as both a symbol of leisure and an important element of socializing the nation's subsequent elites led to the rise of so-called country club sports, which were designed to be and remain socially and racially segregated because of the ramifications of participation.

While more rough-and-tumble team sports, such as football and basketball, have largely integrated in terms of class and color (though less so by gender), the country club sports, and especially tennis and golf, but also field hockey, swimming, and lacrosse, remain largely segregated by those traditional Western markers. Historically, country clubs have been racially segregated "Whites Only" spaces. Even today, because country clubs are mostly private institutions, they have the legal right to prohibit membership based on race, religion, class, and even gender. Many continue to do so, including prominent clubs in cities such as Fairfax, Virginia, and Birmingham, Alabama, and in such exclusive settings as Lexington, Kentucky's The Idle Hour Country Club and the now legendary Augusta National in north Georgia.[13]

Similarly, many clubs have also restricted women's membership. Until very recently, many clubs would not allow women to be members, though they would allow women to attend the club and utilize its vast array of resources as long as they were accompanied by male members. Thus, men could bring their wives and daughters, which, we should add, has less to do with integration and more to do with providing young men of means an opportunity to meet appropriate women suitable for courtship. We note further that at the time of this writing, Augusta National, for all its fanfare and ubiquity as a golf Mecca of sorts, still does not admit women as independent members.

Outside of blatant discrimination, one way to maintain segregation in the country club sports is by keeping them well outside the reach of more modest aspirants by, for example, charging exorbitant fees to join and maintain one's membership. According to ClubCorp, which operates private country clubs across the United States, the cost of exclusivity is fairly staggering: "The initiation fee to join a private club can vary between nothing and $350,000. Annual fees typically range from $3,000 to $15,000. Monthly food-and-beverage minimum at most clubs, which usually adds another $600 to $2,500 *annually*."[14] Thus, for those seeking to enter from outside the established country club set, the cost of doing so is both a financial and a social burden that gives rise to the difficulties of crossing such distinct lines in search of opportunity, as well as offering a further glimpse into the challenges Richard Williams faced as he sought to maneuver his daughters toward life on the professional women's tour.

ON THE SHOULDERS OF GIANTS

Though every successful athlete can point to those shoulders on which they stand in their journey to success, for the Williams sisters it was a most delicate balancing act, to be sure. Racism, sexism, and the intersection of the two continue to plague women's tennis, and neither Venus nor Serena Williams has been spared. Even as certain future hall of fame athletes, this dominant pair of African-American players continue to face headlong the challenge of stepping across the multiplicity of the sociocultural divide as it exists in American sports; but in doing so, they are working from a script that had been penned by a remarkably small number of pioneers who preceded them on the tour.

As was the case in our discussion of country club sports, there were both individual and institutional forces that opened up access for female athletes, including the Williams sisters, and allowed them to enter the elite world of tennis and dominate it. As with most examples of integration, there were heroes who led the way.

For example, when we talk in terms of the integration of American sports—on various levels—most people think initially of Jackie Robinson, who reintegrated Major League Baseball in 1947 more than a half-century after the forced "retirement" of Fleet Walker. There were important figures in tennis as well, especially Althea Gibson, Billie Jean King, and Arthur Ashe. Not only did these individuals break gender and color barriers, but because of their successes, they served as both pioneering figures and powerful advocates for young African Americans like Venus and Serena Williams to aspire to opportunities that had been all but denied to previous generations.

In addition to the sheer courage of these predecessors, there were also two essential pieces of legislation passed that helped to change the landscape in ways that benefited a coming generation: the Civil Rights Act of 1964 and

Title IX of the Education Act of 1972. These laws created legal avenues by which to challenge the segregation of country clubs and, hence, country club sports as highlighted above. For example, despite century-long racial segregation of golf courses, and despite the legality of private clubs to discriminate based on their standings as private rather than public entities, the Professional Golf Association (PGA) used legal means to demand that any club hosting a PGA event must integrate. As a result, even entrenched clubs like Augusta National were forced to admit at least a nominal number of black members, integrating formally in 1990, just seven years before Tiger Woods won his first Masters. We should note as well that other clubs refused to integrate and as a result forfeited their right to hold PGA events, further demonstrating the extent to which the entrenchment of bias remains a part of the larger equation.

Title IX is of course the watershed moment in modern sport, especially in its role in creating spaces for women in this heretofore male-dominated basin. As so often depicted, it simply guarantees that women and girls would have to be given equal access to educational opportunities when it came to matters of public funding, reading:

> No person in the United States shall, on the basis of sex, be excluded from participation in, be denied the benefits of, or be subjected to discrimination under any education program or activity receiving Federal financial assistance.[15]

While Title IX did not provide the legal avenue for integrating clubs or even advocating for equal pay, it did open up many doors of opportunity for girls and young women to play sports despite traditional obstacles or stigmas long since established. In order to meet the requirements of Title IX, high schools and colleges were forced to add women's sports, and many chose to add sports like tennis and golf. The addition of these country club sports to public schools meant that girls and young women had—often for the first time—a chance to learn to play these sports and to compete in them. And yet, while the route to competing at the elite levels in tennis and golf remain, to a large degree, the purview of the country club set rather than the high schools or colleges, the access door was cracked open more than it had been prior to 1972. Many girls and young women have walked through this crack and have gone on to compete at elite levels, including one Cheyenne Woods, Tiger Woods's niece, who plays on the golf team at Wake Forest University and hopes to one day qualify for the LPGA tour, though she is something of an anomaly still both in terms of the route she took and the color line she has to cross to get there.

Strictly in terms of entry into the highly competitive and notably unforgiving world of professional tennis, the distance between potential and actual access remains vast in this setting as well. For example, between Althea Gibson's reign as a premier professional tennis player in the fifties up though the era of the Williams sisters' dominance in women's tennis in the first decade of the twenty-first century, there have only been a handful of African-American women who have gained national and international stature on the world tour, with even fewer coming from outside the country club world.

There is the often overlooked and certainly underappreciated Lori McNeil, who achieved All-American status at Oklahoma State University in the mid-1980s and was a Wimbledon Singles Quarterfinalist in 1986. Before that, McNeil was the National Collegiate Athletic Association (NCAA) Big Eight Athletic Conference Singles Champion in 1982, and by 1987 she was ranked fourth in the world by the Women's Tennis Association (WTA). In 1994 she defeated the defending Wimbledon champion Steffi Graf (7–5, 7–6, 7–5) in the first round, marking the first time in Grand Slam history that a defending champion suffered a first round loss.

Another overlooked African-American woman to predate the Williams sisters was of course Zina Garrison, who made headlines in 1990 at Wimbledon by becoming the first African-American woman to reach a Grand Slam final since Althea Gibson some thirty-two years earlier. Garrison, playing in the era of Tracy Austin, Pam Shriver, Chris Evert, Gabriela Sabatini, and other dominant female tennis players, was plagued by health problems, and she never did reach her full potential before retiring in 1997. But before that, she was ranked as high as fourth in the world in singles, leaving something of a foundation from which another of her demographic profile could one day build.

EXPECTATIONS RELATIVE TO THE COLOR LINE

Moving away from the Williams sisters and the duality of race and gender for a moment, we can see that the enormity of the struggle of the perceived interloping athlete has long been a problematic feature in American life. To be sure, one element of this story of the traversing of the lines that formed around American sports that have long governed sport socially, politically, and racially that rings true across type, across gender, and across the color line itself is the price an athlete pays for the *privilege* of competing at the elite level. In spite of the more modern look of sports today, with its widening range of color, gender, and personality, there remains more than just a mere hint of traditional discriminatory tones that can be found in the makeup of sports' administrations, existing labor practices, and certainly the level of vitriol that continues to cascade from the stands of sporting arenas.

If Harry Edwards's pronouncements of the 1970s rang true then, that the dark faces on the floor represent less the galvanizing of the tapestry of America and more the reracializing of American life through sport,[16] the continued treatment of athletes who exist outside the range of the dominant segments of the population demonstrates how little things have actually changed, and especially at the level of expectations—athletic, behavioral, or otherwise. Sports fans now accustomed to rooting for athletes who do not necessarily share their social, political, or cultural experiences and outlooks have nevertheless come to demand loyalty and devotion while bristling at the hint that an athlete can live a life freely outside the public eye. In this regard, expectations for athletes—and especially African-American athletes—have grown to be suffocating and perhaps even absurd, but they are no less real. And the price for not acquiescing properly is a high one indeed.

In 1981, Patrick Ewing, a future member of professional basketball's hall of fame, was then a student-athlete playing Division I basketball at his father's alma mater, Georgetown University, where he started as a freshman. Highly touted from the start, he was as dominant a college athlete as has existed. And yet, he was subjected to a constant barrage of chides and barbs that strike at the heart of traditional American racial animus.

Indeed, even though he led the Hoyas to a national championship in 1984, and in spite of having taken them to the NCAA finals in 1982 and later in 1985, his own classmates would taunt him on *his home court* by throwing bananas on the floor during the games and otherwise making nearly constant references to his having only recently descended from apes.

Without question, student-athletes of color—young, vulnerable, and typically ill-prepared for the pressure they are about to face—remain visible targets for racial derision, making Ewing less the exception when it comes to public scorn.

As legal scholar Phoebe Weaver Williams has noted in an article entitled "Performing in a Racially Hostile Environment," which paid particular attention to the events surrounding Patrick Ewing at Georgetown:

During the 1982–83 season, students at Providence College held up "Ewing Can't Read" signs. At the Meadowlands, Seton Hall supporters unfurled a banner that read, "Think! Ewing! Think!" while in Philadelphia, Villanova fans wrote "Ewing Is a Ape" on placards. T-shirts were sold at the Big East schools declaring, "Ewing Kan't Read Dis." Several Georgetown games were interrupted by bananas thrown on the floor. Twice during the 1982–1983 campaign, the Hoyas and chief rival St. John's engaged in fistfights partially attributable to the Big East's ultra physical style . . . as well as the racial slurs from St. John's student body. Far too many of the school's white working-class Catholic student body used Ewing as a sounding board for their own latent racist attitudes.[17]

As she further acknowledged as part of an exchange with Ewing: "The point isn't that this season has been degrading to a black man; it has been degrading to any man. On the airplane last week, I asked Pat again how he was holding up. He told me, 'I've grown accustomed to it.'"[18]

Certainly (and certainly disturbingly) characterizations of African Americans and specifically African-American athletes as animals are legion and date back centuries. To be sure, as Jim Crow continued to entrench itself amidst the broader American culture, the scant few African-American athletes who made it into the public eye were typically portrayed as brutish, animal-like, and dangerous. As well-chronicled heavyweight boxing champion Jack Johnson, and, perhaps to a lesser extent (and really for more practical World War II reasons alone), Joe Louis faced a degree of virulence similar to what Ewing did much earlier in the century as exemplified by the many writers who took great pains to chronicle their dismay over the spectre of the dominant physical specimen.[19] Benjamin Lowe, in his book *The Beauty of Sport*, puts it thus: "The athlete, as representative of the 'best' human physique, brings his natural beauty to the sport domain. It is the acceptance of this feature of nature, the athlete as ideal form, based on the equal acceptance that there is beauty in nature, which tends to make it axiomatic that sport is beautiful in natural terms."[20] A similar albeit more muted approach to the images of the African-American athlete continues to exist even today, something that was both glaring and perhaps oddly familiar on the cover of a 2008 edition of *Vogue*, which depicted a snarling, buff, and altogether dangerous looking LeBron James hovering menacingly bestride supermodel Gisele Bundchen who looked the epitome of the vulnerable white maiden.[21]

Though the shot was taken while the two had been playfully cavorting during a shoot (there was a wide range of poses that are much less dramatic inside), and while *Vogue* put out a press release that celebrated James as the magazine's first black man to be featured on its cover, scores recoiled at just how familiar the image was in the context of American life, and primarily it brought to mind the types of images found in the 1933 film *King Kong*, which itself is often tied to the legacy of the panic over Jack Johnson's reign as world heavyweight champion. Images such as these, long since imagined to have disappeared, offered crude depictions of what is today no longer polite discussions of the American Negro. French psychiatrist and revolutionary Frantz Fanon put it this way in his powerful book *Black Skin, White Masks*: "The Negro symbolizes the biological danger. . . . To suffer from a phobia of Negroes is to be afraid of the biological. For the Negro is only biological. The Negroes are animals. They go about naked."[22] And it is these images—both then and now—that allow us to circle back to the Williams sisters who, like Jack Johnson yesterday, suggest the most glaring example of the interloper in this most insular world of professional tennis and the fear that their collective presence engenders.

Indeed, a search for not only images but also depictions of the Williams sisters suggests that they are anything but immune, not from merely criticism, but rather from the racial animus that many simply assume and dismiss as mere relics of a bygone era. A sampling of some of these depictions from a specific section of a self-consciously racist website titled Chimpout, a section of which is seemingly devoted solely to making disparaging comments about the sisters and various members of their family, contains captions that are remarkably well-crafted and thought out in spite of their disturbing nature:

The Williams sisters Vagina and Smegma were eliminated in Olympic competition. In typical nigger fashion they make excuses for their loss. God I hate these two.

is there a more disgusting pair of sheboons on the planet? they are so bad they give niggers a bad name!

"I didn't do what I needed to do," Serena said. "Just didn't work out. . . . I was cruising. There's no reason I should have lost."
     The nigger admits it wasn't at it's [*sic*] best and then says there's no reason it should have lost all in the same sentence.

I'm glad these tennis sheboons lost. If you think those two are bad, their pappy is even worse when it comes to TNB.

If we judged them by the content of their character, they'd be begging us to judge them by the color of their skin

Damn it US fans where was your support??!?! You should have been there throwing bananas and waddymelon at the poor apes.

I hate those to [*sic*] fat bitch SHEBOONS.[23]

But while the above seem at first glance to be extreme and at odds with current standards of social decorum, it is also not unusual to hear either of these champions referred to in such loaded terms as athletic, as playing with a certain degree of flair, powerful, strong, big, and with references to their Negroid features, etc. Such covertly patronizing remarks, while mild by comparison, no less devalue these two African-American female athletes while showing how little regard the culture holds when it comes to matters of the black body and black beauty beyond narrowly confined spaces such as sport. Indeed, in a 2009 column that explored their bodily struggles when compared to the thin, lithe, white, and mostly Eastern European women who make up the bulk of the women's tennis tour, Serena Williams, who since her debut on the circuit has had to defend her body, acknowledged: "Just because I have large bosoms, and I have a big ass [laughter], I swear, my waist is 30 inches, 29 to 30 inches, it's really small! I have the smallest waist, but just because I have those two assets, it looks like I'm not fit."[24]

Of course, these are far from the only instances when the so-called black body has been damned with praise—faint or otherwise. The Williams sisters have had to put up with years of dismissive, condescending commentary regarding their physiques. In contrast, in a piece that seems to extol his features, even LeBron James found himself the subject of some remarkably inane if not insulting commentary when a *Sports Illustrated* cover story referred to his physique as having "raised veins [that] run like tiny interstates up his arms and calves,"[25] as if the somatic motif supersedes any athletic accomplishments.

LIFE INSIDE THE COUNTRY CLUB

The baggage that tends to follow high-profiled, world-class athletes who manage to traverse the country club world comes with other hidden costs beyond the performance expectations. Such baggage is fraught with elements that seem wholly at odds with both competition and the sort of collegiality one would expect through a rather strict adherence to the many myths that seem to govern sports. To further explore this on a more micro level, we reference an interview that took place on June 9, 2011, with an African-American male tennis player, whom we call Ronnie, who competes for a small private liberal arts college in the southeast, and who competed on the United States Tennis Association (USTA) junior tennis circuit. We found that overall, his thoughts about competition, rivalries, jealousies, and racism all fit with what other African Americans in the country club sports world have said about their experiences.

In our discussions, he made it clear that the competition-related expenses of more than fifty thousand dollars a year coupled with the pressure of competing began to take its toll on his health. Ronnie disclosed that the locker room was always tense, and he felt that he was not welcome on the circuit. He went on to say that in addition to feeling snubbed and cast adrift in the locker room and on the courts by his opponents, even other players' parents were both obnoxious and rude to him. When asked if he and his parents went to dinner with other athletes and their parents after matches, his response was that they have never been invited. Moreover, he maintained that when travelling, which can be quite extensive on this junior circuit, he simply looked forward to getting to his hotel room and connecting with his friends via the various electronic options available today.

In reflecting upon the interview, one has to ask how Althea Gibson, Arthur Ashe, Jackie Robinson, and so many others put up with and endured so many barriers—barriers that might include segregation, isolation, denial of access to compete, and so forth—as they pioneered their ways through their respective sports.

These circumstances bring to mind elements of Alan Sillitoe's short story "The Loneliness of the Long Distance Runner." We reference this less as a matter of the arc of the tale, which Sillitoe so nimbly weaves around a young convicted robber who becomes a great cross country runner at the prison school for delinquent boys where he is holed up, but rather because it brings to mind the image of the solitary figure left to toil in his or her thoughts while navigating accordingly.[26]

Literary allusions aside, it is really no great stretch to see that the African American pioneers who did so much for sports, i.e., the Jackie Robinsons and the Althea Gibsons, most assuredly suffered themselves through some solitary moments with long, lonely days, long, lonely nights, and certainly deep, lonely thoughts. Thinking about Ronnie juxtaposed to Sillitoe's brief narrative reminds us of Ernie Davis, the first African American to win the coveted Heisman Trophy. Long before March Madness, ESPN, Twitter, and the like, student-athletes had little visibility. They went to class, they played their sports, and, if they participated in revenue-generating sports, they looked forward hopefully to a professional career.

African Americans in the Ernie Davis era knew their place and were expected to remain there.[27] Jim Brown, Davis, and the more recently deceased John Mackey, all of whom attended and played at Syracuse University, certainly at one time or another knew their place. The point here is that loneliness was merely a portion of the fee that they had to pay in the hope that such experiences would allow them access to the broader social network found through sports. But their stories also reveal their isolation from the social aspects of college that included not being able to live on campus, restricted access to athletic facilities, and the lack of the complete student-oriented social life that mainstream students take as part of their birthright. The toll of such isolation is a high one indeed; and while it alone cannot be the single causal link why many pioneers in sport died young or poor or virtually ignored until it was convenient to remember them posthumously, we also have to wonder how much this had to do with the stresses of being the first to cross a barrier that even then showed that it had little room and even less patience for those who did not belong.[28]

Regarding Ronnie, thus, his concerns about the stresses of playing on the junior tour—the long-distance travel, the eating of unhealthy food on the road, the missing of upwards of forty-five to fifty days of school each year—show the extent to which these matters have yet to be fully fleshed out. Moreover, what Ronnie's story further reveals is that in his particular case, and by extension that of all young interlopers seeking entrance into the world of competitive tennis, up to and including the Williams sisters, there remains an implicit understanding that the country club is not reserved for them any more than it was reserved for Gibson, Arthur Ashe, or even Billie Jean King and Martina Navratilova, if controlling for other types of sociopolitical matters beyond the color line.

RACE AND SPORT

In a more nuanced theoretical assessment of contemporary racism, Bonilla-Silva and Forman argue that in our time, contemporary racism takes on a discursive strategy and tone with whites distancing themselves from blatant racism while still blaming people of color for their own disadvantages. Among the strategies used is the phrase that operates along the lines of "I am not a racist but. . . ."[29]

We argue that this standard of rinsing away the stench of discrimination by proclaiming that racial animus no longer exists in what some have deemed a postracial order is pure fallacy. It also seems to inform so much of the narrative that unravels each time Venus and Serena Williams take to the courts. Indeed, the attacks on their character, their respective games, and their clothes, and the attacks on their family, most specifically those heaped on their father, are remarkable for their vitriol and what it says about us and the question of race even today. From a purely competitive point of view, it lends even further indication of the dominance these two women have over their closest competitors insomuch as they are able to switch off the noise and maintain their composure just long enough to continue to rack up wins. It would appear that when faced with the actual gunshots of Compton, the symbolic gunshots of racism hold very little sway over the competitive excellence that these two young women wield as they strive to win; but beyond the courts, the broader point is that the victories matter less than the legacy of the noise itself.

On this issue of symbolism, Bonilla-Silva offers commentary regarding what he contends are the symbols of race and racialized thinking, symbols that while often missed by commentators, tend as well to underscore the enormity of racism's reach.[30] The extent of the "symbolic racism" which Bonilla-Silva describes is profiled against the backdrop of the sheer depths of the racial antagonisms that were thrown at the Williams sisters and their family to keep them on the far side of the very world they continue to dominate. These antagonisms extend far beyond the acceptable taunts that we have come to expect from contemporary sport fans in America. The argument being made here is to suggest that despite the fact that the American population has become more racially and ethnically diverse, and beyond the fact that different groups are now afforded the opportunity to move into previously white-dominated spaces, new techniques of exclusion and marginalization are being employed in an effort to regulate the opportunities and progress available to racialized underrepresented minority group members.[31] For our purposes such exclusion and marginalization can be viewed directly in the lack of commercial opportunities available to the Williams sisters.

In race relations theory social distance is accorded a place wherein whites disapprove of living next to, working with, or interacting socially with African Americans.[32] These new, symbolic forms of racial antagonisms are harder to detect and harder still to fight. We heard this in Ronnie's voice when he talked about being alone on the junior tennis circuit, and we see it every time Americans cheer a Venus or Serena upset, when we see inferior tennis talent cashing in huge endorsement deals, or when John McEnroe remains fêted for his much ballyhooed meltdowns while Serena Williams can be portrayed as a thug and a misfit and threatened with suspension for daring to challenge a call.

DOMINANCE AND SPORT

Dominance in sport remains a conundrum. Whether in regard to team sports or individual sports, Americans have a fascination with dominance, but it also seems to make them uneasy. How it is defined is often part of the overarching conundrum itself.[33]

In this context, to understand the career achievements of Venus and Serena Williams, and how week after week and year after year they can dominate women's tennis, requires a theoretical perspective that is not embedded within some unexplainable racial and gender characteristics attributed to good performance in sport: race, speed, gender, and height.[34] While important, these do not in any significant way help us to *explain* sport dominance.[35]

What is significant, however, is that Venus and Serena Williams clearly compete in tennis not only to win, but also to crush their opponents. Like Tiger Woods, they play week in and week out against the other strongest players in the field. This is inherent in the structure of tournament play, unlike other sports, e.g., football and especially boxing, where much of the competition is not against the most dominant players or teams. Thus the Williams sisters' motivation can be characterized not simply as a desire to perform well enough to win but, rather, to perform well enough to become totally dominant. The data on their tournament and Grand Slam wins support this belief, and Wimbledon is clearly the most illustrative of this dominance.

Our attempt at explaining the dominance of the Williams sisters in tennis utilizes "Reversal Theory," most often referenced to the work of Professor Michael Apter. Through Apter, we find that the core of the theory is about individual motivation and the structure of mental life. For Venus and Serena Williams, this means—and it has been corroborated—that, mentally, they, more than other players, can focus on the task at hand while letting nothing bother or otherwise upset their concentration.[36]

Another aspect of this theory of the structure of mental life is the ability to craft a deep desire from a basic social-psychological standpoint to overly value winning. This desire is connected to the emotions (some of which we see in Venus and Serena when their opponents challenge them) and, finally, the way Venus and Serena view the world. That is, seeing the world in their own particular way could be framed as a positive form of myopia.

What reversal theory does not account for are experiential statuses, such as racism, sexism, religious bigotry, etc. The explanatory power of the theory is, thus, enhanced when we add these to the model as we have sought to do throughout this chapter.[37]

CLOSING THOUGHTS

The Williams sisters embody every element of the mythology surrounding American sport with one glaring exception: they don't at all fit the profile of the wholesome-looking all-American ideal. The same has been said about other such athletes who have similarly run afoul of the prevailing culture by virtue of their appearance or backgrounds, bringing to mind such controversial champions as Jim Thorpe, Jim Brown, Muhammad Ali, and even Babe Didrikson, all of whom threatened the very core of the American athletic mystique. As one critic reminds:

> With their funky hair, muscular bodies and African-American skin, Venus and Serena Williams are perhaps the most noticeable tennis players in the world right now. Not only are they the most noticeable, but they are also two of the best players . . . Growing up in Compton (south LA), they hardly had the typical country club background that so many tennis stars seem to have. One reason for their success is their strong family bond and drive for success. They are also devoted Jehovah's Witnesses.[38]

To be sure, the story of the Williams sisters remains incomplete. As we enter into this second decade of the twenty-first century, we find that Venus and Serena Williams are still in their collective primes and remain the two most routinely and consistently dominant forces in women's tennis. But as we have also seen, they have paid and will likely continue to pay an exorbitant price for their accomplishments.

Taken far afield by a family that eschewed if not outright ignored the long since established barriers of tennis's country club environment, they may have laid waste to the lie, but in so doing, they have also suffered for their aspirations. And while technically not pioneers, they have been able to accomplish alone and together what so many have thought impossible in this narrowly defined and insular world: excellence amidst the noise of racism and the near-constant barrage of slights, slams, and otherwise egregious assaults from both within and without the courts in a sport that has seen more than its share of phenoms lose their way to the vagaries of instant celebrity.

NOTES

1. John Intini, "Q & A with Richard Williams, Venus and Serena's Famous Father," September 1, 2009, http://www2.macleans.ca/2009/09/01/richard-williams-venus-and -serena's-famous-father-on-creating-champions-his-critics-parenting-and-the-problem -with-tennis/ (June 1, 2011).

2. Bruce Schoenfeld, *The Match: Althea Gibson & Angela Buxton: How Two Outsiders—One Black, the Other Jewish—Forged a Friendship and Made Sports History* (New York: Amistad, 2004).

3. Jacqueline Edmondson, *Venus and Serena Williams: A Biography* (Santa Barbara, CA: Greenwood, 2005).

4. Russell A. Potter, *Spectacular Vernaculars: Hip-Hop and the Politics of Postmodernism* (Albany: SUNY Press, 1995). This cultural definition of "tough" has also been applied to the training regimen first presented to the sisters by their father, Richard.

5. Edmondson, *Venus and Serena Williams.*

6. Delia Douglas, "Venus, Serena, and the Inconspicuous Consumption of Blackness: A Commentary on Surveillance, Race Talk, and New Racism(s)," *Journal of Black Studies* (2011) 20:1–19.

7. *People in the News,* "Venus and Serena Williams: A Perfect Match," CNN Online, September 18, 2004, http://www.cnn.com/CNN/Programs/people/shows/williams/profile .html (July 12, 2011).

8. Earl Woods, *Training a Tiger: A Father's Guide to Raising a Winner in Both Golf and Life* (New York: William Morrow, 1997).

9. Edmondson, *Venus and Serena Williams,* 35. On this last point, and although this is not necessarily the most prudent place to analyze this issue, the long-held specter of the absent African-American father is a long overdue subject as it relates to the African-American family. This, we argue, is a misreading of Moynihan's thesis that has contributed to this problem (Daniel Patrick Moynihan, *The Negro Family: The Case for National Action* [Washington, DC: Office of Policy Planning, US Department of Labor, 1965]). See, especially, Angela J. Hattery and Earl Smith, *African American Families* (Thousand Oaks, CA: SAGE, 2007).

10. Thorstein Veblen, *Theory of the Leisure Class* (New York: Oxford, 2008).

11. Nancy Struna, "Sport and Society in Early America," *International Journal of the History of Sport* 5 (1988): 292–311.

12. Veblen, *Theory of the Leisure Class.*

13. Marvin P. Dawkins, "Race Relations and the Sport of Golf: The African American Golf Legacy," *Western Journal of Black Studies* 27 (2003): 231–235. See also Jeffrey Sammons, "Race and Sport: A Critical, Historical Examination," *Journal of Sport History* 21 (1994): 203–278.

14. "ClubCorp," *Business Week,* November 17, 2003, http://www.businessweek.com/magazine/content/03_46/b3858624.htm (July 18, 2011).

15. University of Iowa, "Landmark Title IX Cases in History: Gender Equity in Sport," n.d., 2006, http://bailiwick.lib.uiowa.edu/ge/historyRE.html (July 18, 2011).

16. Harry Edwards, *Revolt of the Black Athlete* (New York: Free Press, 1970).

17. Phoebe Weaver Williams, "Performing in a Racially Hostile Environment," Marquette Law Scholarly Commons, n.d., 1996, http://scholarship.law.marquette.edu/facpub/171/ (August 1, 2011).

18. Ibid.

19. Al-Tony Gilmore, *Bad Nigger: The National Impact of Jack Johnson* (Port Washington, NY: Kennikat Press, 1975).

20. Benjamin Lowe, *The Beauty of Sport* (Englewood Cliffs, NJ: Prentice-Hall, 1977).

21. Associated Press, "LeBron James' *Vogue* Cover Called Racially Insensitive," *USA Today* Online, March 24, 2008, http://www.usatoday.com/life/people/2008-03-24vogue-controversy_N.htm (July 12, 2011).

22. Frantz Fanon, *Black Skin, White Masks* (New York: Grove Press, 1967).

23. Chimpout, "Williams Sisters Eliminated," August 16, 2008, http://www.chimpout.com/forum/showthread.php?10493-Williams-sisters-eliminated.&s=70b7543f68601bbb3 96ee31848df2bae (July 12, 2011).

24. Jewel Woods, "Venus & Serena Williams: The Politics of Black Beauty," blog, March 9, 2009, http://www.jewelwoods.com/node/12 (July 13, 2001).

25. Chris Ballard, "The Power of LeBron," *Sports Illustrated*, February 2, 2009, http://sportsillustrated.cnn.com/vault/article/magazine/MAG1151216/index.htm (July 15, 2011).

26. Alan Sillitoe, *The Loneliness of the Long-Distance Runner* (London: Plume, 1959).

27. Robert Gallagher, *The Express: The Ernie Davis Story* (New York: Ballantine Books, 2008).

28. Earl Smith, *Race, Sport and the American Dream* (Durham, NC: Carolina Academic Press, 2009).

29. Eduardo Bonilla-Silva and Tyrone Forman, "I Am Not a Racist But . . . ," *Discourse and Society* 11 (2000): 50–85.

30. Eduardo Bonilla-Silva, *Racism Without Racists: Color-blind Racism and the Persistence of Racial Inequality in the United States* (Lanham, MD: Rowman & Littlefield, 2009).

31. See Bonilla-Silva, *Racism Without Racists*. See also W. J. Wilson, *The Truly Disadvantaged: The Inner City, the Underclass, and Public Policy* (Chicago, IL: University of Chicago Press, 1987); Orlando Patterson, *Rituals of Blood: Consequences of Slavery in Two American Centuries* (New York: Civitas, 1999) and "Jena, O. J. and the Jailing of Black America," *New York Times*, September 30, 2007, http://www.nytimes.com/2007/09/30/opinion/30patterson.html (September 30, 2007); and Lawrence D. Bobo and Camille Z. Charles, "Race in the American Mind: From the Moynihan Report to the Obama Candidacy," *Annals: American Academy of Political and Social Science* 621 (2009): 243–259.

32. Earl Smith and Angela J. Hattery, "Race Relations Theories: Implications for Sport Management: A Critical Essay," *Journal of Sport Management* 25 (2011): 107–117.

33. Adrian Bejan, Edward Jones, and Charles Jordan, "The Evolution of Speed in Athletics: Why the Fastest Runners Are Black and Swimmers White," *International Journal of Design & Nature* 5 (2010): 1–13. See also Daniel F. Chambliss, "The Mundanity of Excellence: An Ethnographic Report on Stratification and Olympic Swimmers," *Sociological Theory* 7 (1989): 70–86.

34. Smith, *Race, Sport and the American Dream*.

35. Bejan, Jones, and Jordan, "The Evolution of Speed in Athletics."

36. Michael Apter, *Reversal Theory: Motivation, Emotion and Personality* (London: Routledge, 1989).

37. Earl Smith, *Sociology of Sport and Social Theory* (Champaign, IL: Human Kinetics, 2010).

38. Chevron Carsville, "Tennis Anyone?" n.d., http://www.chevroncars.com/learn/sports/venus-serena-williams (June 2, 2011).

MARION JONES
Equity through Infamy

—ROBERTA J. NEWMAN AND JOEL NATHAN ROSEN

INTRODUCTION

Unlike how it is with other African-American female athletes, there is no shortage of material when it comes to erstwhile track and field star Marion Jones. Newspaper and academic articles, books, both for children and adults, blogs, documentaries, and her many appearances on daytime and nighttime television all chronicle Marion Jones's life and athletic prowess to one degree or another. They span her childhood, from her abandonment by her biological father through her adolescent tomboy tendencies that would become, according to her, the training ground for her development into a world-class athlete who just happened to be a woman, and an African-American woman, at that.

Where once her story was one to be celebrated, however, the majority of more recent Jones-related material that seems to have exploded in the wake of her very public fall from grace reads less as a story of an athletic phenomenon with Horatio Alger overtones than as a disquieting tale of a woman foolishly caught up in a dragnet brought about by the lure of fame and celebrity. In this regard, there has been very little of Jones's life either on or off the track that has been left unexamined. Few seem to look beyond uncritical biography and conjecture into what is by every measure a very real human drama made all the more significant by its sociopolitical underpinnings. Indeed, more so than any of her many medals or her remarkable statistical accomplishments—or really most any other measurement by which an athlete's prowess can be accurately gauged—it is her foibles that stand poised to be her legacy. But in truth, what the story of her rise and fall and perhaps even the more recent attempt at rehabilitating her image demonstrates, more than any of the other factors, is that it is the coalescence of race and sex and expectation that serve as the most important pieces of the puzzle that is Marion Jones.

Jones's fall was indeed dramatic and wholly public, which made it seem all the more real and all the more personal. For a while at least, she belonged to us. She was ours, sport's version of a dream girl. Perhaps it was her million-dollar smile that captivated us all—that and her ability to get from one spot to the next faster than anyone else. She was golden, and she was beautiful, but she also crossed the one line in sport that remains sacrosanct—and she got caught. "Yes, I took a performance-enhancing drug, and I can't go back and undo any of it," she wrote in her 2010 autobiography.[1] From that point on, there have been reassessments on top of reassessments of her life, her motivations, and ultimately her place in the larger sporting narrative.

Her story may be an all-too-familiar account of an athlete who has achieved fame only to free-fall into disgrace, with one major exception: she is a woman. In a culture whose approach and attitudes towards women athletes have typically been at best begrudging and at worst dismissive if not downright hostile, why is it that this woman's story, which is less tragic than it is sobering, demonstrates such resilience, so long after she demonstrably *let us down*, as her fans and admirers suggest?

That a woman who so publicly projected such confidence and was capable of such unprecedented physical accomplishments, with such ease and such poise could so seemingly easily give it all away may strike at the heart of this saga, but only because it underscores so much of the ancillary discussions relative to sport today. Adding by extension the omnipresence of race—more specifically color—to this mix, alongside the vagaries of gender, always a hotly contested topic within sporting circles, makes this a truly American tale, if only because it hits all the highs and lows that we have come to expect in American narratives of the sort: outsider makes good, outsider exposed, outsider forced to plead for absolution before ultimately being shoved back into the shadows, where the outsiders tend to congregate—well out of view. And yet the trajectory of this particular narrative, with all of its public twists and turns, its private anguish, and its undeniable prurience, in a sense leaves Jones's story poised to be one of the most remarkable of its kind in the annals of contemporary sport, if only because through it all, Marion Jones has seemingly managed to lap the field in the most unprecedented of fashions.

THE FORMATIVE YEARS

Marion Louise Jones, who holds dual citizenship in the United States and Belize, was born on October 12, 1975, in Los Angeles, California, to a Belizean mother, dubbed Big Marion, and her African-American husband, George Jones. Her father left the family when Jones was quite young, a matter that would become something of a recurring theme in young Marion's early life, if only because of the instability it created. Nonetheless, her mother, who projected then as now a quite cheerful and industrious demeanor, remained determined to instill in her children the notion that they could never be limited by the typical obstacles to success in America, namely race, class, or gender, in spite of the condition in which George Jones's departure left her young family. In this regard, we can see quite clearly that Big Marion held fast to the immigrant dreams so much a part of the American ethnic experience.

But while Big Marion continued to put her faith in the mythos of the American Dream, her daughter learned at a very young age that dreams and reality rarely line up, as exemplified by the relationship with her father. This is not to say that she suffered from a lack of positive male influence. Certainly, the first most significant man in her young life was her stepfather, Ira Toler, a retired postal worker, who she claims doted on her, perhaps more so than even her mother, with whom she developed over the course of years a cordial, albeit distant relationship. Toler's presence in their lives seems to have been a boon to the family's immediate future, which saw them moving away from one of L.A.'s lower-income neighborhoods into suburban Palmdale, where young Marion and her half brother, Albert, grew up with a significantly higher standard of living than the one to which they had been accustomed.[2]

When she recalls her time with Toler, however, we can see that a much different relationship had developed: "[S]ometimes he showed up unannounced at school with a McDonald's cheeseburger and fries while the other kids were eating cafeteria food." Jones, in return, never allowed her stepfather to get far away: "It was almost like I was living in his back pocket."[3] Unfortunately, Toler would die suddenly of a massive stroke when Jones was just eleven, which in effect changed not only the household, but Jones herself. As biographer Ron Rapoport contends:

> Brokenhearted, she could feel her life changing in ways she did not completely understand. She had yearned for a father figure, and Ira had been that and so much more. He was the man who raised her, who took care of her, who loved her. But now she had to face the fact that despite her love for him, something had been missing.[4]

While such unfortunate turns certainly took their toll on young Marion, the more fashionable, *pop-psycho-mythological* insistence that at the root of her later transgressions was an ongoing search for a father figure seems overly simplistic if not downright infantilizing. As Rapoport would later contend in 2007 in a well-conceived reflection on her rise and fall, these circumstances neither justify nor excuse what would befall her later in her life, claiming that through it all, Jones remained "a strong, determined, intelligent woman who took charge of every aspect of her career."[5]

Nevertheless, one would be hard pressed not to imagine that the changing family dynamics would exact some toll on a young Marion Jones, as well as on the rest of the family. Thus, while outwardly she would learn to project a much tougher façade, most conspicuously in her embrace of and approach to sport, for the most part Jones grew to be quite introverted in virtually every other aspect of her life. Sport, however, would continue to be the one place where she seemed to find refuge.[6]

According to her two autobiographies, as well as a range of other accounts, Jones thrived on competition, especially when it came to squaring off with Albert and his friends, from whom she learned competitive play. That she regularly faced, and routinely bested, the local boys indicated that her burgeoning athletic skills placed her in a unique category from an early age. Indeed, the extent to which her athletic reputation grew can be found early on as she moved up the ranks in local community sports. Her 2000 biography, for example, includes an account of how dominant she had become in T-ball and later in straight-on baseball, where she out-hit, out-threw, and out-ran her mostly male peers. However, she would also note that baseball quickly turned ugly for her when opposing parents, aware of Jones's enormous talent (and perhaps concerned about the gender ramifications of such talent), openly urged the other children to, among other things, throw at the young girl who had taken over the league in such dramatic fashion, which ultimately ended her interest in bat and ball games.[7]

But beyond such unfortunate incidents, when it came to her athletic development, the one constant was her brother, Albert, five years older and himself a budding athlete, who many commentators fail to recognize as the most important "man," as it were, in her young life. She latched on to him in ways that ultimately underscored her emergence as an extraordinary young athletic talent. As she recalls, when Albert would try to sneak out of the house on Saturday mornings, he would find his sister, who took an interest in virtually everything he did, including basketball, riding bikes, and the like, waiting to go with him. Soon, she became "one of the boys," a premier athlete in her own right, and was often among the first selected when they chose sides for games. As Albert would remember, "She was strong, almost as tall as most of my friends, and she never, ever quit."[8]

Though athletically confident, Jones was also socially inexperienced if not downright awkward. On the field, she could be fierce if not relentless, but this rarely translated off it. Indeed, outside of sport, she had few if any lasting friendships. More simply put, despite her growing reputation as a rising young athlete, a star in the making, she lacked both the vocabulary and the skill set to thrive off the field.[9] Regardless, her limited social life did little to otherwise diminish her zeal for competing. In fact it provided her with a baseline from which to embrace and expand upon her burgeoning acclaim. Her speed and athletic abilities were undeniable, and her family as well as her coaches typically described her as a fully confident if not focused young woman, at least when she was at play.

From the very outset, all she seemed to care about was sport and the trappings of celebrity. Surrounded by the celebrity culture of the late 1970s and 80s, she appears to have understood the connection between success and fame. A seminal moment for her came at age eight, when she attended the torch relay of the 1984 Los Angeles Olympics. She recalled that when she returned home that evening, she wrote on her bedroom chalkboard simply: "I want to be an Olympic champion."[10] From this viewpoint, it seems clear that what appealed to her more than athletic success was the acclaim and all the attendant pageantry athletic success could generate.

DOMINANT ATHLETE

While still in grade school, Jones had already garnered a reputation as a fierce if not formidable competitor. She excelled in several sports including basketball, gymnastics, and a range of track and field events. Indeed, her prowess as an up-and-coming factor in women's track and field was initially heralded by her selection at age sixteen as an alternate on the United States' 4 x 100–meter relay team in anticipation of the 1992 Olympics in Barcelona, Spain. Though she would ultimately turn down the offer, choosing instead to remain on the sidelines for the next four years, she was clearly becoming a bold force in American sport, despite the fact that she was still in high school.

In hindsight, her decision to turn down the USOC offer in 1992 may have been more significant than had appeared at first glance. The early speculation was that this decision likely resulted from her mother's refusal to allow her to participate due to poor grades, but Jones had later reported that this was a calculated and conscious decision borne of her competitive desire to be an active participant rather than an inert stand-in who could conceivably win her first Olympic medal without actually participating.[11] As she speculates in her 2000 biography, no coach would rely on an untested sixteen-year-old schoolgirl with a gold medal on the line. Moreover, because alternates—even those who ultimately do not participate—were in line to receive medals if the team were to have won, that was not how she wished to make her initial mark. She writes:

> Ever since I could remember, I wanted my first gold medal to be something that I sweated for. I didn't want anybody giving me one . . . I want to be an Olympic champion. I want gold medals. But when I'm eighty years old and I'm sitting in my rocking chair on the veranda drinking lemonade with my husband, and my grandkids run up to me, I want to be able to show them my gold medals and say, "See this, honey? This is something that I ran for, that I sweated for, that I earned. Nobody handed me this."[12]

Indeed, her depiction of the circumstances surrounding her withdrawal from the team demonstrated a growing self-confidence and an independent spirit that in some ways belied the uncertainty and lingering fears of those early years. It also left little doubt that she was clearly in charge of her surroundings and well aware of the ramifications of her choices.

With the decision to bypass Barcelona behind her, in the days leading up to her high school graduation, Jones, who some continue to regard as the greatest school-aged athlete of any demographic background to ever come from California, received scholarship offers from hundreds of universities and colleges, mostly to run track. To the shock of many, however, she opted instead to play basketball at the University of North Carolina, where as a freshman point guard, the woman they called "Flash" helped lead the Lady Tar Heels to the NCAA Division I women's championship in 1994. It was also there that she would meet fellow Olympic hopeful C. J. Hunter, at the time an assistant coach for the UNC track team, whom she married in 1998 and whose presence in her life would cast a problematic shadow over her career in the years to come.

EMERGING STAR

In retrospect, her basketball career remains a more integral feature of her athletic legacy than many realize, but in some ways, it was also something of an ill-fated dalliance. Already an established collegiate star, she was selected for a spot on the 1996 United States' Women's Basketball Team on the way to the World Games, but during practice, she broke a bone in her left foot, which she would subsequently rebreak while rehabilitating on a trampoline later that same year. Speculation is that she would have likely continued to pursue basketball had it not been for the foot injuries, which ultimately forced her decision to forsake her basketball career in favor of track and field, a move endorsed by Hunter as well, though he also insisted that her return to the track would only be for international rather than collegiate purposes.[13] It is also likely that the injury was both a lesson learned and a cautionary tale, making her all the more determined to rehabilitate the injury properly and rededicate herself to chasing the celebrity of which she dreamed.

Her comeback was as impressive as it was unprecedented. By 1997 she was back competing—and winning—in track meets around the world, this time under the watchful eye of Trevor Graham, a coach of growing renown, who nevertheless brought the specter of what would later come to be known as BALCO into her life. Regardless, it was the 1998 season that provided the impetus for what was to come. That season she completely decimated the competition, taking thirty-seven first-place finishes in thirty-eight tries spread out over five continents, which not only spoke to her prowess on the track, but equally so of her attraction to the celebrity spotlight as she grew into a sport and media sensation on the brink of international acclaim.

Her real celebrity came bursting out of the blocks during the 2000 Summer Olympic Games in Sydney, Australia. Indeed, eight years after walking away from a spot as an alternate on the US Olympic team, and another four after watching her dreams fade due to recurring foot injuries, Jones set her sights on Olympic glory in Australia. Riding high on the wave of those two remarkable seasons, she forecast repeatedly that she would win five gold medals, a feat not accomplished in track and field since 1924 and never by a woman, given that women were traditionally limited by the types of events that were open to them.[14] This was certainly new and exciting ground for everyone, and she remained resolute throughout, telling writers at *Newsweek* nearly two years before the Summer Games: "If I get four golds and a silver I'll be disappointed. A lot of people are like, 'You should be totally happy with that.' No. I'll say this career has been a failure."[15]

While in the Olympic Village the week before the games, she provided *Time* magazine's Robert Sullivan a similar sketch, responding: "I do see it like that—that I'll win. When people are taken aback by that, I'm surprised. I would hope those women you saw racing against me last night are going to the Games to win. I don't know how realistic it is for everybody, but . . ."[16] Of course a media frenzy ensued, making it one of the predominant—if not the dominant—story lines of the coverage of the games. Fans and rivals all watched attentively, if not adoringly, as Jones went on to win her predicted five medals, though to her chagrin, only three of them would be gold.

Her crowning moment came in the 100-meters, which she won in 10.75 seconds with a margin of victory of .37 seconds, the largest since the XV Olympiad held in Helsinki in 1952. What is most astonishing about these is that they were not even close to being her personal bests, which in retrospect seems difficult to explain, given all that would soon transpire. Jones had run a 10.65 in the 100-meters and 21.62 in the 200-meters a year earlier in a meet in Johannesburg. In fact, her performances in Sydney—a 10.75 in the 100-meters, and 21.84 in the 200-meters—seemed almost lethargic when compared to her times shortly after her return to track and field in 1997, which seems unusual given the extent to which her twice-broken foot had stymied her career.[17]

Even more striking than these victories were the discussions and reactions that ensued. Few, if any, in the world of women's sport have ever been given such accolades for their performances up against the enormity of the Olympic games, and especially when held up to the male athletes, who now seemed small by comparison. History has demonstrated that women athletes—more specifically women athletes of color—remain undervalued, but Jones's performances in Sydney, and all those performances that led up to the 2000 Olympics, seemed to have changed the athletic landscape, if only for a moment. There is no denying that given those performances, coming on the heels of the predictions and the media storm they sparked, women's sport seemed to have mattered in a way that it had not throughout its often complicated past.

Indeed, while some female athletes, mostly in tennis and figure skating, have received some measure of acclaim above their peers—beyond even their male counterparts in some cases—the average American has typically ignored women's sport, especially individual women's sport. The exception was US women's soccer, which at this time was ascendant. But there was a fundamental difference between Jones and soccer stars Mia Hamm and Brandi Chastain. While Hamm and Chastain were members of a team, Jones competed on her own. Moreover, the two celebrity soccer players, as befits America's sweethearts, were white and beyond reproach whereas Jones was neither.

Yet, following Sydney, women's sport exploded into relevance. And Marion Jones, centered in the spotlight, seemed to be everywhere. She was not only talented but exceedingly photogenic. Like Chastain and Hamm, as well as the inimitable Florence Griffith Joyner before her, Jones parlayed her appearance into a more central feature of her rise to prominence. Indeed, by now a staple on ESPN broadcasts and in sport-related media in general, she was photographed by no less than Annie Leibovitz for *Vogue*, and she was featured prominently in the IMAX film *Top Speed*. Multinational behemoths such as Nike, Tag Heuer, and Gatorade brought her into their respective folds, while the increasingly ubiquitous "Got Milk" ads garnered her millions, certainly uncharted territory for the overwhelming majority of women athletes, let alone a woman of color.[18]

Among the many concerns that had long swirled about female athletics were issues of recognition, overshadowed as women's sport was when placed up against men's athletics, and any subsequent opportunities to bank on one's accomplishments. This all seemed to change after Sydney—at least for Jones. Charming, charismatic, and tall with rippling muscles and an engaging smile, Jones became the standard bearer for the new female face of power, success, and vigor. And yet, as we have also come to know, along with the trappings of celebrity come consequences, which in Jones's case were first the accusations and later the revelations that all was not right with her. This is when everything changed: her public face, her athletic standards, and, ultimately, her reputational arc. Filip Bondy, writing in the *New York Daily News*, for example, was explicit in his disapproval, stating that once her most public demise became fact, his image of Jones was forever shattered:

> I want to remember [her] as the magical, innocent student athlete at
> North Carolina winning the NCAA basketball championship. She glowed
> that evening, previewing her $1-million smile to the world. Her urine
> presumably was clean and she had the world at her fleet feet. I'd like to
> remember Jones that way. I can't any more. She is a liar and a cheat.[19]

To be sure, Jones's thunderous crash from icon to villain is hardly exceptional in an age that has come to assume that all athletes are somehow frauds. Celebrities fall hard in contemporary life, and certainly international celebrities fall doubly hard. This is what happened to Marion Jones once allegations of impropriety slowly gave way to the hard evidence, followed predictably by the confession and hopes for redemption.

As has long been the case with fallen stars from all walks, the sporting public has seen its share of celebrity meltdowns, most of which stem from incidents related to doping allegations and/or positive tests. Certainly the litany of track and field participants, ranging from Canadian sprinter Ben Johnson to British stars Dwain Chambers and Linford Christie, not to mention Marion Jones's first husband, C. J. Hunter, and her one-time paramour Tim Montgomery, both of whom have been banned from competition for multiple positive tests, gives clear indication of the extent to which drugs have been a huge concern within track and field, which conventional wisdom maintains is the dirtiest of all contemporary sports, distance bicycle racing notwithstanding. And the fact that Jones's alleged malfeasance came to light at the same time as even higher-profiled suspects, including baseball's Barry Bonds and Roger Clemens, seems to underscore that even the most casual conversations about sport include some discussion of drug use. This is probably why so few were surprised, though no less angered, to learn that Jones had ultimately used drugs.

There is no use denying that any athlete caught blatantly and perhaps routinely skirting the rules is clearly in the wrong, but the problem stems from the general consensus that all athletes—not just Marion Jones—are potential cheats and are otherwise undeserving of our admiration as well as the rewards of celebrity. Where this becomes most problematic, however, is in the context of the contemporary athlete, who is painted as superhuman, while at the same time cannot be trusted to uphold the morals and values regarded as unassailable within the parameters of American culture. In this regard, doping, more so than sex scandals or contract disputes or even the odd brush with the law, reminds us that the traditional images presumably found within sport, such as piety, patriotism, and, above all else, notions of fair play, are no longer the default position among sport's critics and watchdogs.

One element of our societal reaction to cheating among athletes that warrants further scrutiny is the extent to which participants of color bear the brunt of public ire. Where once American sport was perceived as an embodiment of the white, Anglo-Saxon, American ideal, the reality of a world where Jack Johnson and Jim Thorpe are no longer the exception but in certain circumstances, most notably in track and basketball, Jones's bailiwicks, the rule, has altered the meaning of sport. Whether it comes in the guise of overt reminders, such as *Sport's Illustrated's* now notorious exposé on the assumed demise of the white athlete,[20] or through more subtle measures such as rule changes that penalize players for the most innocuous-seeming behavior, like what has come to be called, ambiguously, "excessive celebration," American sport has shifted from marking the birthright of the white male to a perceived affront on the still cherished gospel of *Muscular Christianity*.

THE JONES SCANDAL IN CONTEXT

The doping issue appears to mark yet another chapter in an ongoing saga that suggests that those who trespass on such hallowed ground need to be aware of their place and the consequences of their encroachment. Contrary to popular conjecture, Marion Jones's initial run-in with track and field's anti-doping initiatives stemmed from an incident in which she missed a random drug test in high school, which lent traction to the whispers of impropriety that emerged long before those stunning performances in Sydney. The story was that Jones missed a random out-of-season drug test, which led to her being slapped with the standard four-year ban from competition. Claiming that she was out of the country at the time and never received any notification about the required test, which demands that athletes present themselves for testing within forty-eight hours, she learned of her suspension through the media long before she knew of a letter, which was mailed to her coach's office, subsequently signed for, but left unopened until the story broke. Her attorney, the late Johnnie Cochran of the O. J. Simpson "Dream Team" fame, had the suspension overturned, but this episode, along with Jones's knack for surrounding herself with people with direct ties to other suspect users, many of whom were themselves aligned with Victor Conte's now infamous Bay Area Laboratory Co-Operative, or BALCO, combined to create swirls of suspicion and clouds of doubt.[21]

In these circumstances, we can see the traditional expectations at play insomuch as sport's authorities could so easily surmise that there had to be something amiss. While nothing came of this particular episode, it did put her and those around her on notice that the sport's governing bodies were on alert, which again speaks volumes regarding the level of suspicion that not only she but any other presumed interlopers are forced to endure regularly. As both a woman and an athlete of color, she was twice damned and stamped as such from the start of her public career, which left her marked accordingly.

The official story of her drug use and subsequent arrest for lying to federal investigators dovetails with such expectations. In the midst of the 2003 BALCO scandal, her name appeared on several occasions alongside those of Bonds and dozens of other celebrity athletes rumored to be doping. That her coach, Trevor Graham, who came on board at the insistence of C. J. Hunter in 1997, was among those directly tied to the circumstances further placed her in the crosshairs of what had quickly become a major story with significant international overtones. It is also where the story becomes all the more curious given that by all accounts, Jones did not begin to use any of the banned substances until the weeks just prior to the 2000 games. Indeed, she has long since claimed and continues to claim that what she did was to follow Graham's orders to place what she believed was a pill containing nothing more than flaxseed under her tongue, which ultimately turned out to be the

BALCO product known as "The Clear," a story line that oddly enough has been repeated several times by other BALCO clients.

In his 2007 lament aptly titled "This Dream Needlessly Costs Her," biographer Ron Rapoport would surmise that if she is to be believed, what looks to be a calculated attempt to defraud comes off more as a situation in which an athlete and her coach began to recognize the enormity of the task before her. Having long since vanquished her competitors, all that stood between her and Olympic glory were those extraordinarily ambitious goals, which Rapoport, and certainly others, find to have been at the root of her decision process—Graham's role notwithstanding. As he writes:

> I think she and Graham looked at the Olympic schedule and saw that in a period of 10 days she would have to run three races at 100 meters, three at 200 meters, compete twice in the long jump, run heats in the 400- and 1,600-meter relays and then run the relay finals less than two hours apart. I think they decided she would need help. I think they bought into the widespread notion among athletes that steroids would help her recovery time.[22]

Jones may have fallen into both categories. She no doubt needed to be stronger and faster than her competition, and she obviously craved the attention that winning and establishing new benchmarks could bring. And although she was still in her midtwenties during the 2000 Olympics, she also had to know that speed on the track typically is reserved for the young. Given that she was essentially still rehabbing a recurring injury may have also contributed to the circumstances as they occurred, and yet, the latter makes the case for her beginning her drug use during the 1997 season rather than the six weeks from Sydney that continues to be the official story.

What also bears revisiting is her well-established goal orientation that once again reminds us of who was really in charge of Marion Jones's career: Marion Jones herself. To further recount, she had a great deal riding on the 2000 Games. She had consciously passed on the 1992 Olympics, missed the 1996 Olympics due to injury, and likely figured the 2000 Olympics was her best, and possibly last, chance for the sort of Olympic glory she sought and its resulting perks. She had openly touted goals that by any measure were lofty if not unprecedented, and given that the trials that led up to the medal events themselves meant that she was to have been in a nearly constant state of exertion, she had to prepare for the equivalent of several marathons over a very brief period of time in track terms. Given this scenario, Jones would have to have been much less concerned about any loss of youthful vigor and much more focused on her ability to recover quickly enough to perform at high enough levels for each subsequent event to make the medal rounds, which indeed is the one performance advantage that hormones and anabolic steroids can offer users.

RAMIFICATIONS AND OUTCOMES

Without question, her Olympic moment provided Jones with everything she could have wished for herself. Her fame, and with it her fortune, skyrocketed. Her endorsement deals coupled with her likeness reproduced on a Wheaties box were significant on several levels, not the least of which was that her selection meant she had been anointed by the business world as the next golden child despite her role as an interloper.

To be sure, when she no longer could avoid the legal and public scrutiny that had pressed her about not only her steroid use but also the financial wrongdoing resulting from her involvement in Montgomery's check-kiting scheme, which ultimately derailed her celebrity, Jones took to the offensive, including the publishing of an open letter in which she admitted to using steroids in the lead-up to the 2000 games. She proclaimed, "I want to apologize for all this. I am sorry for disappointing you in so many ways."[23] What is also notable about the letter of apology and her attempt to reclaim what was left of her reputation is that after years of public denial, followed by the two perjury counts that landed her in federal prison, she was now willing—almost eager—to confess to everything, which ultimately puts her on an even newer path to celebrity on the talk-show circuit, where she attempted to appeal to a demographic to which she herself belonged: women. Then, once she exhausted this audience, she resorted to making public appearances in front of school groups, further cementing her remarkable about-face by openly touting personal foibles as a means of returning to professional glory.

Yet, despite the fact that her first attempt at resuscitating her reputation came by means of engaging in what might be interpreted as women's work in the contemporary sense, i.e., speaking to women as a woman via the confessional medium of the talk show, followed by her brief foray into professional basketball in a traditional women's league, the WNBA, Jones continues to wear the mark of public disgrace in the public eye.

Ironically, however, her role as an exposed cheat places her in a position for which she had strived all her life: to be, simply, "one of the boys." No longer could she be publicly viewed solely as a female, one whose exploits could be construed as "pretty good for a girl." Rather, it resituated her on the same plane as such iconic figures as Bonds and Clemens. While it is indeed rare, if not wholly unprecedented, for a track star, any track star, no less an African-American female, to be mentioned in the same breath as the likes of other sport luminaries—cheaters or otherwise—these circumstances have proven to mark a most extraordinary turnabout.

Thus, in the cultural milieu such as sport, with all its erected and assumed barriers, Jones, through her failings, has ultimately managed to garner the one element of legitimacy so typically denied female athletes of all walks: equality through infamy by becoming one of sport's most heralded reprobates. In spite of all the noise and amidst all the shouting, hand-wringing, and clothes-rending over the entire scandalous affair, Marion Jones appears to have finally hurdled that last frontier for women in sport as she stands shoulder-to-shoulder with some of sport's most infamous outlaws. Therefore, while hers may indeed be a story of personal distress and great public humiliation, it may also someday prove to be the new litmus test for legitimacy in a world that up to now has historically looked upon women's athletics as little more than a sideshow and footnote to the men and boys for whom competition was thought to have been their once and future birthright.

NOTES

1. Marion Jones, *On the Right Track* (New York, NY: Howard Books, 2010), 134.

2. Marion Jones and Kate Sekules, *Marion Jones: Life in the Fast Lane* (New York, NY: Warner Books, 2004), 28–29.

3. Ron Rapoport, *See How She Runs: Marion Jones & the Making of a Champion* (Chapel Hill, NC: Algonquin Books of Chapel Hill, 2000), 12.

4. Ibid.

5. Ron Rapoport, "This Dream Needlessly Costs Her," *Los Angeles Times*, October 9, 2007, http://articles.latimes.com/2007/oct/09/sports/sp-jones9 (August 11, 2011).

6. Jacqueline Vleck, *Marion Jones: Press Pause*, directed by John Singleton (Bristol, CT: ESPN Films, 2010), television.

7. Rapoport, *See How She Runs*, 3–4.

8. Ibid., 5.

9. Ibid., 7.

10. Maria Newman, "Marion Jones," *New York Times*, November 30, 2009, http://topics.nytimes.com/top/reference/timestopics/people/j/marion_jones/index.html (July 17, 2011).

11. Newman, "Marion Jones."

12. Rapoport, *See How She Runs*, 43–44.

13. Bill Gutman, *Marion Jones: The Fastest Woman in the World* (New York: Pocket Books, 2000), 61.

14. Robert Sullivan, "Meet the Marvelous Marion Jones," *Time*, September 1, 2000, http://www.time.com/time/arts/article/0,8599,53900,00.html (September 24, 2011).

15. Marc Peyser and Alisha Davis, "Sprinting for Gold," *Newsweek*, August 3, 1998, 57.

16. Sullivan, "Meet the Marvelous Marion Jones."

17. "Marion Jones Biography." USA Track & Field Online, April 30, 2007, http://web .archive.org/web/20070621193541/http://www.usatf.org/athletes/bios/Jones_Marion.asp (September 24, 2011).

18. See, for example, Ron Rapoport, "This Dream Needlessly Costs Her"; Ira Berkow, "Sports in Our Times: Years Later, Jones Feels a Link to Owens," *New York Times*, February 9, 2001, http://www.nytimes.com/2001/02/09/sports/sports-of-the-times-years -later-jones-feels-a-link-to-owens.html (September 14, 2011); and Lance Pugmire, "Out of the Money," *Los Angeles Times*, June 23, 2007, http://articles.latimes.com/2007/jun/23/ sports/sp-marion23 (September 14, 2011).

19. Filip Bondy, "Marion Jones Drags Others into Selfish, Steroid Mess," *New York Daily News*, October 6, 2007, http://www.nydailynews.com/sports/more_ sports/2007/10/06/2007-10- 06_marion_jones_drags_others_into_selfish_s.html (September 6, 2011).

20. S. L. Price, "Special Report: What Ever Happened to the White Athlete?" *Sports Illustrated*, December 8, 1997, http://sportsillustrated.cnn.com/vault/article/magazine/ MAG1011593/index.htm (August 2, 2011).

21. Rapoport, *See How She Runs.*

22. Ron Rapoport, "This Dream Needlessly Costs Her."

23. Mark Starr, "Tarnished Glory," *Newsweek*, October 5, 2007, www.thedailybeast.com/ newsweek/2007/10/04/tarnished-glory.html (August 13, 2011).

PAIRED HEROINES

Chris Evert and Martina Navratilova on the Global Stage

—KATHLEEN A. BISHOP

INTRODUCTION

The reputations of Chris Evert and Martina Navratilova are forever joined together in the minds and hearts of tennis fans and still celebrated the world over. The pair will also be forever celebrated in the record books. Arguably, they shared the greatest rivalry in all of sports. Muhammad Ali and Joe Frazier fought three times; Björn Borg and John McEnroe competed in fourteen finals. On the other hand, Evert and Navratilova played eighty matches over sixteen years, sixty of which were finals.

In the best of these historic rivalries the athletes differ dramatically both on and off the athletic field, but, even more importantly, the greatness of the opposing player pushes each competitor to far greater heights than either would have reached alone. In no pairing is this more the case than with these two superstars. Evert—the icy cool blond, all-American baseliner—and Navratilova—the dark, Eastern European with the wicked temper and dangerous south paw serve—were a study in contrasts and a tennis fan's dream matchup.

In literary analysis there exists a term that applies equally well to these two tennis greats. "Paired heroines" are characters who contrast in marked and basic ways. This concept was a staple of nineteenth-century romance, and examples abound. One instance of the concept of paired heroines would be the Munro sisters, the fair Alice and the raven-haired Cora, in James Fenimore Cooper's *The Last of the Mohicans*.[1] The two young women are tied together in the novel, but they could not be more different. They are a study in contrasts, and, as with Paired Heroines in general, the totality is a richer, greater whole than the separate parts. Cooper's *Leatherstocking Tales* deals with the loss of innocence that accompanied the United States' conquest of the continent, the loss of the Edenic world of the indigenous peoples of the Americas.

This earlier American fall from grace is paralleled in the loss of innocence that accompanied the roiling struggles of the 1960s and 70s. Evert and Navratilova were born half a world apart, but both were to grow up in a rapidly changing international scene. The transformation of the global arena was vast and rapid: the Vietnam War, student protests, the decline of Communism, the civil rights struggle, feminism, the fight for gay rights symbolized by the Stonewall Riot in New York City, and much more forever transformed the political and social landscape. The world of sports was of course dramatically caught up in all of this. The institution of Title IX in the schools (which mandated equal funding for girls' sports programs) in 1972 and the earlier birth of the open era in tennis in 1968 were followed by Billie Jean King's fight for equal rights for women in tennis. These social and cultural changes, along with the first real coverage of professional sports on television, ushered in a golden age for the two talented young women who were destined for induction into the Tennis Hall of Fame in Newport, Rhode Island.

Obviously, men and women have always lived according to different sets of societal rules that dictate what is normal and desirable regarding behavior and appearance. In sport, these gender constructs are magnified many times over because of the intrinsically aggressive, i.e., male nature of athletic competition. In the case of Evert and Navratilova, the opposing tensions attached to being proper, feminine young ladies versus prototypical American "winners" paved the way to a plethora of complications that the two young players had to negotiate, in addition to all the usual challenges of growing up. The fact that Evert and Navratilova are personally so opposite in so many ways only serves to emphasize the difficulty of being a woman in America.

BEGINNINGS

Their paths to the Tennis Hall of Fame were as varied as the women themselves. Christine Marie Evert was born on December 21, 1954, in Ft. Lauderdale, Florida, one of Jimmy and Colette Evert's five children. By all accounts her youth was nearly idyllic, and, like most future champions, she ventured onto the clay courts very early. As fate would have it, her father was a teaching pro at the local public courts at Holiday Park Tennis Center (now the Jimmy Evert Tennis Center), and she began playing at the age of five.[2]

Jimmy Evert had played tennis on a full scholarship at Notre Dame, and then competed on a national level. Growing up in depression-era Chicago, he developed a staunch work ethic and impassive style that he conveyed to his five children. As Evert tells it now, she was not thrilled to be practicing daily at so tender an age, but she soon developed fast friendships at the courts, and before long, Holiday Park was her favorite place to be.[3]

Since she was so diminutive, young Chris couldn't manage to hit the standard backhand; instead she used both hands, a trademark shot that would decimate countless opponents in the decades to come, and spawn a generation of pony-tailed imitators, the most notable being Tracy Austin. Indeed, their first meeting at Wimbledon in 1977 (which Evert won 6–1, 6–1 in forty-nine minutes) was termed the Looking Glass War.[4]

Tennis was a family affair for the Evert clan, and Jimmy Evert had just the right temperament to encourage his daughter's natural talents to blossom without turning into a smothering taskmaster like so many tennis fathers who have followed in his path in subsequent years.[5] He was certainly stern and sometimes rigidly enforced discipline. In her 1982 autobiography Evert recalls missing the Beatles' debut on *The Ed Sullivan Show* because they didn't take the stage until 8:45, and bedtime for the Evert children was 8:30—with no exceptions.[6] But he was also, without question, a caring, loving dad, who always preferred to take a backseat in Evert's professional life.

As further proof of Jimmy Evert's self-effacing style, he continued in his teaching capacity at the local public courts for nearly fifty years, long after his daughter was the reigning queen of the tennis world. The rigor he enforced at this public facility has been compared to elite tennis academies, and besides Chris, he produced many other professionals, eight of whom went on to compete at Wimbledon (e.g., Harold Solomon and Brian Gottfried).[7]

At fifteen, Chris Evert made what can only be described as one of the most spectacular tennis debuts in history when she was unexpectedly asked to join the field at a professional tournament in North Carolina. In the opening round she beat clay court specialist Frankie Durr of France, 6–1, 6–0. In the second round she faced off against Australian Margaret Court, who was already a tennis legend, having just completed a Grand Slam (winning the Australian Open, French Open, Wimbledon, and United States Open in one calendar year). Amazingly, the ninety-pound teenager beat the six-foot, twenty-eight-year-old Court in two tie break sets. Although she did not have her first tournament win until she was sixteen, Evert went on to reach the final in North Carolina, which she lost in straight sets to Nancy Richey, but she had made an entrance to be remembered.[8] Even at this early age, she exhibited the cool, calm, collected demeanor that would soon earn her the moniker "The Ice Princess." Throughout her early career, Evert's reputation vacillated between the pony-tailed all-American girl, alternately "Chris America" or "Miss American Pie," and the emotionless and cerebral backboard from Florida.

All the while, and certainly unbeknownst to Evert, on the other side of the globe her future rival was growing up behind the Iron Curtain in the small town of Revnice, Czechoslovakia. Martina Navratilova was born in Prague on October 18, 1956, into an athletically inclined family. Navratilova's maternal grandmother had some success playing in Czech national tennis tournaments, and her mother was a professional ski instructor.[9]

Although living under the Communist regime was challenging in many ways, she and her half sister, Jana (named after their mother), had a very happy childhood. Jana senior and Martina's stepfather, Miroslav, who together raised the two girls (Martina's birth father died when she was nine), were avid recreational tennis players, and some of Navratilova's earliest memories are of watching them play on the Czech red clay courts. Early lessons from her step-father when she began playing at the age of six, which later continued under the watchful eye of tennis pro George Parma, along with the Communist government's support for sports in general, created a favorable atmosphere to nurture the young girl's obvious talents. Soon Czech tennis great Jan Kodes took Navratilova under his wing, and at sixteen she won her country's national title.[10]

In 1973 Navratilova traveled to the United States for the first time. From the beginning she exhibited a fascinating combination of disparate aspects: guarded and suspicious at times, overtly emotional at others. Although it was all very new and overwhelming at first, the teenager took to America, quickly growing to love the country and its inherent freedoms.

The young Czech was especially enthralled by the spell of American fast food, and she gained twenty pounds in the first six weeks. In general, Navratilova loved pretty much everything about her newfound home. In her 1985 autobiography, *Martina*, she writes, "I'm not a mystic about many things . . . but I honestly believe I was born to be an American . . . things never really felt right until the day I got off the plane in Florida to play in my first tournament . . . and it felt right."[11]

Navratilova made headline news at the 1975 United States Open in New York City when she made the difficult decision to defect after losing to her American rival Chris Evert in the semifinal, 6–4, 6–4. She was nineteen years of age. Although the Czech Tennis Federation had been an asset to her early progress as a child prodigy, as she climbed the world rankings, the government began to clamp down on her freedom, attempting to dictate where and when she traveled on the tour, and with whom she associated, not to mention taking a large chunk of her winnings.[12]

As a result, she came to the painful conclusion that she must permanently sever her relationship with her homeland. International relations between the East and West were still relatively tense in the 1970s, and as Navratilova tells it, the actual process of deciding to live in the United States was quite terrifying. In the days following her defection, she was escorted everywhere by the FBI, and she literally feared that at any moment she could be drugged and spirited away by Communist agents and returned—permanently—to behind the Iron Curtain, perhaps never being permitted to play international tennis again, not to mention the possible dangers her family might face. This last point was especially frightening since her parents had long withstood pressure to join the official Czech Communist Party.[13]

Navratilova was prevented from seeing her family for four years until 1979 when they also defected and joined her in Dallas where she had bought her first home. She did not actually travel to Czechoslovakia again until her triumphal return home as a member of the United States Federation Cup Tennis Team in 1986 . . . with teammate Chris Evert at her side. The Communist government had reluctantly agreed to Navratilova's visit in order to be able to host the lucrative Fed Cup tournament. The world's number one player's name was absent from the program, and during the course of the match the public address system referred to her as the "other player." In an emotional victory she defeated Hana Mandlikova and received a standing ovation from her countrymen.[14]

Like Evert, Navratilova had been successful from a young age. Within a year of arriving in the United States she had beaten Margaret Court in Australia, and although she lost her first match to Chris Evert on March 22, 1973, at the Akron Open, she soon beat her for the first time in a third set tie break (3–6, 6–4, 7–6) at the 1975 Washington, D.C., Virginia Slims event. Although she did not win her first final against Evert until 1976, Navratilova would go on to eventually dethrone the reigning queen while simultaneously revolutionizing the game of tennis for both women and men, with her groundbreaking physical training regime. But it was Evert who had the earliest sustained success in the game.[15]

THE RECORD BOOKS

Evert and Navratilova played a total of eighty times over sixteen years from 1973 to 1988, sixty of these matches being for titles. At one point, Evert was ahead in their matchups by a wide margin of 14–2, and the years ahead brought many exciting, hard-fought battles with the two tennis greats exchanging the number one ranking seventeen times. In 1984 they were deadlocked at thirty matches apiece; but on November 7, 1988, they would play their final match, and Navratilova's victory was her forty-third over Evert, who wound up with thirty-seven victories in their head-to-head matches.[16]

Chris Evert's record is more than impressive, and in many categories will probably never be surpassed, especially on clay. She had a 125-match winning streak on that surface from 1973 to 1979. Her career total win-loss margin is 1309–146, and in 1974, it was 103–7, a single season record. Evert won at least one Grand Slam title every year for thirteen consecutive years, a record for both women and men. Her career victory percentage was .900, the best in tennis, and Evert won 154 career singles titles, surpassed by only one woman: Martina Navratilova.[17]

Navratilova, cited as "one of the greatest female athletes of all time" by the International Tennis Hall of Fame, won 74 consecutive matches in 1984, which remains a record to this day. Over her career she won 167 singles titles (and 177 doubles crowns), more than any woman, or man, in history. Perhaps her most astounding statistic is the longevity of her success: Navratilova played her last professional match on the tour with famed doubles specialist Mike Bryan (twin brother of Bob Bryan). They won the 2006 U.S. Open mixed doubles title at Flushing Meadows in New York City; Navratilova was forty-nine years and eleven months old.[18]

The excellence of the competitive rivalry of the "Celestial Twins of the Centre Court"[19] is borne out by the statistics (see Figure A). Evert and Navratilova amassed an impressive collection of titles that indisputably puts them among the all time tennis greats. This is especially true in their performance in the four "slam" events, the Australian Open, the French Open (Roland Garros), Wimbledon, and the United States Open.

In her illustrious career Chris Evert collected eighteen Grand Slam victories in singles and three doubles titles. Martina Navratilova's record in the majors is nothing short of astonishing. She was a winner on all surfaces and achieved victories in all four of the Grand Slams, amassing eighteen singles titles, along with thirty-one doubles and ten mixed doubles crowns. Her greatest triumphs came on the hallowed courts of Wimbledon where she competed in twelve singles finals, winning nine times.

Figure A

	Evert	Navratilova
Australian Singles Titles	2	3
Finalist	4	3
Doubles Titles	x	8
French Singles Titles	7	2
Finalist	2	4
Doubles Titles	2	7

	Evert	*Navratilova*
Wimbledon Singles Titles	3	9
Finalist	7	3
Doubles Titles	1	7
U.S. Singles Titles	6	2
Finalist	3	3
Doubles Titles	x	7
Total Combined Titles	21	45
Total Singles Titles	18	18[20]

THE EVERT PUBLIC PERSONA

In America the line between public and private has always been porous; nowhere is this more true than in the celebrity-laden culture that permeates professional sports. This characteristic of lives on display is especially true of individual sports like boxing or figure skating. This is also the case with professional tennis, but there is an additional, albeit unique, element present in the DNA of tennis having to do with its long history rooted in country clubs and private tennis centers that are, by their very nature, exclusive, judgmental, hierarchical, and, most importantly, very social.[21]

There is no question that of the two players, Evert and Navratilova, the young Floridian was better equipped in many ways to deal with the very special demands placed on athletes off the field or court, having been born and raised in the United States and having the additional benefit of basically growing up on the courts of Holiday Park Tennis Center.

Chris Evert also had the tremendous advantages bestowed upon her by nature. Yes, she was a gifted athlete, both physically and especially mentally, but she was also a marketer's dream client, a killer competitor and also the all-American girl next door: beautiful, blond, . . . and "feminine."[22] Chris Evert was a commodity. When Dave Anderson of *The New York Times* covered the 1975 U.S. Open semifinal between Navratilova and Evert, he was obviously less impressed with the tennis Evert played than with the fact that she was Jimmy Connors's girlfriend and, in his opinion, able to remain so girlish even as she defeated the, implicitly, man-like jock from behind the Iron Curtain:

At the age of 20, she is now the world's most dominant female tennis player. But part of her appeal is that she always looks like a female. Her long fingernails were polished a pale pink. She wore a small diamond on a gold chain around her neck and silver earrings, pierced. Against her streaked blond hair and golden tan, her eyelashes were so dark they appeared to have been dipped in an ink well.[23]

In this sense she had what many might claim to be an *interesting* (my italics) love life. Evert has been married or engaged to be married four times to equally powerful, good-looking, marketable professional athletes, beginning with Hall of Famer Jimmy Connors when they were still teenage phenoms.[24] They were engaged and planned to marry in 1974 (although they later cancelled their plans). In that year they each captured the Wimbledon Singles title, as well as the public's imagination, when they attended the annual Wimbledon Ball together and took the floor for the traditional dance as the reigning champions. Cover photos and stories of the "Love Double" appeared around the world.

Five years later Evert married handsome British tennis star John Lloyd, becoming Chris Evert-Lloyd for the duration of their eight-year union. A year after her divorce from Lloyd, Evert's close friend and rival Martina Navratilova introduced her to the dashing Olympic Alpine downhill racer Andy Mill in Aspen, Colorado. They were married in 1988 and had three children together: Alexander James, Nicholas Joseph, and Colton Jack. They divorced in 2006 with Evert paying Mill a multimillion dollar settlement. Evert's third, and most recent, marriage was to golf megastar Greg Norman in 2008. The marriage lasted a mere eighteen months, with Norman surprisingly remarrying less than a year later. Speculation as to the cause of their divorce continues.

At the beginning of her career, from the outside looking in, it seemed that Chris Evert had a fairy tale life, replete with handsome princes, beauty, success, and universal acceptance. However, Evert remembers a very different scenario. Although to the public she appeared to be an object of adulation and the ultimate insider, she actually was, for a period in the midseventies, reviled and shunned by the top women on the United States Tennis Association tour. Of course much of it was pure envy of her success on the court, her good looks, and her crossover appeal to the wider American public; but matters were complicated due to the internecine strife going on within women's professional tennis, which was in its infancy and experiencing major growing pains.[25]

At first Evert was resented because she was consistently getting to the final rounds of tournaments, and, as an amateur who could not accept prize money, she was taking money away from the professional women. She sensed "resentment" from the other players, and felt they viewed her as the "enemy"; the other girls would give her "dirty looks" in the locker room. In the other players' views, Evert was cool, detached, and unfriendly. As is often the case, Evert was, as she tells it, just a shy kid overwhelmed by all of the attention and excitement. This kind of hazing is difficult to deal with in the best of circumstances, but it was magnified many times over by the birth of the women's tour.[26]

Whether it was coincidence or destiny, Chris Evert entered the game at the very juncture when a small group of players, led by Billie Jean King, decided to push for a breakaway women's tour, a necessary and inevitable consequence of the grossly disproportionate prize money paid to female athletes. The proverbial last straw came with the 1970 Pacific Southwest Championships where the women's trophy brought $7,500 and the men's $60,000.[27]

With the backing of Virginia Slims, a small pool of women, including King and Rosie Casals, began a separate women's circuit, which competed with the USTA women's tour. Evert chose to continue playing USTA events, along with other stars like Evonne Goolagong and Virginia Wade. As a result of this decision, Evert was even more ostracized than before by most of her fellow players. She saw it as an impossible situation, as she wrote in her 1982 autobiography:

> [I was] a pawn in the power game between the USTA and the women.
> ... If I played USTA-sanctioned events instead of the Women's Lob
> circuit [i.e, the Virginia Slims tour], I was considered a scab outside the
> union. If I agreed to play the Slims events as an amateur, I risked being
> suspended from all future USTA junior events and was ridiculed for
> robbing the pros of their prize money.[28]

Whether her decision was the right one or not is debatable. She did what she believed she had to do, but she was on the wrong side of history, and within the year the new tour was sanctioned and the rebels were reinstated by the USTA.

Although she continued to be an outcast in the tennis world, she remained a darling of the public, but this too changed with the 1972 Wimbledon tournament. The British tabloid press is notorious for its viciously full and uncensored coverage of the rich and famous. This of course is never truer than during the Wimbledon fortnight, the annual celebration of the English championships, when even devout footballers and cricketers—and their fans—become avid tennis aficionados. BBC television coverage of "The

Championships" as they are called is, by law, all day, every day of the tournament on multiple channels.

In the ensuing forty years, press coverage has, in general, globally become much more intrusive and controversial, as is tragically illustrated by the role the paparazzi in Paris played in the death of Princess Diana in 1997. But in 1972, the young Chris Evert was entirely unprepared in every way for the firestorm that broke out around her in London. The foundation had been laid when she defeated England's star player, Virginia Wade, at that year's Wightman Cup.[29] Paradoxically, the famously reserved British found Evert's demeanor cold and haughty, labeling her the Ice Lolly (i.e., lollipop). Evert says, "I suddenly became 'Little Miss Cool,' 'The Ice Maiden,' and 'The Ice Dolly' to the British media. None of the nicknames were [sic] flattering."[30]

NAVRATILOVA—THE NEW WOMAN

As evidenced by Chris Evert's many experiences in the complicated and multifaceted world of the celebrity athlete, the road is difficult even under ideal conditions—even for the golden girl from Florida. How much more challenging was the journey for the other half of the Paired Heroines of tennis?

Ever the opposite in so many ways, Martina Navratilova faced an array of challenges as she entered upon the world stage. She was already sure to be perceived as "Other" due to her Eastern European upbringing as a Communist behind the Iron Curtain. If Chris Evert presented the perfect package to the Americanized global market, Navratilova was the polar opposite. Dark and brooding, at turns distrustful and apt to have inappropriate emotional outbursts, the chubby young Czech was the ultimate outsider. As columnist Johnette Howard put it:

> They were reduced to broad caricatures: Evert the so-called Ice Maiden versus the shrieking, head-clutching, blunt-to-the-bone Navratilova, or "Navrat the Brat." Chrissie the girl next door vs. Martina the lesbian outsider. Chris America vs. Navratilova the Communist defector, the iron curtain Amazon whose forearm veins stood out in bas-relief.[31]

All of these perceived negative attributes would be challenging to overcome in the best of circumstances, but Navratilova was hiding a secret that was becoming increasingly burdensome personally and difficult to conceal: her true identity as a homosexual. Although she had a boyfriend as a teenager in Czechoslovakia with whom she had an intimate relationship,

Navratilova always knew, from a very young age, that she had special feelings for other girls and women, which she only much later learned to label as "gay" or "lesbian."

As Navratilova began to travel widely on the international tennis circuit, and after defecting in 1975, she felt a newfound freedom to explore her feelings for other women. Like Evert, over the ensuing years, Navratilova had numerous high-profile relationships with glamorous people such as socialite and former beauty queen Judy Nelson, a married mother of two with whom she lived for eight years until 1991, and previous to this she had a three-year relationship with acclaimed writer and gay icon Rita Mae Brown, author of *The Rubyfruit Jungle*. That relationship ended in 1981.

Navratilova was also linked with famous sports figures such as golfing great Sandra Haynie, an older woman who mentored her for a period in the late seventies; but it was her 1981 meeting with basketball star Nancy Lieberman, a relationship whose personal dimensions continue to confound, that transformed Navratilova from a very good tennis player into a superstar who would rewrite the books on what a female athlete could achieve and be.[32]

In its formative years, the professional women's tennis tour was composed of a relatively small circle of players who traveled together from city to city. They shared life together both on and off the court. Chris Evert was one of the first women to reach out to the young Eastern European when she was new to America and the circuit, and the two would form a lasting relationship, which has endured to this day. As their bond grew, they spent many hours together, traveling, sharing meals, practicing, and eventually playing doubles together, culminating in their capturing the 1976 French Doubles title.[33]

The problem was, in this pair, Navratilova was always runner-up, both competitively when they faced off in singles and in the real world. As ubiquitous albeit well-respected sports commentator Frank Deford said in 1986, Navratilova was identified as "the bleached blond Czech bisexual defector."[34] Navratilova felt that members of the press, in general, were far more "snide" about female athletes, and that personally it was impossible to compete with one of the "Osmonds," a reference to the popular singing family whose wholesome, fresh-faced persona makes this comment a glaring swipe at Evert's similar public image.[35] To be sure, Evert consistently projected a larger-than-life, wholesome, all-American image, and Navratilova just counted herself lucky to be included in her circle. But everything, including their close-knit relationship, changed dramatically in 1981 when she met Lieberman, who transformed the way Navratilova interacted with the world, starting with Evert.

Lieberman stressed that Navratilova was simply being too nice. She would have to learn to have the "killer instinct" if she wanted to be a winner. She explained to her new charge that it was impossible to have a friendly lunch or dinner with archrival Chris Evert and then go out on the court and not just beat her, but destroy her, as she must do. Lieberman effectively ended Navratilova's friendship with Evert for a period of several years as she stressed that Navratilova had to wear her "game face" any time she was in public, and especially any time she was around Evert. Although time has healed those wounds, Evert experienced the change as a shocking alteration in her friend's behavior. In an article in the *New York Times,* Evert said, "She [Lieberman] taught Martina to hate me. And while that's not the same as physical harm, I think you could call it emotional abuse."[36]

In her reinvention of Navratilova, Lieberman developed for her an all-inclusive fitness regime that encompassed not only the standard tennis drills and practice sessions, but also weight, speed, and agility training, as well as cross training that included other sports like basketball. She also stressed a total life approach to competition that incorporated sports psychology and then revolutionary ideas about diet and sports. The plan was more than successful and Navratilova became the prototype for the new female athlete.[37]

To accomplish this huge undertaking, Lieberman brought in a wide variety of experts to assist, including ophthalmologist Dr. Renée Richards, a transsexual who was already famous, and controversial, for having competed professionally on the women's tennis tour. The newly formed group quickly became known through wide media coverage as "Team Navratilova." They attracted a lot of attention, most of it quite unflattering. As Howard explains, "Navratilova was routinely marginalized as the lesbian with the outrageous entourage in tow. For eight years her partner was a divorced Texas beauty queen and mother of two. One of her coaches was a six-foot-two transsexual ophthalmologist, Renée Richards."[38]

Although Nancy Lieberman, for a time, cast Evert in the role of hated enemy, it was only through Navratilova's long-time, close-knit relationship with Evert that she was able to benefit from her new coach's advice. In a sense, Lieberman was teaching Navratilova the lessons about on- and off-court demeanor that Jimmy Evert had taught his daughter all those years before at Holiday Park Tennis Center. Lieberman was actually asking Navratilova to be more like Evert emotionally in order to beat the champion at her own game, something she could easily model since she had watched Evert first-hand through their close friendship together on the tennis circuit.[39]

Through physical, mental, and emotional work, Navratilova was transformed into a cocky, unbeatable juggernaut that dominated the women's game for years to come. To this day, Evert still bristles when she recalls the way the newly confident Navratilova would arrogantly strut about the court, slapping her thigh angrily if she missed a shot, even if it was an impossible get.[40] Navratilova developed the attitude, not seen again on the women's tour until the debut of the Williams sisters years later, that any match, on any surface, against any opponent, was hers to win or lose. The tennis player on the other side of the net was almost irrelevant to the equation.[41]

IMAGE AND THE MARKETPLACE

Of course the swagger that resulted from Navratilova's domination on the tennis court did not translate well to the world of advertising and the increasingly lucrative endorsement packages that were fast becoming the road to crossover superstardom in the larger society. Select athletes could become household names and gain entry to the American cult of celebrity that brought with it international recognition and incredible financial rewards that tennis champions of the past, like Margaret Court or Rod Laver, could never even have imagined.

In the twenty-first century the opportunities available to athletes have multiplied exponentially. A case in point is Maria Sharapova, the Russian-born beauty who is as talented as she is marketable. As Eric Wilson points out, "One does not become the highest paid female athlete in the world without recognizing that the greatest potential for earnings comes not from winning championships, but from endorsement deals...." Sharapova, twenty-four, made "$24.5 million from June 2009 to June 2010, according to Forbes, about $4 million more than her nearest competitor, Serena Williams."[42]

Chris Evert's virtually predictable marketability in many ways was the prototype for today's superstars. She secured key endorsements with top tennis equipment and apparel manufacturers like Wilson, Converse, and ellesse, as well as general market products like Lipton Tea. Although by Evert's own account, she is not as squeaky clean as people think, perception is everything, and to this day her numerous endorsement deals have remained strong.[43]

Americans in particular seem to perversely enjoy building up celebrities to unnatural heights only to tear them down. Sexual scandals, gay sexual scandals, can be especially viral, as evidenced by the married Billie Jean King's explosive palimony scandal in 1981, when she was sued by her former secretary, Marilyn Barnett. King lost key endorsements for a Wimbledon clothing line, a Japanese apparel company, a hosiery line, and a jeans contract to the tune of $1.5 million, an enormous figure at the time.[44] The revelations sent shock waves throughout the tennis world, and the effects were devastating, not only for King, but for tennis as a whole. World Team Tennis lost key sponsorships, and within a year Avon had dropped the women's tour.[45]

In the midst of the turmoil, Navratilova, as a young gay woman, struggled to maintain her focus on tennis, but she was of course swept up in it all, and her sexual orientation cost her dearly in the marketing world. Even her coach, Nancy Lieberman, was tainted by association, and her career suffered as a result. In a 1994 *New York Times* article Robin Finn said that "on the endorsements front, she [Navratilova] was an orphan. Commerce preferred Evert, and still does. . . ."[46] In point of fact, Navratilova never really put the whole thing behind her until after her retirement, which is when she first began to collect significant endorsement packages, a not uncommon trajectory found throughout the history of female athletes writ large.

THE BEST OF RIVALS AND THE BEST OF FRIENDS

Although Evert and Navratilova have been retired from the women's tennis tour for years, they remain connected to tennis and to each other. Among other ventures, Evert is currently a contributor to *Tennis* magazine, and Navratilova works throughout the year as a television commentator for several networks, as does Evert.[47]

Their rivalry was truly one for the ages. In the ensuing years nothing has even come close to matching the longevity, competitiveness, and sheer drama of this pairing of titans. The only other comparison in the last decade could be the Williams sisters, who have dominated the women's tennis game, and are only now entering the twilight of their careers as they reach thirty. But their matchups were very different—uncomfortable is the word that comes to mind—uncomfortable for the two siblings and equally uncomfortable for fans to witness. Rather than being rivals, the Williamses were more like the corulers of the tennis realm.

Socially, the legacy that Evert and Navratilova left is still being felt and still being played out on the world stage. Because they are so different in so many ways, the juxtaposition of characteristics that they presented crystallizes the notion of diversity. To be a woman in the twenty-first century is not any one thing. One can be a traditionally feminine heterosexual female or a strong, proud lesbian, or any combination of the two, and still be a woman, still be a winner.

The passage in June 2011 of the New York State bill legalizing gay marriage proves how far as a society we have come and how far we have to go. Women athletes in America have long fought against negative stereotypes, from the days of Babe Didrikson, who was accused of not being a real woman because of her athletic prowess, to Althea Gibson, who broke through racial barriers. A more recent example of the continuing struggle would be the homophobic remarks of tennis champions Lindsay Davenport and Martina Hingis directed against Amelie Mauresmo, the French star, who is a lesbian. Hingis, notoriously, is quoted as saying that "Sie ist ein halber Mann" ("She is half a man").[48]

Today, Evert and Navratilova are personally closer than they were at any prior juncture in their lives. Truly, they are the quintessential paired heroines in the parallel journeys that ultimately knotted their lives. Moreover, they remain well aware that they share a bond that is unique and profound. Each completes the other, and they both feel that no other human can understand their lives in quite the same way as they, and only they, do. As Frank Deford has said in his typical grandiloquence, "Together they form a complete whole. There has never been a rivalry like it in women's sports. You could even leave out the qualifying gender and be correct."[49]

Or as Navratilova herself would couch it, "I'm so happy I was one half of a whole,"[50] a pairing that only in the years beyond their athletic dominance has begun to be understood and appreciated by the public.

NOTES

1. James Fenimore Cooper, *The Last of the Mohicans* (New York: Bantam, 1981).

2. *The Evert Era*, Tennis Channel, n.d., 2008.

3. Ibid.

4. Frank Deford, "She Won, But Is She No. 1," *Sports Illustrated On-Line*, December 28, 1981, sportsillustrated.asia/vault/article/magazine/MAG1125119 (July 29, 2011).

5. Some infamous examples of the tyrannical tennis father: Peter Graf, Stefano Capriati, Damir Dokic, and Jim Pierce, who would scream obscenities from the stands, and by Mary Pierce's own account, would routinely beat her after bad match performances or even subpar practice sessions. More recently documented examples include Maria Sharapova's relationship with her father, and on the men's side of the game, Mike Agassi, as written in Andre's autobiography, *Open* (New York: Harper Collins, 2009).

6. Chris Evert Lloyd with Neil Amdur, *Chrissie, My Own Story* (New York: Simon and Schuster, 1982), 43.

7. *The Evert Era.*

8. Johnette Howard, *The Rivals: Chris Evert vs. Martina Navratilova: Their Epic Duels and Extraordinary Friendship* (New York: Broadway Books, Random House, 2005), 15–16.

9. Martina Navratilova with George Vecsey, *Martina* (New York: Fawcett Crest, 1985), 6.

10. *Signature Series,* "Martina Navratilova," Tennis Channel, n.d., 2009.

11. Vecsey, *Martina,* 2.

12. *Signature Series,* "Martina Navratilova."

13. Ibid.

14. Frank Deford, "Yes, You Can Go Home Again," *Sports Illustrated,* August 4, 1986, 22–28.

15. Vecsey, *Martina,* 105.

16. Howard, *The Rivals,* 279–281.

17. Amdur, *Chrissie,* 227–228.

18. Bonnie DeSimone, "Act II of Navratilova's career ends with a win," ESPN.com, 2006, http://sports.espn.go.com/sports/tennis/usopen06/news/story?id=25 78105 (November 12, 2011).

19. Richard Evans, "Celestial Twins of the Centre Court," *The Times* (London), March 18, 1986.

20. Dennis J. Phillips, *Women Tennis Stars: Biographies and Records of Champions, 1800s to Today* (Jefferson, NC: McFarland & Company, 2009), 85–89.

21. This is also true of golf. One need only think of the Tiger Woods debacle of 2010 to illustrate the vicious and swift nature of the punishment of transgressions, especially of a sexual nature.

22. This is not to say that Evert didn't face an uphill battle in fighting persistent stereotypes. In a 1981 article, Frank Deford wrote, "Even now in the all-American world of Ft. Lauderdale, Fla., a male is considered more of a man if he's an athlete, but a woman athlete is perceived to be less of a female." "Love and Love," *Sports Illustrated,* April 27, 1981, 72–88.

23. Dave Anderson, "The Chris and Jimmy Romance Revival," *New York Times,* September 6, 1975, 13.

24. Evert also had serious romances with Jack Ford, son of President Gerald Ford, and Hollywood heartthrob Burt Reynolds, not to mention relationships with various celebrities too numerous to mention here.

25. Howard, *The Rivals,* 253; Eunice Oh, "Chris Evert and Greg Norman Split," *People On-Line,* October 2, 2009, people.com/people/article/0,,20309956,00 (July 29, 2011).

26. Amdur, *Chrissie,* 59.

27. Jon Henderson, "Hard work and glamour make women's tennis shine," *Observer On-Line,* June 22, 2008, guardian.co.uk/sport/2008/jun/22/wimbledon.tennis3 (July 29, 2011).

28. Amdur, *Chrissie,* 61.

29. The Wightman Cup, which pitted Great Britain against the United States, was an annual women's team tennis event, similar in structure to the Davis Cup or Federation Cup, which ran from 1923 to 1989.

30. Amdur, *Chrissie,* 76.

31. Howard, *The Rivals,* 5.

32. Vecsey, *Martina*.

33. Ibid., 111; Lisa Lax and Nancy Stern , *30 For 30 Series*, "Unmatched," ESPN, n.d., 2010.

34. Frank Deford, "A Pair Beyond Compare," *Sports Illustrated*, May 26, 1986, 80.

35. Lax and Stern, "Unmatched."

36. Robin Finn, "Violence, Evert Says, Has to Do with No. 1," *New York Times*, January 21, 1994, B11.

37. Howard, *The Rivals*.

38. Ibid., 6.

39. George Vecsey makes the point that, in general, women are more civil, both on and off the court. "Male athletes, by contrast, are much more catty. Witness the disdain between Jimmy Connors and John McEnroe and the way Andre Agassi dissed Pete Sampras in his recent book. Bill Russell and Wilt Chamberlain did stay respectful, even when Russell won the titles, but Joe Frazier still hates Muhammad Ali. . . ." Quote is in "The Best of Rivals and Best of Friends, Then and Always," *New York Times*, August 30, 2010, F10.

40. Lax and Stern, "Unmatched."

41. Navratilova was truly the forerunner to the supreme female athletes who take the court today: "They're stronger, bigger, faster, better trained and pushed above all by the example of the Williams sisters. Serena, glorious and muscle bound, and Venus, long-limbed and tall, have redefined the sport around power. Years ago, tennis writers used to call Martina Navratilova, listed at 5-foot-8 and lean, a giantess with popping veins because other women seemed weaklings by comparison." Michael Kimmelman, "Women Who Hit Very Hard and How They've Changed Tennis," *New York Times Magazine*, August 29, 2010, 26.

42. Eric Wilson, "Maria Sharapova Extends Her Reach," *New York Times*, May 26, 2011, E1.

43. Finn, "Violence," B11.

44. Nancy Spencer, "America's Sweetheart," *Journal of Sport and Social Issues*, Vol. 27, No. 1, 16.

45. Vecsey, *Martina*, 236.

46. Finn, "Violence," B11.

47. Among other ventures Navratilova appears on the Tennis Channel and BBC; Evert is on ESPN and BBC.

48. Derrick Whyte, "Tennis: Storm over man-sized Mauresmo," *Independent Online*, January 30, 1999, independent.co.uk/sport/tennis-storm-over-mansized-mauresmo-1077214 (July 29, 2011).

49. Deford, "A Pair," 80.

50. Lax and Stern, "Unmatched."

"RAINDROPS ON A WINDOW"

Race and Sex and the Framing of the Sheryl Swoopes Narrative

—LISA DORIS ALEXANDER

INTRODUCTION

In 2002 when a *New York Post* article erroneously hinted that New York Mets catcher Mike Piazza was gay, one sportswriter wrote that his coming out "would have only been the biggest sports story of the year, probably the biggest in many years."[1] Subsequently, sportswriters spent a lot of time and column inches speculating about the consequences of a high-profile team–sport athlete coming out of the closet during his or her career. It was assumed that there would be a media frenzy followed by fans' rejection, loss of sponsors, and a relatively quick end to said athlete's career. Given this story line, when Women's National Basketball Association (WNBA) superstar Sheryl Swoopes announced, just three years later, that she was in a relationship with a woman, one would have assumed that the media would have been all over the story.

Sheryl Swoopes is the epitome of sporting excellence, having achieved every accolade a basketball player can earn. Swoopes was a high school All-American, was named the Union College Player of the Year, led Texas Tech to two South West Conference (SWC) titles and the 1993 NCAA Championship while being named Most Valuable Player.[2] After she was called a "female Michael Jordan . . . a point scoring machine as prolific as the women's game had ever known,"[3] there were no opportunities for Swoopes, or any other woman, to play hoops professionally in the United States. In 1996 she helped the United States win gold in the Atlanta Olympic Games, and one year later she became the founding member of the Houston Comets, one of the inaugural teams of the WNBA. The Comets won four WNBA championships as Swoopes racked up three MVP awards and was eventually named to the WNBA All-Decade Team.[4] Finally, in what has become the end-all-be-all of professional sports, Swoopes became the first woman to have a basketball shoe named after her—the appropriately named Air Swoopes by Nike.[5] By any measure, Swoopes is a superstar.

Prior to Swoopes's announcement, however, fortunately or unfortunately, depending on one's point of view, her revelation was not met with the frenzy sportswriters had anticipated. John Ryan of the *San Jose Mercury News* wrote, "Let's face it: on the list of shocking headlines, 'WNBA player is gay' falls somewhere between 'Romo took steroids' and 'Steinbrenner is angry.'"[6] According to Jemele Hill of the *Montreal Gazette*, "If a star athlete admits being gay, you'd think it would hit the mainstream like an egg smashes into a windshield . . . Only Sheryl Swoopes's disclosure she is a lesbian isn't egg-to-windshield. It's raindrops on a window, and more pebbles than [a] ton of bricks."[7] Granted, Swoopes was not the first lesbian to come out during her athletic career; tennis players Martina Navratilova and Amélie Mauresmo and WNBA players Sue Wicks and Michele Van Gorp each came out while they were still active. Swoopes's announcement made her the highest profile U.S. team–sport athlete to come out during his or her career, but the news was treated like a nonstory. In a perfect world, consensual relationships between adults would not be cannon fodder for talk radio, tabloids, and news broadcasts, but that is not the world in which we live. If society is so obsessed with celebrity relationships, especially same-sex ones, what would account for the lack of interest in Swoopes's announcement?

Herein, I will argue that Swoopes's status as an African American, as well as the historical misperceptions regarding female athletes' sexual identity, suppressed the hype usually associated with an announcement of this type. As I suggest, far more attention would have been paid to her announcement had she been white and/or male. At the same time, Swoopes's importance is not limited to her sexual identity; the ways in which her entire career has been framed speaks to larger issues surrounding race and gender.

LADIES FIRST

One of the reasons why Swoopes's announcement was met with yawns and crickets has to do with emphasized femininity, which, according to theorist Mimi Schippers, "consists of the characteristics defined as womanly that establish and legitimate a hierarchical and complementary relationship to hegemonic masculinity and that, by doing so, guarantee the dominant position of men and the subordination of women."[8] To further expand Schippers's larger point, emphasized femininity privileges those traits that make men's positions of authority and power over women seem natural and necessary. This emphasized or idealized form of femininity includes characteristics such as "being emotional, passive, dependent, maternal, compassionate, and gentle"[9] and is usually typified by women who are white, upper class, and heterosexual.[10] For example, it is easier to keep women out of positions of power and authority if all women are framed as passive and dependent.

One of the problems the WNBA and other female professional sports leagues face is that the characteristics of emphasized femininity are in direct contrast to the qualities female athletes need to do their job effectively—compassionate and gentle are not two words usually used to describe great athletes. Because emphasized femininity and athleticism are seemingly contradictory, female athletes are often framed as masculine and/or lesbian, labels that have followed female athletes for decades. If the WNBA wanted to successfully market its game, it had to find ways to highlight a fairly specific form of femininity because the player's athletic activities and muscular bodies contrast with society's definition of ideal womanhood.

When the inaugural WNBA began in 1997, Swoopes was framed as one of the league's poster children, particularly in terms of her status as a mother. Though Swoopes was the first player to sign a contract with the WNBA, she spent the first two months of the opening season on injured reserve because she was pregnant, but the superstar also made headlines when she returned to the court six weeks after giving birth to her son.[11]

Indeed, the WNBA took the opportunity to showcase the maternal side of the league by turning Swoopes's pregnancy into "a press bonanza, with soft news stories about maternity in general, balancing baby with basketball, and the generous sacrifice of Swoopes's husband, Eric Jackson, to stay home with the baby."[12] *Working Mother* magazine featured Swoopes as one of only two women of color on the "Moms We Love" list, and the blurb was quick to point out that Swoopes refused to sign onto the U.S. Olympic team until it agreed to pay for her son and his babysitter to accompany her to Australia.[13] This move emphasized the fact that motherhood was Swoopes's primary focus and de-emphasized her role as an athlete.

And yet, Swoopes wasn't the only player whose maternity was prioritized and made available for public consumption. In 2009 the official WNBA website featured an "Ask Olympia" section where fans could submit questions to Utah Stars center Olympia Scott-Richardson, and as Sarah Banet-Weiser points out, the overwhelming majority of questions concerned Richardson's recent pregnancy.[14] When Cleveland Rockers star Suzie McConnell Serio made her WNBA debut, the Lifetime Network, which televised the game, placed a microphone on her seven-year-old son so that the viewing audience could hear his comments about his mother's return to the court.[15]

To be sure, focusing on a player's maternity reinforces traditional gender roles, diminishes her status as an athlete, and, because each of the women was married, helped frame the WNBA as a heterosexual space.[16] This focus on the nuclear family not only reinforced the idea that the WNBA was a heterosexual space where women could be wives, mothers, and professional, but it branded the WNBA into what Banet-Weiser deems a "family-oriented, moral game."[17] This type of framing is construed as keeping women's priorities firmly planted within the domestic sphere and pushes the player's athletic accomplishments to the back burner. The more time and column inches spent discussing a player's role in her home means that less time is spent discussing a player's role on the court, which sends the message that there is little need to take anyone's game too seriously. Despite their status as professional athletes, players are being framed in what appears to conform to traditional gender roles. Adding to this effect, because of the traditional stereotypes regarding black women's sexuality, framing the WNBA's predominantly black workforces in terms of traditional gender roles led to some unintentional outcomes.

Critical race theorist and black feminist scholar Kimberlé Crenshaw argues that analyzing race and gender separately would not be equivalent to the analysis of their intersectional relationship because, as she posits, "the intersectional experience is greater than the sum of racism and sexism."[18] This means that analyzing race, class, gender, and sexuality separately is an inadequate method of analysis and that analyzing these factors together, since they intersect with each other where power relations are concerned, provides a more complete analysis. Under normal circumstances, then, highlighting a basketball player's maternity in conjunction with—and in some cases more than—her skill on the court would be discussed solely as a not-so-subtle form of patriarchy.

It is true that the focus on motherhood does make clear the differences between male athletes and female athletes and certainly privileges the NBA over the WNBA—though Swoopes was applauded for her swift return to action after maternity leave. In contrast, it is inconceivable that players like LeBron James or Kobe Bryant would miss six games let alone six weeks for paternity leave. The WNBA highlighted the maternal side of its players for a multitude of reasons, not the least of which was because, according to black feminist scholar Patricia Hill Collins, league officials "realized that its profitability might suffer if the league was perceived as dominated by lesbian ballplayers [so the league had] to ensure that the 'mannish' label applied to lesbians, female athletes, and Black women as a group would not come to characterize the WNBA."[19]

The fact that the majority of WNBA players were going to be black women was a reality that could not be ignored, a matter that arguably led the league to frame someone like the aforementioned Suzie McConnell Serio as "the good white girl" to "(re)establish what can be seen, valued, and desired."[20]

This was a way to downplay the league's majority black workforce and the stigma of female athletes as *mannish*. Focusing on the player's maternity within a nuclear family was another way of avoiding the "mannish" label and is problematic for several reasons. At the same time, because femininities are raced and classed, the effects of this framing are not that simple.

As mentioned earlier, emphasized femininity is usually reserved for white, heterosexual, upper-class women, and this framing pushes women of different races, ethnicities, sexualities, and class statuses into pariah femininities. Women who are framed within these pariah femininities are problematic from a societal standpoint[21] and they are "stigmatized and sanctioned"[22] through the use of controlling images. According to Collins, controlling images of black women usually take two forms: the bitch and the bad black mother. The bitch presents the African-American woman as "aggressive, loud, rude, and pushy,"[23] while the bad black mother (BBM) is "abusive . . . neglect[s] their children either in utero or afterward [and] are stigmatized as being inappropriately feminine because they reject the gender ideology associated with the American family ideal."[24] By emphasizing the players' roles as married women with children while holding players like Swoopes and Scott-Richardson up as the ideal working mothers, the WNBA challenged the controlling images usually associated with black women and tried to counter the notion that black women broadly and the women in the league more specifically were unfeminine.

Showcasing black motherhood and nuclear black families can be a source of empowerment for both the players involved and the audience being exposed to these images. As Melissa Harris-Lacewell pointed out in her defense of Michelle Obama's decision to be the "mom-in-chief," highlighting black motherhood

> subverts a deep, powerful, and old public discourse on black women as bad mothers . . . In the modern era, black mothers have been publicly shamed as crack mothers, welfare queens, and matriarchs. Black single motherhood is blamed for all manner of social ills from crime to drugs to social disorder. And black mothers are often represented in popular culture and the public imagination as domineering household managers whose unfeminine insistence on control both emasculates their potential male partners and destroys their children's future opportunities.[25]

The WNBA marketed Swoopes and others as phenomenal players, wives, and mothers for almost twelve years which, though still problematic, showed that the WNBA would not perpetuate the racist controlling images usually associated with black mothers.[26] The WNBA could have focused primarily on the player's athletic ability in the same way that the NBA and other male sports leagues promotes its players, but, unfortunately, that did not happen. Framing WNBA players as married working moms may have helped put a more nuanced and realistic spin on black motherhood and black families, but it also affirmed traditional gender roles for women and sent a clear message that the players were heterosexual.

"HOT SEX ON A PLATTER"[27]

Emphasizing their players' home lives and maternity was one way that the WNBA attempted to market itself as a heterosexual space. Another equally effective way of emphasizing heterosexuality is through the sexualization of female athletes. Sexualization manifests itself when more emphasis is placed on an athlete's sexuality or physical attractiveness than on her athletic ability. One need only to peruse *Sports Illustrated*'s swimsuit issue to see this form of sexualization in action where arguably this type of sexualization both trivializes female athletes and robs them of their "athletic legitimacy."[28] This observation did not stop the Sports Sponsorship Advisory Service from telling female athletes to "play the sex appeal card to attract more media coverage and therefore more sponsorship."[29] Arguably the continuous sexualization of female athletes serves as a backlash against the increasing number of women and girls participating in sports because that sexualization can diminish athletic accomplishments and ostracize female athletes who do not conform to mainstream society's definition of attractive.

Judging female athletes by their looks instead of their athletic ability allows audiences to view these women more as sex objects than legitimate athletes, a framing which, if pervasive enough, can put the legitimacy of the entire sport into question. In the mid-1990s, women's tennis's most popular and highest earning player was Anna Kournikova despite the fact she never won a singles tournament. Kournikova earned her popularity and endorsements because she played up her sex appeal.[30] It is not surprising that athletes with mainstream sex appeal would secure endorsements, but being sexy does not influence what happens on the court. Or does it?

On the June 29, 2009, episode of ESPN's "Pardon the Interruption," Michael Wilbon reported that Wimbledon officials scheduled *attractive* unseeded players on the prestigious Centre Court while *less attractive* top seeded players, such as Dinara Safina and Serena Williams, were scheduled on the side courts.[31] Despite the fact that they expressed disappointment with the decisions, neither Wilbon nor cohost Bob Ryan was surprised at this news, though both expressed genuine shock at the idea that Serena Williams was not considered attractive enough for the Centre Court. In this instance looks helped to decide which athletes were promoted and which weren't. By all appearances, attractiveness (or the perception thereof) supersedes athletic ability.

Since the WNBA is a team sport, it is more difficult to put the sexy ahead of the athletic; however, that does not mean that the league did not try to bring the sexy to women's basketball. On the contrary, according to Patricia Hill Collins, the WNBA chose to highlight

> a certain kind of sexuality that simultaneously avoids images of the muscled woman or the sports dyke and that depicts the women as sexually attractive to men (in other words as heterosexual). For example, during its first season in 1997, early marketing of the league featured Lisa Leslie and Rebecca Lobo, two women whose facial features, long hair, and body types (Leslie was a model) both invoked traditional images of femininity.[32]

Swoopes, like several other WNBA players, embodied this heterosexual ideal. As Darcy Plymire and Pamela Forman point out, in her advertisements for the league and her sponsors, Swoopes "embodied traditional modes of feminine dress and comportment [and was] portrayed as a 'shopaholic' in an ad for the Discover card."[33] At the same time, Swoopes was never pitched as a sex symbol in the same way that Kournikova was. There is no way of knowing whether the framing was a conscious decision on Swoopes's part, a lack of necessity due to her proven talent, or a racially constructed definition of sexy that would be out of reach for Swoopes and other women of color. While most would argue that it is in a sport's best interest to highlight their *best* players as opposed to their prettiest players, the use of sex appeal to sell sport, much like the discussion on maternity, is not as simple as it appears.

The aforementioned discussion between Michael Wilbon and Bob Ryan shows that the mainstream definitions of sexy are not uniform. As mentioned earlier, framing female athletes by their sex appeal instead of solely on their athletic ability is problematic; however, there is room for empowerment within this practice. The embrace of female athletes and framing them as sexy give women and girls a healthier body image toward which to strive rather than the images of pop stars and supermodels usually framed as the epitome

of femininity and sexiness. Former *New York Times* style editor Holly Brubach made the following argument:

> It's one thing to allow that the muscular body constitutes a new ideal
> for women—that it is in fact beautiful. But the truth is that, despite the
> anxieties it provokes, it's also sexy. Muscles bestow on a woman a grace
> in motion that is absent from fashion photographs and other images in
> which the impact resides in a carefully orchestrated, static pose. Muscles
> also impart a sense of self-possession—a quality that is unfailingly
> attractive. This is not sex appeal conferred on a woman, as it's conferred
> on supermodels and sex goddesses. The athlete has come by her powers
> of attraction honestly. Other women's valiant attempts to make them-
> selves beautiful—even when they succeed—are no match for the athlete's
> evident pleasure in her own articulate body.[34]

Sexualizing women, whether they are athletes or not, is still problematic;
however, highlighting strong and fit female bodies can also be empowering.
When World Cup champion Brandi Chastain posed nude for *Gear* magazine,
she argued that "the photo did not objectify [my] body . . . Hey, I ran my
butt off for this body. I'm proud of it."[35] Olympic swimmer Jennifer Thompson made a similar argument when she appeared topless in a 2000 issue
of *Sports Illustrated*. It is true that both Chastain and Thompson are white,
blonde, and heterosexual, and because of that, they represent the Western
heterosexual female ideal,[36] but they aren't the only women using sex appeal
to their advantage. As discussed earlier, Serena Williams has done an excellent job of balancing her athletic talent with her athletic body. In 2009, Williams was ranked number one in the world, won the Australian Open and
U.S. Open, and earned $14 million dollars in endorsements—more than NFL
players Peyton Manning and Tom Brady and NBA star Kobe Bryant.[37] Those
endorsement dollars are arguably due to a combination of her tremendous
professional achievements as well as her beauty. Unfortunately, having to rely
on physical beauty instead of pure athleticism presents a double standard for
female athletes and presents an extra hurdle for women who do not conform
to the characteristics mainstream society views as desirable.

In 2009, *ESPN The Magazine* began offering an alternative to *Sports Illustrated*'s swimsuit issue. Instead of featuring seminude female models, *ESPN*
created the body issue featuring nude and nearly nude female *and* male athletes. The issue not only showcased how sexy athletic men and women can
be, but also further expanded the definition of sexy by including photos of

men and women of color (who have not always fit into the mainstream definition of sexy). The athletes included triathlon champion and amputee Sarah
Reinersten, professional poker players Scotty Nguyen, Jennifer Harman, Phil
Hellmuth, and Daniel Negreanu, and U.S. Olympic softball team member Jes-
sica Mendoza, who was eight months pregnant at the time of the shoot and
commented, "I try to get young girls to see themselves as beautiful and to not
feel insecure about their bodies . . . The more we can get more realistic bodies
in front of them, the better."[38]

Though the issue featured multiple players from a wide range of sports,
only one WNBA player, Cappie Pondexter, posed for the issue. ESPN writer
Alyssa Roenigk argues that this is because the league "cling[s] to the idea that,
because women have fought long and hard to even the playing field, they've
moved past the need to use sex appeal to sell their game."[39] Moreover, Roenigk argues that the WNBA's uninspired TV ratings do not support this line
of thinking. In some respects Roenigk is correct. The average attendance at a
WNBA game was 8,039 in 2009 while the average viewership was 269,000;
however, both of those numbers were up from the previous year, while the
future attendance projections look promising as well.[40] Still, there is a host of
reasons why WNBA viewership is low, including the fact that the majority of
games are on cable, and there is no guarantee that sexualizing WNBA players
will bring the league's attendance and ratings closer to NBA numbers, which
averaged 1.7 million viewers in 2010 (but were flat from the previous year).[41]
The WNBA is faced with a complicated dilemma; it can highlight the physical
attractiveness of its players in an effort to increase the game's exposure and
revenue, which would reinforce the idea that women's sports need sex appeal
to function. On the other hand, the league can continue to focus purely on
the game and hope it can find other ways to grow the game before the NBA
withdraws its financial support.

WHERE ARE ALL THE WHITE WOMEN AT?[42]

In much the same way that femininities are raced and classed, sexualities are
as well. One of the reasons why Swoopes's announcement should have made
headlines but strangely did not has to do with the fact that while mainstream
American popular culture has multiple examples of white lesbian celebrities, there are a miniscule number of African-American celebrities who
have same-sex partners and who are public about their relationships. The
discussion of how race and sexuality intersected when it came to Swoopes's
announcement was largely muted. In her article in ESPN *The Magazine*,

Swoopes opined, "I mean, you have Ellen DeGeneres and Rosie O'Donnell, but you don't have your well-known gay African American who's come out. Not to my knowledge. I know it's not accepted in the black community. I know I'll probably take a lot of flak."[43]

It is almost taken as a given within popular culture that blacks are more homophobic than whites. According to bell hooks, this perception stems from the fact that "there is a tendency for individuals in black communities to verbally express in an outspoken way antigay sentiments."[44] In 2008 when California passed Proposition 8, which overturned the California Supreme Court's ruling that same-sex couples have a constitutional right to marriage, many pointed to exit polling that found that 70 percent of blacks voted for the measure, which appeared on the surface to be the final push the measure needed to succeed. While blaming Prop 8 on black communities made for good headlines, it ignored the fact that black communities make up approximately 6.2 percent of California's population and accounted for only 10 percent of the vote.[45] In other words, blaming black voters for the referendum's passage ignores the millions of white voters who supported the measure. Indeed, one of the more recent studies analyzing black attitudes toward homosexuality found that while blacks are more likely than whites to condemn homosexuality, even when controlling for factors such as religion and education, "blacks are more likely than comparable whites to favor gay civil liberties, to support gay employment rights, and to favor a law prohibiting antigay discrimination."[46] Regardless of whether heterosexism and homophobia in black communities are overstated, given how rare out black celebrities are in popular culture, Swoopes's announcement should have elicited some discussion on race and sexuality. Unfortunately, that did not happen.

Very few sportswriters discussed Swoopes's racial identity within the context of her sexual identity. Only a handful acknowledged that sexuality *and* race were parts of her identity. Liz Roberts of the *New York Times* mentioned that Swoopes was "the first high-profile African-American basketball player to come out as gay."[47] The *New York Times*' Selena Roberts wrote, "There is no diminishing the importance of each female athlete who publicly declares she wants to love freely in a homophobic culture, to live truthfully in a society divided on gay rights. Somewhere, a girl may feel less alone and less of an outcast because someone like Swoopes—an African-American woman—has further diluted the taboo."[48]

It seems as though there is an inability to embrace intersectionality, which means that individuals will be reduced to whichever portion of their identity is the most convenient to digest at any given moment. As clinical psychologist Connie Chan pointed out, "[I]ndividuals who declare a sexual identity may become primarily identified in those terms [and] when they do, it can overshadow their racial/ethnic identity."[49] This erasure of Swoopes's racial identity also begs the question: is mainstream America "ready" for LGBT people of color who are out?

Arguably Swoopes's "triple jeopardy" of identities (i.e., being black, a woman, and a lesbian) could be another reason why the story did not gain the traction it should have. Because mainstream discourse about sexual orientation assumes that the entire LGBT community is white,[50] Swoopes's announcement did not fit the narrative. Because black LGBT people have been ignored by academics and popular media,[51] it was easy, at least from a media exposure standpoint, to push Swoopes into the proverbial closet. *Sun Reporter* writer Huel Washington said as much in his column when he stated that "some of the people who now know could have been fooled all of the time [sic] and they would have been happy to see the women continuing to play basketball each year and not worry about which ones are lesbians and which ones aren't."[52] The tone of the piece intimated that life would have been better for everyone if Swoopes had kept her sexuality to herself. But Washington's point of view ignores the history of black women and the closet, of which Dave Zirin noted:

> For African-American women athletes, especially in the WNBA, the closet can be a cavernous, lonely, chamber of depression. Many come from small Southern towns and communities where homophobia is as thick as the humidity. They then go to college programs where learning to stay in the closet can be as much a part of the coaching drills as lay-up lines and the three-person weave. Swoopes's courageous stance has the potential to begin to move that weight in the other direction. It also has the potential to reach out to young African-American lesbians, made to feel like the twenty-first-century version of Ralph Ellison's *Invisible Man*.[53]

But is Zirin's analogy apt? Did journalists turn Swoopes into the proverbial invisible woman? Did they forget her racial identity? Would the story have been bigger if a white female athlete had come out? What makes the erasure of Swoopes's race even more disappointing is that this was not the first time that race, gender, sexuality, and sports collided.

In 2003, Los Angeles Sparks forward Latasha Byears was ostracized by the WNBA after being investigated for the sexual assault of a teammate. Though the commentary surrounding Swoopes and Byears was drastically different, one thing was similar: the intersections of race, gender, and sexuality affected how the mainstream media framed them.

In the popular imagination, if Sheryl Swoopes was the Michael Jordan of the WNBA, Latasha Byears was Dennis Rodman. If Swoopes's job was finesse and scoring, Byears admitted, "My job was to do the dirty work." And if Swoopes did not think of herself as a lesbian until she met her partner, Byears was out from day one.[54]

In essence, sportswriters *e-raced* Byears's racial identity when she was accused of sexual assault and run out of the WNBA. She filed suit for wrongful termination. According to Byears, on June 5, 2003, she threw a party to celebrate the Sparks's receiving their championship rings, and the next day, she was informed about the allegations, which were to be followed by her suspension the very next day, and, finally, her outright release by the franchise on June 10. While these events unfolded, Kristine Newhall and Eric Buzuvis found parallels in the Byears saga with that of others struggling through the vagaries of the sport/sex conundrum, noting that in their coverage of Byears, sportswriters

> never suggested that racial stereotypes about sexually aggressive Black men or sexually promiscuous Black women could have played any role in the rape charges brought against her or in her subsequent dismissal from the team and exile from the WNBA. Again, the myth of a color blind and race-evasive society obscured the intersecting role of race in the alleged discrimination experienced by an openly gay player commonly perceived as a "thug" and a "pimp."[55]

To make matters even worse, very few sportswriters made any correlation between how Jerry Buss, owner of the Sparks and the Lakers, treated Byears and Kobe Bryant, who was facing his own sexual assault charges during the same time frame. And yet ESPN's Scoop Jackson highlighted the hypocrisy when he wrote two years later, "Same accusation, same drama, same sport, same time, same organization, same owner. Totally different treatment. While Kobe was able to 'do his thing' during the investigation of his alleged sexual assault, Latasha wasn't able to do jack."[56] What is more egregious about the situations is that Byears was never charged with a crime, but despite this, she was summarily dismissed by the Sparks. Bryant on the other hand *was* charged, though the Lakers stood by him through the very public hearings and the subsequent settlement and apology. Part of this difference certainly has to do with money and celebrity status, a combination that impacted how Bryant and Byears were treated so differently in spite of some of the more glaring similarities of their circumstances:

> Bryant is a marquee player—so famous beyond the arena that, like Arnold or Oprah, he is widely known by only his first name. He sells millions of dollars' worth of tickets and merchandise for a big-time sports franchise. Byears generated no discernible income for an unprofitable enterprise, and she had already made some other missteps on and off the court. What's more, in its effort to project a wholesome, family-friendly image, the WNBA is more sensitive to bad press than is the NBA, which could field a pretty decent All-Star team of players who have rap sheets.[57]

Whether the deferential treatment stemmed solely from celebrity or not, Byears sued the organization for discrimination based on gender and sexual orientation and used Bryant's treatment to further her argument. It certainly begs the larger question of whether the WNBA would have rushed to judgment if Byears had been white or if she had not been an out lesbian. Arguably Byears's dismissal was a combination of all of these factors, and the case was ultimately settled.

While Swoopes and Byears are similar in terms of racial, gender, and sexual identities, their stories were framed in drastically different ways. Part of this discrepancy stems from the fact that these women conform to very different controlling images associated with their racial and sexual identities. Much has been written about black athletes, their relationship with mainstream media, and questions surrounding who is praised and who is vilified. Sportswriter Steven Travers argued that "most whites love to like blacks. It makes them feel good. It helps convince them that racism is not what it used to be. What is not on the surface, however, is that most whites love to like *certain kinds* of blacks."[58]

Swoopes is very much the type of black athlete mainstream society could embrace. Prior to her announcement, she was not known for making any political and/or controversial remarks, and as mentioned earlier in this piece, she was framed as a relatively wholesome working mother who wasn't a threat to anyone. Byears, on the other hand, was among the "new jack athletes" who, according to author Thabiti Lewis, "with their tattoos, cornrows, rap albums, black self-expression, dissing, taunting, celebrating achievement in unnec-essarily creative manners [are framed] as egomaniacs, villains [or] hostile foreigners who must be purged from the American imagination, strangers in their own country."[59] While the concept of the "new jack athlete" has typically been discussed in relation to black masculinity, Byears's persona fits many of the characteristics sportswriters despise about new jacks. According to Lewis, new jacks are *unmanageable* black stars with their own minds and outlook on the world; "they lack a traditionally defined political edge, value self-expres-sion, embrace outlaw culture and follow the credo of hip-hop culture, which is about being 'real niggaz.'"[60]

Prior to the sexual assault accusation, Byears embraced outlaw culture by having several run-ins with law enforcement: she had to sit out her first WNBA game because of a DUI. Byears *kept it real* (my italics) during her second year in the league when she bounced a ball off the face of an opposing player during a game. After that incident Byears was suspended for two games and in the online forums, WNBA watchers started calling her a thug.[61] Like many male new jack athletes, Byears uses tattoos as a form of self-expression, and in a July 2003 interview with *GQ*, the outspoken Byears admitted that when she was younger, she wanted to be a pimp.[62]

The same characteristics that make Byears a new jack and, therefore, a pariah in the eyes of many sportswriters, also made her the one thing the WNBA tried to distance itself from: an outspoken lesbian. Byears spoke openly about how team management did not want her speaking to LGBT publications and urged her to use discretion when going to nightclubs.[63] That advice was summarily ignored. If there are *acceptable* personas for black celebrities, there are also *acceptable* personas for lesbian celebrities, and les-bians of color must find ways to navigate both sets of controlling images. Swoopes was deemed acceptable and while her story was not given the atten-tion her status warranted, she was not treated like a pariah in the manner Byears was.

LESBIANS NEED NOT APPLY

Though discussing WNBA players' roles as athletes and mothers falls into the gray area of reaffirming patriarchal notions of femininity yet challenging the idea of black women as bad black mothers, there is little doubt that this fram-ing sought to define all of the players as heterosexual. One of the reasons why Swoopes's announcement about her same-sex relationship was ignored has to do with the fact that "stereotypes about female athletes being lesbians are pervasive in the world of sport."[64] In other words, since many people believe that female athletes are lesbians anyway, there was no need to call attention to Swoopes's announcement. The WNBA's focus on maternity and emphasized femininity was an effort in part to dispel the myth that all female athletes are lesbians. Unfortunately, in their zeal to affirm heterosexuality, the WNBA effectively silenced its lesbian players and coaches and neglected its lesbian fan base. In essence, according to *The Advocate*'s Michelle Kort, "lesbians are the six-ton elephant in the room—the one you're not supposed to notice."[65]

Swoopes was asked after her announcement whether or not the WNBA put pressure on the players to remain closeted, to which she replied, "I don't know if I'd say it puts pressure on them, but I think as players, as athletes, we feel like it's not something they want us to do."[66] This thought process would explain why someone like Latasha Byears was advised not to speak with LGBT magazines.

In a separate interview Swoopes was asked whether she thought the WNBA tried to hide the lesbian presence within the league, to which she replied, "I'd probably say I agree with that to a certain degree, and then I also have to say that I don't agree with it. First of all, the WNBA, they know about me. They've known for the past five years . . . I think everybody in the WNBA, they're OK with it—I just don't know if they know how to market it, where other people would be OK with it."[67] It seems as though the league has developed a sort of "don't ask, don't tell" policy when it comes to lesbians in an effort to make its product more palatable to middle America and to the NBA, which underwrites the league.

IT DOESN'T COUNT UNLESS A MAN DOES IT

It seems fairly obvious that one of the primary reasons why shrugged shoulders were the main reaction to Swoopes's announcement was because she's a woman. When discussing Swoopes, columnist after columnist remarked that it was "easy" for a lesbian to come out, and that heterosexism and homophobia in the sporting world will not change until a male athlete comes out. According to Malinda Lo and Ross Forman of *Curve Magazine*, "[T]he historic nature of [Swoopes's] coming-out seemed at times to be ignored as news outlets quickly focused on why male athletes rarely come out. This reflects both a long-standing stereotype that female athletes are likely to be gay, thus it's not a newsworthy story, and sexism in the sports world in general, which often minimizes women's achievements."[68]

Instead of engaging with what Swoopes's announcement meant to her, the WNBA, and the sporting world in general, sportswriters focused on male athletes. Jim Rome made the argument that Swoopes "is in a fringe professional sports league and is anything but a household name in this country. [Male athletes] have a lot more to lose because they have a lot more at stake. Bigger league. Bigger profile. Bigger dollars. Bigger backlash. Bigger ball. Bigger everything."[69] *Los Angeles Times* columnist Bill Plaschke said on ESPN's *Around the Horn*, "Sadly, I don't think it's going to make much of an impact because, for whatever reason in this country, lesbians are viewed differently than gay men. There's not the stigma against lesbianism that there is against gays and men. Especially in athletics."[70]

In tandem with such sentiment, Jemele Hill of the *Montreal Gazette* made the argument that "the only way we're going to address homophobia in sports is if Peyton Manning, the NFL's MVP last season, makes a similar disclosure. Or Brett Favre. Or Michael Jordan."[71] And yet another writer asked the question "how would the world turn if a prominent, well-respected male athlete announced during the prime of his career that he was gay? Would everyone applaud his courage or turn their backs in disgust? Though Swoopes opened the door slightly, the male athlete who announces he's gay while still playing will tear the roof off."[72]

In interviews with Swoopes, the conversation inevitably turned to whether a male athlete would follow in her footsteps, to which she replied, "In my lifetime? No. I think high-profile male athletes feel like they have so much more to lose than to gain. People asked me if I was worried about losing endorsements and stuff. My answer was no."[73] Arguably a male team-sport athlete coming out during his career would be a bigger story; however, that does not diminish what Swoopes did.

By continually making the point that a gay male athlete would lose everything if he were to come out, sportswriters and columnists are inadvertently helping to keep gay athletes in the closet. It has been argued elsewhere that the intense media scrutiny and almost constant surveillance that professional athletes endure "forces athletes to regulate their behavior regardless of their sexual orientation, and helps to keep gay and bisexual players in the closet during their careers. The media scrutiny might also help explain why players are more willing to come out after they have left professional sports [because] the need to discipline/control their behavior diminishes."[74] Because no male U.S. team-sport athlete has ever divulged his homosexuality during his career, no one has any evidence to suggest that he would lose endorsements if he came out.

Swoopes herself mentioned that she did not fear losing her endorsement deals and that she has the support. In fact, Swoopes became a spokesperson for Olivia Cruises and Resort, a lesbian-centered business, upon her announcement and kept the endorsements she already had. At the same time, stating that a WNBA player would have an easier time coming out than an NBA, MLB, or NFL player perpetuates a double standard between male and female athletes and ignores the consequences lesbian athletes and coaches have faced when they do come out. The entire idea that having out gay and lesbian players would have a substantial impact on sport culture is a misnomer, according to former NBA player John Amaechi, who came out after he retired:

> A gay sportsman coming out just isn't going to have the impact you think. Young people are mostly already won over in terms of LGBT human rights, and those with the real power aren't going to be swayed by an athlete, because they aren't swayed by the hate crimes statistics, they aren't swayed by the genuine love of gay couples and they aren't swayed by the logical argument for equality.[75]

Though sportswriters seem to be eagerly anticipating the day when a gay male team-sport athlete comes out, as Amaechi points out, there is no guarantee that the announcement will have any impact outside the sporting world.

PARTING SHOTS

In 2009 Sheryl Swoopes found herself on a forced hiatus. While most assumed she retired, in fact, no team offered her a contract. In 2011, Swoopes returned to the WNBA by signing with the Tulsa Shock and in addition made headlines for another reason: her relationship with Alicia Scott had ended and Swoopes was engaged to a gentleman named Chris Unclesho. Like her announcement in 2005, Swoopes's relationship status did not make too many waves. ESPN. COM's Michelle Voepel noted, "Swoopes didn't seem to want to have—for lack of a better way to put it—a 'coming out as straight again' interview. She wasn't renouncing homosexuality or saying she wished she hadn't said what she did in 2005."[76] Swoopes's relationship status could open a discussion regarding the fluidity of sexuality, a notion popularized in the 1940s by Alfred Kinsey, or, and probably more likely, lend credence to the conservative notion that sexuality is a choice, homosexuality and bisexuality can be "cured," and because of that, LBGT persons do not deserve civil rights. On the other hand, it is possible that Swoopes' engagement will be swept even further under the rug than her same-sex relationship. Sheryl Swoopes's career is an interesting case study for analyzing the ways in which race, gender, and sexuality intersect in sport. By any measure, Swoopes is one of the most accomplished basketball players in history. In a society that is obsessed with the personal relationships of actors, singers, politicians, and athletes, Swoopes announcing that she was in a same-sex relationship should have been big news.

It is possible that the muted coverage of Swoopes's announcement is due to the continued mainstream acceptance of same-sex relationships, but, unfortunately, given the current political climate, that explanation seems too optimistic. Instead, sportswriters used Swoopes's race, gender, and sexuality to lessen the impact. The erroneous yet ingrained assumption that most, if not all, female athletes are lesbians conspired with the belief that coming out only matters if you are a (white) male athlete.

The WNBA highlighted marquee players like Swoopes and their nuclear families as a way to counter the perception that professional female athletes are all lesbians. On the one hand, this framing worked against the controlling images of black women as bitches or bad mothers; on the other hand, it lent credence to the idea that lesbians were somehow bad for the league's image and pushed its lesbian players and coaches deeper into the closet. The majority of sportswriters were so busy waiting with bated breath for a male professional athlete to come out of the closet that they dismissed the Swoopes story when it was right in front of them.

The decreased scrutiny Swoopes encountered could be a good thing insomuch as she was able to live her life and continue her career without the heightened media attention. And it would be tempting to conclude, as some sportswriters have, that lesbians and/or people of color would have an easier time coming out than white gay men; however, that overlooks the fact that women and people of color are more vulnerable to the economic and political discrimination faced by LGBT communities in the United States. This view also does not take into account the personal costs that coming out can have on individuals, nor does it address the fact that having parts of one's identity ignored or dismissed can take a toll as well.

What Swoopes's situation implies is that sportswriters are not that interested in female athletes unless they are being sexualized. Beyond that, it seems obvious that sportswriters are not that interested in lesbian athletes. Moreover, a black lesbian female athlete will continue to be treated as invisible, which, as Adreana Clay argues, "can be detrimental to Black lesbian identity and community."[77]

Would Swoopes's announcement have garnered more attention if she were white? There is no way to answer that question until a white team-sport athlete of Swoopes's stature comes out. As the earlier quote from John Amaechi points out, having gay and lesbian athletes come out will not eliminate heterosexism and homophobia any more than increased exposure to black athletes will eliminate racism.

Having more prominent black lesbians come out would certainly help on a micro level by providing role models for young women and girls, but what effect—if any—this would have on the macro level is unknown. What is clear, however, is that it is inconceivable that black lesbian athletes might have to wait for an end to racism, sexism, and heterosexism to get the attention and respect they deserve.

NOTES

1. Gerry Callahan, "Issue Too Big to Come Out," *Boston Herald*, May 24, 2002, 119.

2. Hazel Smith, "Sheryl Swoopes: 'The Michael Jordan of Women's Basketball'" *New York Beacon* May 1, 1996, http://www.proquest.com.proxy.lib.wayne.edu/ (May 5, 2010).

3. Michael Knisley, "Swoopes' Dreams," *Sporting News* 219, no.21 (1995), 53.

4. Richard Deitsch, "Q&A Sheryl Swoopes," *Sports Illustrated* 104, no. 26 (2006), 29

5. Kimberly Kimmel, "Sheryl Swoopes: Determination Is the Name of Her Game," *Listen* 58, no.1 (2004) 17.

6. John Ryan, "Swoopes Comes Out; WNBA Star Says She's Gay," *San Jose Mercury News*, October 27, 2005, http://www.proquest.com.proxy.lib.wayne.edu/ (May 17, 2010).

7. Jemele Hill, "Openly Gay WNBA Player No Surprise: The Only Way Homophobia in Sports Will Be Addressed If a Male Star Comes Out," *The Gazette*, October 30, 2005, http://www.proquest.com.proxy.lib.wayne.edu/ (May 17, 2010).

8. Mimi Schippers, "Recovering the Feminine Other: Masculinity, Femininity and Gender Hegemony," *Theory and Society* 36, no. 1 (2007): 94.

9. Vikki Krane, "We Can Be Athletic and Feminine But Do We Want to: Challenging Hegemonic Femininity in Women's Sport," *Quest* 53 (2001): 117.

10. Vikki Krane, Precillia Y.L. Choi, Shannon M. Baird, Christine M. Aimar, and Kerrie H. Kauer, "Living in Paradox: Female Athletes Negotiate Femininity and Masculinity," *Sex Roles* 50, no. 5/6 (2004): 316.

11. Betsy Lowther, "Moms We Love," *Working Mother* 25, no. 2 (2002): 46.

12. Sarah Banet-Weiser, "Hoop Dreams: Professional Basketball and the Politics of Race and Gender," *Journal of Sport and Social Issues* 23 (1999): 414.

13. Lowther, "Moms We Love," 46.

14. Banet-Weiser, "Hoop Dreams," 415.

15. Mary G. McDonald, "Queering Whiteness: The Peculiar Case of the Women's National Basketball Association," *Sociological Perspectives* 45, no. 4 (2002): 383.

16. As an aside, it seems ironic and somewhat counterintuitive that the WNBA does not provide child care for its players on a league-wide basis. See, for example, Jennifer L. Metz, "An Inter-View on Motherhood: Racial Politics and Motherhood in Late Capitalist Sport," *Cultural Studies<->Critical Methodologies* 8, no. 2 (2008): 274.

17. Banet-Weiser, "Hoop Dreams," 415.

18. Kimberlé Crenshaw, "Demarginalizing the Intersections of Race and Sex: A Black Feminist Critique of Antidiscrimination Doctrine, Feminist Theory, and Antiracist Politics," in *Feminist Legal Theories*, ed. Karen J. Maschke (New York: Garland Publishing Inc., 1997), 24.

19. Patricia Hill Collins, *Black Sexual Politics: African Americans, Gender, and the New Racism* (New York: Routledge, 2004), 136

20. McDonald, "Queering Whiteness," 387.

21. Schippers, "Recovering the Feminine Other," 95.

22. Ibid.

23. Collins, "Black Sexual Politics," 123.

24. Ibid., 131.

25. Melissa Harris-Lacewell, "Michelle Obama, Mom-in-Chief" *The Nation*, May 5, 2009, http://www.thenation.com/blog/michelle-obama-mom-chief (May 23, 2010).

26. McDonald, "Queering Whiteness," 383.

27. Title of a 1992 song by the hip-hop group A Tribe Called Quest. Song can be found on the soundtrack to the film *Boomerang* starring Eddie Murphy and Halle Berry.

28. Alina Bernstein, "Is It Time for a Victory Lap?: Changes in the Media Coverage of Women in Sport," *International Review for the Sociology of Sport* 37 (2002): 422.

29. Audry Gillian, "Sex Appeal 'Pays in Sport,'" *The Guardian*, August 27, 1999, http://www.guardian.co.uk/uk/1999/aug/26/audreygillan (February 2, 2011).

30. Victoria Carty, "Textural Portrayals of Female Athletes: Liberation or Nuanced Forms of Patriarchy," *Frontiers* 26, no. 2 (2005): 138.

31. Michael Wilbon and Bob Ryan, "Babes-Only on Centre Court," *Pardon the Interruption* (Washington, D.C.: ESPN, June 29, 2009).

32. Collins,136.

33. Darcy C. Plymire and Pamela J. Forman, "Speaking of Cheryl Miller: Interrogating the Lesbian Taboo on a Women's Basketball Newsgroup," *NSWA Journal* 13, no. 1 (2001): n.p.

34. Holly Brubach, "The Athletic Esthetic," *New York Times Magazine*, June 23, 1996, Academic OneFile. Web., http://find.galegroup.com/gtx/infomark.do?&contentSet=IAC-Documents&type=retrieve&tabID=T004&prodId=AONE&docId=A150507641&source=gale&srcprod=AONE&userGroupName=lom_waynesu&version=1.0 (June 21, 2010).

35. Robert Sullivan, "Goodbye Heroin Chic. Now It's Sexy to be Strong," *Time*, July 19, 1999, 62.

36. Carty, "Textual Portrayals," 138.

37. Alyssa Roenigk, "For Sale By Owner," ESPN, October 9, 2009, http://sports.espn.go.com/espn/news/story?id=4540728 (September 4, 2010).

38. Michael McCarthy, "First Look: In ESPN's Magazine, Showing Skin Is No Issue," *USA Today*, September 30, 2009, http://www.usatoday.com/sports/2009-09-28-espnmag-body-issue_N.htm (September 4, 2010).

39. Roenigk, "For Sale by Owner," n.p.

40. Vin A. Cherwoo, "Attendance, TV Ratings on Rise Again for WNBA," *Yahoo! Sports*, August 12, 2010, http://sports.yahoo.com/wnba/news?slug=ap-wnba-positivesigns (September 4, 2010)

41. "NBA Ratings, Viewership, Flat Compared to Last Year," *Sports Media Watch*, January 8, 2010, http://www.sportsmediawatch.net/2010/01/nba-ratings-viewership-flat -compared-to.html (September 4, 2010). Numbers are for ESPN viewership.

42. Quote from *Blazing Saddles*, directed by Mel Brooks (1974; Los Angeles, CA: Warner Home Video, 1997), DVD.

43. Sheryl Swoopes and LZ Granderson, "Outside the Arc," *ESPN The Magazine* 8, no. 22, November 7, 2005, 124.

44. bell hooks, "Reflections on Homophobia & Black Communities," *Outlook* 1, no. 2 (1998): 23.

45. Sherry Wolf, "Why Prop 8 Passed in California: The Myth of the Black/Gay Divide," AlterNetm November 18, 2008, http://www.alternet.org/election08/107474/why_ prop_8_passed_in_california:_the_myth_of_the_black_gay_divide/ (June 10, 2010).

46. Gregory B. Lewis, "Black-White Differences in Attitudes Toward Homosexuality and Gay Rights," *Public Opinion Quarterly*, 61, no. 1 (Spring 2003): 69.

47. Liz Robbins, "Swoopes Says She's Gay, and Exhales," *New York Times*, October 27, 2005, 1D.

48. Selena Roberts, "Homophobia Is Alive and Well in Men's Locker Rooms," *New York Times*, October 28, 2005, 1DL.

49. Connie S. Chan, "Don't Ask, Don't Tell, Don't Know: Sexuality Identity and Expression Among East Asian–American Lesbians," in *The New Lesbian Studies: Into the Twenty-First Century*, ed. Bonnie Zimmerman and Toni A. H. McNaron (New York: The Feminist Press, 1996), 92.

50. Keith Boykin, *One More River to Cross: Black and Gay in America* (New York: Anchor Books, 1996), 87.

51. Ibid.

52. Huel Washington, "Sports Pace; Really Sheryl, Did You Have To?" *Sun Reporter: Lifestyles*, November 3, 2005, http://www.proquest.com.proxy.lib.wayne.edu/ (June 27, 2010).

53. Dave Zirin, "Sheryl Swoopes: Out of the Closet—and Ignored." *Tennessee Tribune*, November 10, 2005, http://www.proquest.com.proxy.lib.wayne.edu/ (June 27, 2010).

54. T. J. Quinn, Christian Red, and Michael O'Keefe, "Battle of the Same Sex: Byears Outs WNBA Conflict on Gay Issue," *Daily News*, October 30, 2005, Sports, 94.

55. Kristine E. Newhall and Erin E. Buzuvis, "(e)Racing Jennifer Harris: Sexuality and Race, Law and Discourse in Harris v. Portland," *Journal of Sports and Social Issues*, 32, no. 4 (2008): 358.

56. Scoop Jackson, "Hard Time with Latasha Byears," ESPN.COM, September 8, 2005, http://sports.espn.go.com/espn/page2/story?page=jackson/050907&num=0 (July 15, 2010).

57. Sandra Kobrin, Jason Levin, "The Glass Closet," *Los Angeles Times*, August 21, 2005, http://articles.latimes.com/2005/aug/21/magazine/tm-byears34 (July 15, 2010).

58. Steven Travers, *Barry Bonds: Baseball's Superman* (Champaign, IL: Sports Publishing L.L.C., 2002), 254.

59. Thabiti Lewis, "Looking for Jackie and Mike: Race, Sport, and Contemporary American Culture," in *Blacks and Whites Meeting in America: Eighteen Essays on Race*, ed. Terry White (Jefferson, NC: McFarland & Company, Inc., 2003), 102.

60. Lewis, "Looking for Jackie and Mike," 103–107.

61. Korbin and Levin, "The Glass Closet," n.p.

62. John Barr and Dave Lubbers, "After Battling Back, Byears Finds Home Again in WNBA," ESPN.COM, July 10, 2010, http://sports.espn.go.com/wnba/news/story?id=2513119&lpos=spotlight&lid=tab3pos2 (July 15, 2010).

63. Ibid., n.p.

64. Quoted in Victoria Canty, "Textual Portrayals of Female Athletes: Liberation or Nuanced Forms of Patriarchy," *Frontiers* 26, no. 2 (2005):143.

65. Michele Kort, "Gay in the WNBA," *The Advocate*, no. 951 (2005): 50.

66. Malinda Lo and Ross Forman, "Most Valuable Lesbian: One Year After Coming Out, WNBA Star Sheryl Swoopes Is Happy, Proud, and in Love," *Curve* 16, no. 8 (2006), http://www.proquest.com.proxy.lib.wayne.edu/ (May 5, 2010).

67. Anne Stockwell, "She Is Our Champion," *The Advocate*, no. 951 (2005), http://www.proquest.com.proxy.lib.wayne.edu/ (May 17, 2010).

68. Lo and Forman, "Most Valuable Lesbian," n.p.

69. Quoted in Dave Zirin, "Sheryl Swoopes: Out of the Closet—and Ignored," *Tennessee Tribune*, November 10, 2005, B1.

70. Quoted in Zirin, "Sheryl Swoopes," n.p.

71. Hill, "Openly Gay," n.p.

72. Erika P. Thompson, "Swoopes Is Gay; Will Male Athlete Come Out Next?" *Recorder*, November 4, 2005, A1.

73. Deitsch, "Q&A Sheryl Swoopes," 29.

74. Lisa Doris Alexander, "Are We There Yet? Major League Baseball and Sexual Orientation," in *The Politics of Baseball: Essays on the Pastime and Power at Home and Abroad*, ed. Ron Briley (Jefferson, NC: McFarland & Company, Inc., 2010), 76.

75. "Towelroad Interview: John Amaechi," *Towelroad*, August 22, 2010, http://www.towleroad.com/2010/08/towelroad-interview-john- amaechi-.html (September 4, 2010).

76. Michell Voepel, "Swoopes, 40, as Passionate as Ever," ESPN.com, July 1, 2011, http://sports.espn.go.com/wnba/columns/story?columnist=voepel_mechelle&id=6732292 (July 1, 2011).

77. Andreana Clay, "Like an Old Soul Record: Black Feminism, Queer Sexuality and the Hip-Hop Generation," *Meridian* 8, no. 1 (2007): 55.

FLORENCE GRIFFITH JOYNER
Sexual Politician in a Unitard

—YVONNE D. SIMS

INTRODUCTION

In her all-too-brief career, Florence Griffith Joyner, or Flo Jo, as she came to be known, marked the embodiment of the sport-celebrity that has come to dominate the more contemporary sport landscape. Her tragic and sudden death from a seizure in 1998 may have ended her life prematurely at the age of thirty-eight, and perhaps well before the whiff of the steroid scandals that would befall many of her contemporaries would taint her as well. Then again, with a public career that in all would span a mere ten years, the sports world nevertheless would embrace her. Flo Jo's flair for the dramatic and playful flaunting of convention left a void that has yet to be completely filled.

To be sure, Florence Griffith Joyner grew to become this inimitable character—this Flo Jo. She harnessed her femininity in a way that African-American women athletes had yet to do, which would win her scores of admirers among the general populace. At the same time she drew nearly as many detractors from those dismayed that she was trading in substance for style with the potential for setting back the various constituencies she seemed to represent, and perhaps most of all women of color. And yet, the circumstances of Griffith Joyner's life and her subsequent legacy are not that easily couched, for as readily as one can argue that her embrace of femininity set back the cause for gender equality, others have argued that such an embrace of her sexuality struck a blow against racialized conceptions of femininity. On this latter point, Leslie Heywood observes, "In a world that still disconnected the idea of female beauty from sports and which tended not to portray black women as beautiful, Flo Jo's beauty received national attention."[1] Heywood goes on to suggest that she helped to reclaim African-American femininity from its place along the contested margins of American life and brought it front and center with no hint of either hesitation or reluctance.

By hitching her magnetic and charismatic personality to her athletic accomplishments, Florence Griffith Joyner grew to become a contributor—if not something of a bold force—in more modern discussions of the sexual power of women at a time when such traditional debates continued to find

146

themselves devoid of context, let alone content. Moreover, by doing so in the male-dominated sporting terrain, she helped to breathe life into stagnating discussions that were poised to dismantle myths about beauty, womanhood, and femininity in not only sport but in the broader social environment writ large. That she could do so against the omnipresence of the color line added a dimension to this discussion that served to ratchet up the level of contestation, which ultimately seemed to place her, albeit briefly, at the center of these debates if only because of her willingness to serve that role by virtue of the persona she created. And for these reasons alone, it stands that while hers is a mixed legacy, it is also one that in retrospect cries out for a more thorough investigation.

Indeed, while scholarly interest in her life remains notably sparse, even in the years following her death, the vast array of more popular depictions of Florence Griffith Joyner have come to mark the predominant cache of what we know of this distinctive if at times dazzling public entity. Certainly her career was of the sort that in virtually every fashion seems tailor-made for the popular media, given its seemingly insatiable thirst for the more prurient and certainly animated exploits of celebrity rather than measured, more calculated discussions typically found in scholarly circles. Running from this serves little purpose toward these ends, and thus, accordingly, rather than attempt to weave sparse bits of academic commentary alone into a more proper review of her time in the public eye, I will instead be looking primarily—though not solely—at these types of popular sources that underscore the extent to which Florence Griffith Joyner's iconic status ran headlong into the cultural spirit of its age.

DEEDEE

The seventh of eleven children, Florence Griffith Joyner was born Florence Delorez Griffith to Robert and Florence Griffith on December 21, 1959, in Mojave, California (roughly ninety miles north of Los Angeles), where they lived until 1964. Tired of the isolation of desert life, however, Florence Griffith was thought to have left her husband and moved her family into the Watts section of Los Angeles, where she hoped to further nurture her children's creativity in spite of the difficult circumstances of ghetto life.[2]

Often taken under the wing of her grandmother, who worked as a beautician, DeeDee, young Florence's childhood nickname, was a curious youngster who used her budding creativity as a means to develop a most visible independent streak and a personality that showed a remarkable flair for the dramatic. Whereas most children would be happy to blend in with their peers, DeeDee seemed determined to stand out and be noticed. As Griffith herself recalled in an interview for *Sporting News*, "We learned something from how we grew up. It has never been easy, and we knew it wouldn't be handed to us, unless we went after it."[3]

And noticed she would be! She rode to stores on a unicycle. She trained a pet rat. And once she was even asked to leave a mall when she arrived there with a pet snake around her neck. In the midst of all this, she attempted many things, including developing an interest in fashion, which she demonstrated in her sewing together some of her own clothes as a means to dress her Barbie dolls, something that would later serve her well in her adult life.[4]

As much as her childhood experiences aided in the development of her distinctive personality, her childhood also marked the genesis of her athletic prowess. She took part in handstand competitions with her siblings and neighborhood kids, and she also ran potato-sack races in a local park. She further developed her trademark speed and quickness when, of all things, she and her siblings were encouraged to chase jackrabbits when they would visit with their father in his desert home, earning her yet another nickname, "Jackrabbit."[5]

As these and other similar experiences continued to help mold her effusive personality, she also began to take the next steps in what would mark the nexus of her adult legacy when, by the age of seven, she started running track under the watchful eyes of volunteers at the Sugar Ray Robinson Youth Foundation (SRRYF). The SRRYF program's design aimed to enhance the lives of the inner-city youth in the Watts community, which seems to have had a great deal of impact in terms of young DeeDee's transition from active child to a more disciplined athlete. Indeed, she was soon to become the best in her age group in the 50- and 70-meter dashes, and by the time she reached the middle and higher grades, she competed in a national championship, the Jesse Owens National Youth Games, and eventually broke records in the sprints and long jump at nearby Jordan High School.

Upon graduating from high school in 1978, she enrolled at California State–Northridge, where she helped the university win the 1979 national championship in track and field under the guidance of her coach, the now legendary Bob Kersee. Financial concerns, however, forced her to withdraw from school, and she worked as a bank teller for nearly two years before returning to school in 1980, which by this time found Kersee leaving the Northridge campus and moving on to an assistant's position at UCLA.[6]

The option of staying where she was without her coach or following Kersee to UCLA offered challenges for Griffith that contained both athletic and academic components. Indeed, transferring would mean staying with her exceedingly influential coach, but it also meant a change in majors, a difficult aspect of her decision often (and perhaps more typically) ignored, but that she recalled later in an interview with *Sports Illustrated*: "I had a 3.25 grade point average in business, but UCLA did not even offer my major. I had to switch to psychology. But my running was starting up, and I knew that Bobby was the best coach for me. So, it kind of hurts to say this [*sic*], I chose athletics over academics."[7] But she also continued to blossom at UCLA, winning her first individual title in the 200 at the 1982 NCAA championships, followed by a second place finish the next season and a fourth place at the World Championships in Helsinki later that year as she prepared for a run at the 1984 Olympic team.

LOS ANGELES TO SEOUL

In 1984, the world was introduced to Florence Griffith in part through her performances in the Los Angeles Olympic Games. Performing in her hometown, Griffith won a silver medal in the 200-meter dash, but in spite of her on-track success, it would be her fingernails, long, curled, and polished with brilliant colors, that would subsequently engage the media's interest. The media began to look beyond her athletic abilities, putting instead on display her unique fashion sense and her dynamic if not larger-than-life persona.

By her later standards, the 1984 Olympics presented a more conventional looking DeeDee, but the media stood poised nonetheless. Beyond her distinctive display, however, further evidence of Griffith's rise amid the other stars of track and field also began to take shape in Los Angeles, where running with and against the likes of other truly great sprinters, including Evelyn Ashford-Simpson and Valerie Briscoe-Hooks, she had proven she belonged. But, perhaps ironically, the very thing that had begun to galvanize the public was also playing havoc with her budding career as she was left off the team's sprint-relay team in spite of her trial times because her coaches feared that her exceedingly long nails posed a potential problem for an event in which dropping the baton during the hand-off was a disqualifying offense. In this regard, it would appear that the coalescence of her rise as track star co-mingled with her growing look and celebrity appeal were already at odds and threatened to derail her future aspirations—at least in part.[8] Still, the

Los Angeles Games were something of a coming out party for Griffith, who looked to the 1988 Olympics in Seoul to continue the progress she made in Los Angeles.

The lull between Olympic years, however, saw real life intervene once again. She returned to teller work, though she also took on side jobs doing hair and nails, all of which left little time for training, much to Kersee's dismay. But it was also during this stage that she began dating Al Joyner, himself an Olympic gold medal winner in the 1984 triple jump competition and part of a family track dynasty that also featured his sister Jackie Joyner. Her association with the Joyners seems to have kept Griffith's spirit for competition alive amid the banality of these interim years. They would marry in 1987, the year after Jackie Joyner married Griffth's coach, Bob Kersee, spreading the dynasty out all the much further.[9]

With the 1988 Olympics coming closer to reality, however, the newly rechristened Florence Griffith Joyner trained hard and had her first major success since returning to track in 1987 at the world games in Rome, where she won a silver in the 200 meters and a gold on the 400 sprint relay team.[10] Over the next several races, and in anticipation of 1988, she won two more gold medals in the 100 and 200 sprint races. Continuing to work with Kersee, Griffith Joyner increased the rigidity of her training schedule in preparation for the Seoul Olympics. She focused on lowering the world record in the 100 (set by Evelyn Ashford-Simpson), which she did from 10.76 to 10.49. This achievement ultimately catapulted her from national to truly international stardom.

The sports world, already on notice from the Los Angeles games, was also by now fully overtaken by her engaging persona, though it remained equally apparent that her outward appearance was swiftly overtaking her athletic talent in the public eye. That appearance remained a subplot to much of her record-smashing achievements on the track. She was now a long way from her childhood in the Mojave Desert and Watts, transforming as she had into a woman who was as fierce on the track as she was bold and courageous elsewhere. And it was in this regard that her private and public personas blended on the track and perhaps more so off it as she finally made the visible transformation from the child DeeDee to the woman that became Flo Jo.

WOMEN ATHLETES AND CELEBRITYHOOD

In "The Sports Hero Meets Mediated Celebrityhood," media scholar Leah R. VandeBerg examines the construction of the hero in sports and women athletes' places within that particular narrative. She offers a conceptual overview of what a hero is before turning her lens to sports where, she claims, women athletes are rarely categorized as heroes despite their records. VandeBerg writes, "Missing from most mainstream discussions of heroes are *female* heroes or heroic narratives featuring women as anything other than victim or trophy," a matter that would make Flo Jo's explosion as an international sensation all the more intriguing.[11]

As has been debated throughout this collection, despite their accomplishments, most women athletes remain on the periphery of media coverage and are largely invisible both in terms of their athleticism and any resulting marketing opportunities. This is particularly true in the case of African-American female athletes. The few who attain visibility do not receive half as much attention from the media as either hero or celebrity as do their male counterparts, given the nature of the construction of masculinity and the emphasis on heterosexual machismo as it continues to dominate the sports marketplace. We see them, to be sure, but in many ways, they are presented to us collectively as oddities or at the very least human interest stories somehow separate from the rest of the athletic community, as it were. Where men—even black men—can be viewed through this prism of genuinely competitive individuals who have sacrificed and made the art of sport something to be admired, the admixture of race alongside the specter of gender seems to render the black female athlete a footnote or, worse even, a trespasser.

By most accounts, however, Flo Jo, because of her talent as well as her sex appeal, shattered such impenetrable standards quite readily. While conquering many existing track and field records, her look and her flamboyance against the backdrop of her athletic talents seem to have contributed significantly to her ability to transcend traditional heroic boundaries, as her media coverage, most of which was positive, if not glowing, peaked between 1987 and 1989. That coverage included four *Sports Illustrated* covers, then certainly the gold standard by which athletic reputation was measured. And yet, her publicity, unlike that of other stars of the era, was not solely linked to on-field accomplishment but rather tied directly to the ancillary elements that she brought by virtue of her lavish looks and quirky personality traits that so lit up the cameras and engaged the public. She was the epitome of both sex and athletic prowess—the sexy successful female sprinter captivating so many with a range of personal elements and physical dimensions.[12]

Here, it is important to note that the demographics for sports-related media content are largely male and heterosexual, which would account for the success that many publications and programs were finding through their coverage of her. Thus, while having a uniquely attractive and successful woman athlete on the cover may have translated into market shares, it must be said as well that this left others to wonder if there was substance that went along with the style when it came to the ubiquity of the burgeoning Flo Jo mystique.

What is undeniable, however, is that at the time, few women of color, irrespective of most factors, had come close to the level of coverage translating into marketability that Griffith Joyner enjoyed throughout this stretch. Venus and Serena Williams, while significantly younger and of a decidedly different age than Griffith Joyner, have made some albeit limited inroads into that corner of Madison Avenue. But in spite of their on-court dominance, which has far and away exceeded Griffith Joyner in terms of both success and longevity, they remain far outside the mainstream when compared to others on the women's tennis circuit who have generally cashed in on their fame and looks. In contrast to the arc of Flo Jo's rise in status, the differences between her and the Williams sisters often come down to the sheer vitriol behind media depictions and reactions. Because the Williams sisters do not fit the Eurocentric model of feminine beauty and comportment (which will be discussed more later), they are more apt to be scrutinized in a negative way for their presence than Flo Jo. She tended toward a more openly sexual and feminine demeanor as suggested by her flowing hair, makeup, and those one-legged unitards that simply screamed sex, which, I suggest, has as much to do with how African-American femininity is defined as it does with any other factor.

As discussed elsewhere in this collection, part of the negativity surrounding the Williams sisters relates to their physical makeup coupled with the fact that they excel in a traditionally conservative sport that has largely rejected the few high-profile, African-American women who have enjoyed success on the professional tour. Moreover, the Williams sisters did not excel using the traditional route of taking lessons from an expensive coach and attending private tennis schools. Instead they learned the sport from their father, Richard Williams, who had no formal training in tennis. Added to this, they are clearly the dominant forces in a sport where historically it has been nearly impossible for African Americans in general to make major inroads, with the exceptions of Althea Gibson, Arthur Ashe, and, to a much lesser extent, Zina Garrison.

In contrast, track has had a much longer and more productive relationship with African-American females that spans decades and multiple stars. Thus, while the Williams sisters and those who precede them in tennis could continue to be seen as interlopers of sorts, Griffith Joyner's ascendancy into the upper echelon of track came with very little of the traditional slings and arrows that we see in the more insular world of what Smith and Hattery claim to be the country club sport scene.[13] Thus, winning without backlash and winning with the sort of flair and joie de vivre that Griffith Joyner would display on and off the track afforded her inroads into the popular culture that simply could not exist for women in most other corners of American sport. In essence, flamboyance and African-American women track stars would not as likely be viewed as such an anomaly, even in this regard. Nor did it hurt her image that, in spite of her obvious African features, she nevertheless stood out amidst her contemporaries insomuch as she managed to fit a much more Eurocentric image of the feminine ideal.

JEZEBEL IN SPANDEX

Much as in film, talent and presence combine to separate a star from a performer's peers, and Florence Griffith Joyner as Flo Jo had a plethora of both. As one of the most famous and important African-American woman performers, Josephine Baker gave audiences what they wished to see in terms of Africa as a primitive continent—wild, untamable, and very unfamiliar to Europe. Ultimately, Baker became one of the first international stars and, unlike her contemporaries of the 1920s in Hollywood, such as Marlene Dietrich, Norma Shearer, and Bette Davis, she was her own star-making machine as opposed to a studio creation.

Flo Jo enjoyed a similar status beyond track. For example, Simon Barnes, author of "Stardom: The Ultimate High for Flo-Jo," notes that Griffith Joyner saw herself not as a fast runner, not as a well-made female, not as a flashy dresser, but as a celebrity virtually from the start and certainly in the aftermath of the Seoul games. As he suggests:

> People turned their heads not because she was beautiful, but because she was a star. Even if you had never heard of her, you only had to look at her to see that she was a star. Her need to be looked at made people look at her ... if she had never done anything, never run a step, never left home ... she would have been a star in the local supermarket, a star in a local bar.[14]

In essence, she was a star even without being elevated to Flo Jo, and in this regard, Griffith Joyner was to track what Baker had been to theater.

Carrying this notion a bit further, Griffith Joyner's charismatic Flo Jo persona harkens back to the way African-American women have long been portrayed in the media. Many parallels exist between Griffith Joyner's public presentation and those two enduring stereotypes of African-American women in stage and film—Jezebel and Mammy. Mammy, aged and desexualized, does not fit in this case, so it is more prudent to focus on the Jezebel character in the case of Flo Jo.

Light complexioned African-American women with Eurocentric features, including such luminaries of yesteryear as Nina Mae McKinney and later the inimitable Dorothy Dandridge, were favored to play the so-called Jezebel role, which was that of the highly sexualized and highly aggressive woman who demands much yet stops at nothing in her quest. The Eurocentric ideal of beauty that permeates this character, while informing a great deal about how African-American femininity is to be judged, has certainly reached beyond the stage and into the main currents of popular culture, where it can be found in sports, yet another arena where the intersectionality of race, ethnicity, and gender gets viewed. As much as African-American women have struggled to eradicate stereotypes based on physical and personality features, these features have remained part of American racial lore and have come to symbolize how others define African American femininity.

Just as the "Exotic Other," certainly the embodiment of Baker's success, was more palatable to audiences in film, Flo Jo's image, spawned as it was in sport, transitioned much more easily into celebrity circles, which, one can argue, continue to rely quite heavily on the Jezebel stereotype to serve as the public face of African-American femininity. Flo Jo seemed quite at ease in using her sex appeal both on and off the track, which translated well not only for her popular appeal, but also in terms of endorsements and other such opportunities. And yet, in choosing this route, i.e., celebrity through the existing cultural norms, she fulfilled the role as the "Exotic Other" in sports. As she continued to climb the ladder of celebrity, she found herself more and more on the receiving end of the star treatment and its subsequent financial rewards that eclipsed most of her contemporaries, including her more athletically renowned sister-in-law, Jackie Joyner-Kersee, who strictly in terms of athleticism and performance was the superior athlete.

Her sexuality, thus, conveyed itself in a manner that commanded as much (or perhaps even more) attention for her persona than her speed did. Nowhere is this made more clear than in the pictures that surface of Griffith Joyner in Seoul. In these photos, she wore a one-piece suit that covered nearly her entire body but left her ankles showing. She simultaneously wore the traditional sprinter's outfit and crowned the ensemble with her long hair flowing behind her as she sprinted to the finish line. More graphically, the shots themselves suggest that Griffith Joyner was fully aware of the media attention, which is made even more apparent in the ways that she seemed to delight in talking as much about her style as she did about her performances on the track.

In highlighting the differences between Flo Jo and Jackie Joyner-Kersee, kinesiologist Margaret Carlisle Duncan examined thirty-three photographs of Griffith Joyner as compared to twenty-five for Joyner-Kersee. Not surprisingly, Duncan concluded that the latter did not receive as much attention as her more glamorous sister-in-law. And she concluded that while both were great in their respective specialties, Flo Jo's physical attractiveness in the more obviously Eurocentric sense tilted the spotlight in her favor.[15]

In presenting her argument, Carlisle Duncan adopts a theoretical model that looks at the underlying meanings that are suggested through photographic images. She notes that when the subject of a photograph is an athlete, meanings are suggested by that person's physical characteristics, and most specifically one's age, race, facial appearance, body type, clothing, makeup, and a range of gender-related attributes. She maintains that the athlete's physical appearance is the instrument through which sporting victories (or tragedies) are achieved while indicating that as athletes' bodies bear the marks of physical conditioning, i.e., muscles, bulk, smoothness, or leanness, they also tend to manifest themselves in revealing poses that leave little to the imagination. Those poses offer the illusion that they are in fact virtually undressed when participating, which is certainly more true in some sports (swimming, basketball, gymnastics) than in others (football, hockey, lacrosse).[16]

Many articles closely scrutinized Griffith Joyner's physique juxtaposed to her athletic performance, though there is also more than a strong hint that the degree to which her body informed her broader reputation took on more sexualized significance, especially as commentary moved toward her attire. In this regard, however, one can argue that her fashion sense can also be construed as a symbiotic matter, one that followed her throughout her career and became in essence a part of her overall bodily image. For example, her outfits at times seemed uncomfortably tight and certainly revealing, and her flowing hair and curling nails seemed as if they could actually be distractions if not outright obstacles to her competitive successes. But the sensual images of Flo Jo running down the other sprinters—with her sleek figure and raven hair blowing in the wind, with those extravagantly long, lavishly polished nails, and one-legged, brightly colored, lycra-to-lace outfits—are as much a part of her legacy as her one-time designation as "fastest woman alive."

Without question, Griffith Joyner's look was unique and added to the interest in her—both on and off the track. As one commentator reminds us, when she would wear that trademark one-legged body suit, spectators in the stands and those watching at home could see a flash of Flo Jo's leg as she bolted past her competitors to reach the finish line, adding a degree of prurience to the more typically staid, desexualized traditions normally associated with the sports world, and a matter rarely lost in the corporate sector.[17]

THE CAMERA'S GAZE

To be sure, the extraordinary cache of Griffith Joyner–related photographs reinforces a sexuality that nearly eclipses her athletic accomplishments. Carlisle Duncan cites an example of Griffith Joyner on a 1988 cover of *Newsweek* with the caption "The Best and the Brightest" in which she is wearing her usual runner's outfit but with shorts that are extremely short and leave a portion of her buttocks exposed. This photograph, Carlisle Duncan contends, invites the reader's gaze and focuses it upon a particular female body part, which, in this instance, is Griffith Joyner's thigh.[18] Moreover, it is indicative of the degree to which sexuality informs the vast majority of the Flo Jo images as they exist on film and in popular discourse.

Still another photograph shows her carrying the American flag after one of her races while the camera's gaze seems to be directed at her genital area. Again, Carlisle Duncan suggests that this seeming fascination with more sexual portions of Flo Jo's body underscores how sexuality can take on another meaning, depending on the angle of the camera and perhaps even the person behind the camera.[19] For African-American women in general and Griffith Joyner in particular, such photographs certainly stand poised to feed into the stereotype of African-American women's sexuality as presented in part by the Jezebel myth. Such images are once again reminiscent of the "Exotic Other" and are particularly dangerous in light of the historical and cultural perceptions formed of African-American women initially in literature and advertisements, but later in film, television, and print media.[20]

The emphasis on illuminating Griffith Joyner's femininity is oddly contrary to how African-American women athletes have been previously seen, or rather not seen. Wilma Rudolph provides an excellent contrast in that she shattered the 100-meter record in 1960 but was afterward virtually ignored in all but the smallest circles for the barriers she broke as an African-American woman.

Sports Illustrated's Kenny Moore notes that while Rudolph, who was fêted in the African-American community and certainly a very attractive woman by any imaginable standard, also found no means with which to capitalize on her success in the commercial sphere,[21] something that was just as difficult for other African-American champions, male or female (the image of Jesse Owens racing horses and motorcycles for cash certainly comes to mind here). Endorsements for African-American women athletes would have been particularly sparse in 1960, to be sure. Despite Rudolph's historic achievements, the largest obstacle for her was that she did not fit the Eurocentric model of beauty.

Then again, even Griffith Joyner's own transformation as a commercial success was an uneven one, in spite of the media's fascination with her. This further suggests that the one constant in her popular appeal was her sexuality, which she could bank on by portraying herself—consciously or otherwise—as the "Exotic Other," and which she certainly epitomized on the track. As Heywood posits, by willingly portraying the "Exotic Other," Flo Jo demonstrated that African-American women could be beautiful in a sport not known for grace and poise and capitalize on their looks accordingly.[22]

STEROID ALLEGATIONS

In spite of her appeal, sexual and/or otherwise, no substantive discussion of Florence Griffith Joyner can exist without some mention of the steroid allegations that followed her even into death, harkening once again the role that her body plays in the majority of discussions about her. And yet, in discussing these allegations, it is also important to place them in their proper context.

To be sure, in this modern athletic age, it has become standard that any athlete whose accomplishments far and away exceed expectations (which hers clearly did) has to be cleared of wrongdoing in terms of any hint or allegations of cheating behavior, regardless of whether the assumptions come laced with fact or are purely conjecture. Certainly, there have been some cases in more recent years in which the circumstances that have befallen one athlete or another have to do with a failed test of some sort, e.g., Ben Johnson in sprinting and Floyd Landis in cycling. On the other hand, this more reactive response to convict those who may have transgressed in the public eye in the court of public opinion shows that in the case of athletes who have been cleared by laboratories and in some cases even courts, the charge tends to linger much longer than the weight of any evidence.

Certainly, when an athlete achieves what Griffith Joyner had, and in such a brief span, i.e., three Olympic golds and one silver by her twenty-eighth birthday, there is going to be speculation, which in many ways was hastened by her tragic death at thirty-eight. Those circumstances harken back to football's Lyle Alzado, who proclaimed—without evidence—that the brain tumor that was killing him was self-inflicted as a result of his protracted use of anabolic steroids and human growth hormone (HGH).[23] And yet, what is perhaps even more noteworthy about Griffith Joyner is the extent to which her more positive media attention actually mitigates the extent to which the persistent speculation marred her legacy. Thus, while speculation continues in earnest regarding her alleged steroid usage, the media in general liked her, and for that reason alone, or at least so it would appear, many seem reluctant to tear her from her celebrity perch.

What makes her ability to have weathered such a storm all the more remarkable is the extent that gender and race usually play in terms of an athlete's ability to survive such allegations. Professor Tom Cassidy of South Carolina State University puts this particular aspect of Griffith Joyner's legacy in just such a context. He claims, among other things, that when it comes to allegations of doping among athletes of color, the public reaction seems to come from a more sexualized place—as if the woman is somehow being sexually promiscuous by acting in such a fashion. In this, he identifies an element of the time-honored sexual double standard that reinforces a uniquely gendered notion that suggests that men who cheat do so out of a misplaced sense of competitive zeal, which on a strictly competitive level excuses or at least mitigates their culpability somewhat. On the other hand, women, who are continued to be seen as guests in competitive sport, cheat because they lack the capacity to compete otherwise. As a result, they are often treated far more harshly if for no other reason than that it stirs up many of the inherent prejudices that have long kept women at best along the periphery of sport.[24]

Cassidy's observations, while certainly borne of speculation, nevertheless give us leave to ponder this divide even further. One can make the case that because of such double standards, women athletes are more closely scrutinized and held to a higher standard than their male counterparts, specifically because women do not belong. In today's climate, the slightest hint of enhancement—steroidal or otherwise—is enough to derail the career of many athletes. But for women athletes, the fall seems all that much more extraordinary, as evidenced by Marion Jones. At the time of this publication Jones was making the rounds in an attempt to rehabilitate her now devastated reputation through a calculated, albeit expected, array of public apologies followed by service that seems both to infantilize, as well as further cheapen, her legacy as one of track and field's most heralded champions.

To be candid, it seems unlikely that Marion Jones will ever regain credibility, let alone her legacy. She has paid the price through the stripping of her medals and with jail time, which says as much about the vagaries of celebrityhood in sports as it does about the specter of cheating itself. Moreover, as exemplified in the Jones scandal and its resulting fallout, something that continues to ring true in cases involving nonwhite athletes is the extent to which they tend to be viewed far more negatively for their transgressions than white athletes. Race and ethnicity certainly underscore these circumstances, but we also cannot discount the role of gender here either.

In this regard, what this state of affairs means for Griffith Joyner's reputation is perhaps all the more fascinating. While some may mention her in terms of a possible doping link, it has not tarnished her legacy as much as one might expect, which is a distinction that in and of itself is little short of remarkable. Had she lived, it is likely that there would have been further investigation by sports journalists and others, particularly in light of the past decade or so when so many athletes—past and present—are either testifying before Congress concerning performance-enhancing drugs or appearing on news outlets to discuss their usage or both. On the other hand, Griffith Joyner's ability to transcend such allegations is based in no small part on her ability to charm the populace in ways that extend beyond the wildest expectations of most every other African-American woman in sport.

Such was her hold over the sporting public, which in essence is as much her legacy as her record-breaking athletic accomplishments or her flair for the theatrical. Thus, for every article—then as now—that mentions Griffith Joyner and steroids in tandem, there are many more that focus on her iconic appeal. She was and still is a hero to many in spite of assertions that her continued iconic status can be explained as a misplaced case of collective nationalism.[25] Thus, while she did not completely escape the shadow of doping, her image as a celebrity melded with her athletic accomplishments. That image continues to provide cover for her amidst the most scurrilous hint of wrongdoing.

A CHALLENGING LEGACY

The fact that an African-American woman athlete could reap this much positive attention demonstrates the power of Griffith Joyner's "Flo Jo" persona. Historically, the mere mention of African-American women and sexuality usually suggested at best something derogatory if not outright despicable. Florence Griffith Joyner was somehow able to harness the power of her athletic abilities and hitch them to her undeniable sexual magnetism, making it all the more palatable to a much more generalized audience while making it all the more profitable in terms of commercial success and widespread popularity. Thus, while she was able to challenge, if not shatter, the image of the "Exotic Other" stereotype by embracing it, she was also able to, in the words of one commentator, "emblemize a robust African-American female sexuality."[26] That she could manage to do so in life, as well as in death, with the cloud of drug use hovering about her is all the more testament to her unique celebrity status.

Florence Griffith Joyner's reputation as such is embedded in sports history. Her persona as both the fastest woman in the world alongside the flamboyance that helped earn her the Flo Jo brand remains a part of sports popular culture and in some ways makes her a very difficult figure for a subsequent generation of budding athletic celebrities to emulate. Indeed, while Marion Jones was once the best hope to overtake Flo Jo as the track world's most endearing celebrity, it now seems unlikely given the extent of the scandal that has all but destroyed her credibility as both an athlete and a symbol of the power of the modern African-American woman. But this also reinforces the extent to which Florence Griffith Joyner was unique. As her contemporary Evelyn Ashford-Simpson once acknowledged, "She was just on another level."[27] After these many years following her death, there is little evidence that suggests that her image is anything but intact.

In all, it is difficult at best to ascertain where Florence Griffith Joyner fits within the larger sports world. Though she has been eclipsed, at least athletically, by a subsequent generation of female stars, her personal brand—her signature style—remains in an arena that has historically shown itself to be unforgiving on its best day and downright menacing, if not disturbing, on others.

NOTES

1. Leslie Heywood, "Florence Griffith Joyner and the Making of Contemporary Women's Sport," November 1, 1998, http://www.mesomorphosis.com/articles/heywood/florence-griffith- joyner-and steroids.htm#ixzz1MwRW816d (May 15, 2011).

2. Kris Schwartz, "Flo Jo Made Speed Fashionable," ESPN.com, n.d., http://www.espn.go.com/classic/biography/s/Griffith_Joyner_Florence.html (June 10, 2010).

3. Ibid.

4. Ibid.

5. Ibid.

6. Ibid.

7. Kenny Moore, "Very Fancy, Very Fast: U.S. Sprinter Florence Griffith Joyner Is Certainly Eye Catching—If, That Is, You Can Catch Her," *Sports Illustrated* Online, September 14, 1988, http://sportsillustrated.cnn.com/olympics/features/joyner/flashback1 .html (July 10, 2011).

8. Schwartz, "Flo Jo Made Speed Fashionable."

9. Moore, "Very Fancy, Very Fast."

10. Schwartz, "Flo Jo Made Speed Fashionable."

11. Leah R. VandeBerg, "The Sports Hero Meets Mediated Celebrityhood" in *Media Sport*, ed. Lawrence Wenner (London and New York: Routledge, 1998), 137.

12. Ibid., 138.

13. See Smith and Hattery's discussion in Chapter 4 of this book.

14. Simon Barnes, "Stardom: The Ultimate High for Flo-Jo," *The Australian*, September 1998, 21.

15. Margaret Carlisle Duncan, "Sports Photographs and Sexual Difference: Images of Women and Men in the 1984 and 1988 Olympic Games," *Sociology of Sport Journal* 7 (1990): 22–43.

16. Ibid., 28.

17. Anise C. Wallace, "Next Stop, Madison Avenue," *New York Times* Online, October 27, 1988, http://www.nytimes.com/1988/10/27/sports/next-stop-madison-avenue.html (July 13, 2011).

18. Duncan, "Sports Photographs and Sexual Difference," 30. This image can be viewed on www.Amazon.com/Newsweek-Magazine-Florence-Brightest-September/dp/ B004VA626M.

19. Ibid.

20. Ibid., 28.

21. Kenny Moore, "The Spoils of Victory: For Florence Griffith Joyner, Olympic Prowess and Smashing Looks Have Been Lucrative, But at the Cost of Her Running," *Sports Illustrated*, April 10, 1989, 51.

22. Heywood, "Florence Griffith Joyner and the Making of Contemporary Women's Sport."

23. Joel Nathan Rosen, *The Erosion of the American Sporting Ethos: Shifting Attitudes Toward Competition* (Jefferson, NC: McFarland & Co., Inc., 2007). Also see Lyle Alzado and Shelley Smith, "I'm Sick and I'm Scared," *Sports Illustrated*, July 8, 1991, 21–27.

24. Thomas Cassidy (professor of English, Department of English and Modern Languages, South Carolina State University) in discussion with the author, October 2010.

25. Bryan E. Denham, "Performance-Enhancing Drug Use in Amateur and Professional Sports: Separating the Realities from the Ramblings," *Culture, Sport, Society* 3 (Summer 2000): 63.

26. Cassidy, discussion.

27. Tim Layden, "Florence Griffith Joyner (1959–98)," *Sports Illustrated*, September 28, 1998, sportsillustrated.cnn.com/vault/article/magazine/MAG1014086/index.html (October 26, 2012).

RACING INTO THE STORM

Roberta Gibb, Kathrine Switzer, and Women's Marathoning

—OREN RENICK AND LEA ROBIN VELEZ

INTRODUCTION

It was 1964—Freedom Summer. The nation was in turmoil. The civil rights movement, the Vietnam War, and social unrest spawned upheaval and conflict. It seemed the country was experiencing an internal temper tantrum of opposing forces and against all of the pent-up inequalities that had existed far too long.

The unrest cut deep into the jugular of the country, and did not seem to leave any facet of life unscathed, including sports. Against this backdrop, two female runners, Roberta Gibb and Kathrine Switzer, emerged as the symbols of equal access for women in the world of marathon competition, and together they challenged traditional feminine roles that had been entrenched for centuries.

Roberta Gibb, as far as she was concerned, was not part of any struggle. It was 1964 when Gibb first witnessed the Boston Marathon. The Boston native was mesmerized with the sport and believed as an athlete, not a feminist, that if she wanted to run, she could. However, life was not that forthright and simple in the 1960s. It was not until February 1966, when Gibb applied to run the Boston Marathon, that she slammed headfirst into the locked gate of sexism. Race officials denied her entry because she was not a man. That injustice, that denial of her rights and the rights of all women who wanted to run and reach their potential as athletes, ignited a fire in Gibb that thrust her into a role she had not imagined. She had become a pioneer in women's distance running.

Gibb ignored the all-male tradition of the Boston Marathon and ran unofficially in the 1966 race. In 1967, Gibb again ran in the Boston Marathon, but this time she was not the only female runner. Kathrine Switzer ran as K. V. Switzer, number 261. Switzer began the race without the officials' knowledge that she was a woman. She ran until an official was alerted to the news that a woman was running with a number. That official, Jock Semple, grabbed Switzer in an unsuccessful attempt to remove her from the course. A journalist photographed the struggle, and the picture of that incident was seen around the world and ignited a fury for fairness for women runners. Switzer went on to become the first official female to complete the Boston Marathon.[1]

That incident in 1967 made Switzer the symbol of the struggle for women to be recognized as legitimate athletes. The incident in and of itself was not earth-shattering, but Switzer's run became something of a tipping point—or, as one author put it, that "little thing that can make a big difference."[2]

Switzer's race was not without controversy from her peers. Roberta Gibb believed the climate was warming for women to run before Switzer's "illegal" entrance into the sport. Gibb blamed Switzer for making the running scene even more difficult for women.[3]

With the pivotal runs of the forerunners Gibb and Switzer, equal access for women runners became a united cry for justice. Gibb and Switzer, each in her own way, were soldiers in the marathon battlefield for equal access in the sixties, running for the rights of all women. This was a cry that could no longer be quieted by age-old myths of the shrinking violet woman and the image of the weak, incapable female. This was also against the tenets of how women were supposed to act and challenged traditional feminine roles and the roots of feminine learning ideologies.

ROBERTA GIBB

In developing a passion for distance running, Roberta "Bobbi" Gibb breached what writer E. J. Tisdell called "the values of the dominant culture."[4] Those values spelled out what was appropriate for women and what was not, and breaking through the gender barrier in sports that were historically the domain of men went against the grain of what was commonly accepted as feminine behavior. Aggressiveness and competition were masculine tendencies, while nurturance and passivity were labels worn by females.[5] In other words, women were expected to commune and cooperate, not compete. But Gibb's love for running fueled her desire to be recognized as a legitimate competitor.

Born in 1943 and growing up in the suburbs of Boston, Gibb didn't think of her zeal for running as unfeminine or extraordinary.[6] In the summers, she raced around the neighborhood, challenging boys and girls. Gibb stated, "I have always been active. When I was growing up, if I saw a green grassy field, I had this uplifting sense of joy. I would run across it with my arms up in the air. I couldn't help myself. It was a love of life."[7]

During high school, Gibb spent afternoons running the wooded areas near her home, not with any sense of competition, but simply for the joy of running. Gibb continued running after graduating from high school in 1962. She entered Tufts University School of Special Studies in Boston; there her boyfriend, a member of the Tufts cross-country team, urged her to begin running distance until she began making her eight-mile commute to the university on foot—running.[8]

Observing the runners in the 1964 Boston Marathon made Gibb know she wanted to experience that event. She stated, "Here were people running on the earth, and they had such a sense of themselves . . . I could see their faces. I just decided I was going to run the race. It wasn't for prize money. I didn't even realize at that point women weren't allowed to run."[9] Gibb said her decision to run was not competitive, but more of a choice to participate in a sport she loved.[10]

In the summer of 1965, with her parents in England, Gibb put her puppy into her Volkswagen bus and drove across the country to California. She ran the terrain along the way from grassy fields and open plains to mountainous areas and sandy beaches. She had planned to run the 1965 Boston Marathon, but she sprained her ankle badly and had to wait until 1966.[11]

By then, Gibb, who had married navy man William Bingay on February 5, 1966, in California, continued to run in nurse's shoes since there were no running shoes for women.[12] She wrote to the Boston Athletic Association for an application to enter the Boston Marathon since it was the only marathon she knew, but she was shocked when Will Cloney, the race director, wrote her back and said women were not physiologically able to run twenty-six miles. Moreover, citing the existing rules governing women's track events, he also claimed that the rules of international sports did not allow women to run anything more than sprints. That had become the standard in athletic circles in 1928 when nearly all distances above 200 meters were dropped from the women's ledger following the feigned uproar over a rather innocuous result of an 800-meter race in that year's Amsterdam Olympic Games. No less than the legendary sportswriter John Tunis was moved to remark that when the race was over, "Below us on the cinder path were 11 wretched women, 5 of whom dropped out before the finish, while 5 collapsed after reaching the tape," none of which was true nor close to accurate. Still, the outcry sealed women's athletic fate for the next three decades.[13]

That was history that Gibb would not accept, and rather than dampen her determination, the age-old myth of female compliance instead of competition (which was at the heart of Cloney's response) spurred it. "I was stunned," Gibb said. "All the more reason to run."[14] Cloney reminded her that women and distance running were not compatible. Such remained the prevailing attitude toward women in sports, "a forum in which girls [were] not made to feel welcome."[15] All of this was news to Gibb, who had been running ten, twenty, and even forty miles at a time.[16]

Apparently, no one in the Boston Marathon hierarchy remembered Great Britain's Violet Piercy, who was the first woman to be timed officially in a marathon in 1926.[17] But Boston Marathon officials were about to encounter and remember another determined woman marathoner, Roberta Gibb.

Gibb would later write in her brief memoir *To Boston with Love* that she had heard the marathon was open to every person in the world. She said that it had not crossed her mind to consider herself different from the other runners. Her outrage turned to humor as she considered how many preconceived prejudices would crumble when she ran along for twenty-six miles. Gibb thought once people knew women could run marathon distances, the field would naturally open up.[18]

Gibb further emphasized that "[t]his was all the more reason for me to run in the race—because they had something to learn. They thought the world was flat, so I was going to teach them it was round."[19] Gibb realized at that moment she was running for much more than her own personal challenge. She was running to change the way people think. She was running to dispel the false belief that was keeping half the world's population from participating in sports, let alone the broader participation to be found in the modern world.[20]

In her memoirs, Gibb continued to claim that it was a catch-22 since you can't prove something you're not allowed to do. She reasoned that if women could do what was thought impossible, what else could women do, or for that matter, what else could anyone do that is thought impossible.[21]

The Boston Marathon of 1966 was not going to pass without Gibb's presence, even though she could not get an official entrance. She took the bus to Boston, arriving the day before the race. She did not know what to expect since she was going against the social norm. She suspected she might be arrested or at the very least thrown off the course.[22]

KATHRINE SWITZER

Kathrine Switzer, a joint resident of New York and New Zealand, was born January 5, 1947, and began running as a youngster before running was something women did. She ran laps around her family property until she was running a mile, two miles, and then running just for the joy of it. She went on to play field hockey at Lynchburg College where she was a standout because of her running ability. Also, while at Lynchburg, Switzer ran the mile with the Lynchburg men's track team.[23]

Switzer continued her mission of running and competing in sports, but since she was not impressed with the athletic ability of the women at Lynchburg, she decided to transfer to another university. She felt she was able to compete in running and other athletics more seriously after she transferred to Syracuse University.[24]

In what would become a controversial yet groundbreaking decision in 1967, Switzer pursued her running by registering as K. V. Switzer for the all-male Boston Marathon. She began the first "official" run for a woman in that event without incident before being spotted by the now-infamous and bellowing figure of Jock Semple, the race official who not only tried unsuccessfully to physically remove her from the course but would in effect become the face of male resistance in this particular domain.[25]

Switzer stated that being able to run the marathon opened people's consciousness to what a woman could do.[26] After her inaugural run at Boston, she ran more than thirty marathons, won the 1974 New York City Marathon, and was ranked sixth in the world in 1975. More than that, though, Switzer has been an advocate for other women in her sports marketing, communication, and fitness efforts.[27]

More than twenty years ago Switzer created the Avon International Running Circuit for Avon Products, Inc., which gave even more credibility to women's distance running. This afforded women all over the world the opportunity to participate in running. In 1980 Switzer managed to shut down the streets of London for the Avon International Marathon, which was the first of its kind in the annals of modern sport.[28]

Through such efforts, Switzer is credited in large measure for making the women's marathon an official event in the Olympic Games with the first women's Olympic marathon in 1984.[29] Her efforts have received acclaim over the years, and she continues to be a spokesperson for women's sports. In July 1998 Switzer was inducted as part of the inaugural class into the National Distance Running Hall of Fame. In 2000, *Runner's World Magazine* named Switzer Runner of the Decade (1966–77) and one of the visionaries of the century.[30]

In 2004, *MORE* magazine launched a women's-only marathon for those over forty. Switzer and legendary marathon runner Grete Waitz were spokespersons for the event.[31]

GIBB'S AND SWITZER'S FIRST MARATHON RUNS

It was a warm day as the approximately five hundred men assembled for the 1966 Boston Marathon, but Gibb had a blue hooded sweatshirt pulled tight around her face, hiding her long blonde pony tail. She wore a pair of her brother's shorts over a black swimsuit and had to hide in the bushes. She did not have an official number nor the respect due an athlete of her ability. She had to wait until the gun sounded and the five hundred men began to run before she could dash into their midst as an unacknowledged runner. Behind her she heard the words, "You are a girl!" When she turned her head around and smiled, one of the men, noting the hot day, told her to take her hood off. Another male runner added, "It's a free road."[32]

The male marathoners, as a group, did not seem upset by Gibb's presence. Surprise was the primary reaction. Eleven miles into the race, one runner recalled, "I was humming 'The Girl from Ipanema' to myself, trying to get hopped up with a little rhythm. Then this girl scooted by. I thought I was hallucinating."[33]

"I hadn't intended to make a feminist statement," Gibb said. "I was running against the distance, not the men, and I was measuring myself with my own potential."[34] Gibb ran the race, but was forced off the course a few feet from the finish line. Her time would have been 3:21:40.[35] She had become the first woman to run the Boston Marathon, but it would be six years before women were "official" runners and given numbers.

Sports Illustrated of May 2, 1966, quoted Will Cloney, the man who had denied Gibb's official entry as saying, "Mrs. Bingay did not run in the Boston Marathon. She merely covered the same route as the official race while it was in progress. No girl has ever run in the Boston Marathon."[36] Moreover, that same issue of *Sports Illustrated* also lamented the fact that Gibb's run "unfortunately took some of the luster from the group triumph of the Japanese, who were truly exceptional." The attitude of the time is summed up in the article "A Game Girl in a Man's Game," with the subtitle "Boston was unprepared for the shapely blonde housewife who came out of the bushes to crush male egos and steal the show from the Japanese."[37]

In 1967 Gibb again ran the Boston Marathon unofficially without a number as she had in 1966. Her unofficial time of 3:27:17 shed nearly six full minutes off her previous efforts, which in distance running is no small feat.[38] But when she crossed the finish line this time, instead of being pushed aside by officials, she was met by a roar of approval from the crowd. One hour after Gibb finished, Kathrine Switzer crossed the finish line.[39]

Switzer's run, however, took a polar opposite turn next to Gibb's own experience, given the ruckus that ensued. While Gibb simply took the discrimination in stride and went about her business, Switzer seemed to be a magnet for rather dramatic controversy. This is perhaps best exemplified in the oft-told encounter with Jock Semple, whose open disdain and subsequent behavior almost got him beaten up by a man nearly twice his size! Indeed, the ruckus that ensued once Semple jumped from the officials' truck, grabbed Switzer, and shouted (in his thick Scottish brogue), "Get the hell out of my race and give me that number," followed by "You are in big trooooouble,"[40] was met by her quite perturbed and annoyed linebacker boyfriend who tossed Semple aside like an old sack, which gave Switzer and her team even more incentive to not only finish the race but to do so competitively. And yet, for all the bluster and spectacle brought about by that now-infamous encounter, it would also appear that every condemnation of both Gibb and Switzer played right into the hands of what they and other activists sought throughout that turbulent period.

While the audio remains fascinating, it is the images that have become part of the legacy of women's sport. Indeed, the photos of Switzer's midrace attack were flashed around the world and are listed in Time-Life's *100 Photographs That Changed the World*.[41] The photographs became banners. Women seemed more galvanized than ever after being presented the injustice of inequality expressed by the photograph. Such images helped to fuel the feminist movement in the late 1960s and early 1970s and the formalization of women's equal rights via Title IX.

To be sure, while it had no direct effect on what Gibb and Switzer accomplished, Title IX, nonetheless, codified in part their campaign to demonstrate that women had as much right to compete as men. Title IX also broke the authority of institutions and athletic officials to keep women out of athletic competition in educational institutions with federal funding. And yet, while this was to be a watershed moment, there was still a great deal to be done.

Switzer made peace with Semple a year later at the starting line of the Boston Marathon when he boisterously threw his arm around her shoulder, turned her toward a camera, and said, "C'mon, lass, let's get a bit o' notoriety." The picture ran in the papers the next day and was captioned, perhaps ironically, "The End of an Era."[42]

SIMILAR AIMS WITH DIFFERING APPROACHES

Without question, Switzer with her "official" number and Gibb in her "unofficial" run both helped pry open that door that had been stuck closed by sexism and misconceptions concerning the female athlete. These two women helped pry open the same door with very different methods. They wanted the same results, but it was also apparent that they disagreed—sometimes vehemently so—about how those results should be attained. It also bears reexamination of the activists and enthusiasts who came before them and offered them something of a jumping-off point for their later exploits.

One such organization was the Road Runners Club of America (RRCA), which became a reality on February 22, 1958, and was a spark that helped ignite women's long-distance running. RRCA established the first events for male and female recreational joggers called "Run-For-Your-Life," which became known as fun runs.[43] These runs were not under the jurisdiction of the Amateur Athletic Union (AAU), which did not allow women to run more than 1.5 miles. In 1965, the RRCA held its first National Women's Cross Country Championship even though the AAU strongly objected to the event.[44]

In 1959, before RRCA instituted the first National Women's Cross Country Championship, Arlene Pieper ran the grueling twenty-six-mile course up Pikes Peak and then back down in 9:16.[45] This run made the little-known Pieper the first woman to officially finish a marathon in the United States.[46] Somehow, attitudes did not change significantly after the Pieper run. There were still allegations that women could not run long distances, and that they would impair if not outright damage their reproductive systems, an ideology whose origins can be traced to mid-nineteenth-century discussion of sport. Beyond that, some even thought such exploits were little more than feminist-driven publicity stunts, making it that much more difficult for women athletes to gain anything close to a firm footing in the overarching sports world. Or as Betty Desch, head of the women's physical education department at the State University of New York at Stony Brook in the 1970s said, "When I went to college in the '30s, we were taught that competition was dirty."[47]

Without question, Gibb and Switzer were breaking myths as well as records in their controversial runs. Ensconced in the world of competitive runners, they became the antitheses of the roles and images that women were expected to portray: nurturers and caregivers, wives and mothers, and a gender for which "webs of connections" rather than the manly rigors of competition should be enough.[48] As noted by feminist learning scholar Elizabeth Hayes, the process of socializing women emphasizes "collaboration, support and affiliation."[49]

Gibb and Switzer are intertwined in the history books as the first "unofficial" and "official" female runners in the Boston Marathon, but their approaches and philosophies were very different. Gibb, who quietly slipped in under the radar, has been referred to as a bandit, while Switzer acted in a more bold if not brazen fashion, first through a bit of well-conceived subterfuge and then by tapping into the resulting publicity brought about through her quite public confrontation. Their different approaches also mirrored the different schools of thought on the social roles women should be taught to occupy. On one hand, women's orientations have long been thought to center on relationships and "sharing feelings and communicating empathy."[50] The other side of such expectations was a more radical approach as found in the feminism embodied by figures such as Gloria Steinem and Betty Friedan, who called for, if not demanded outright, equality in the workplace, home, sport, and other social spheres.

Gibb didn't necessarily want to "rock the boat," as it were. She was obviously more attuned to the feelings of race officials and went about her business accordingly. Switzer, however, embracing a more challenging feminism growing more prominent during the times, confronted what she believed to be an unjust system by entering races in the manner that she did. Among her detractors for such brazenness was Gibb herself, who found Switzer's actions objectionable if only for their chicanery, though to this day, Switzer believes her actions were warranted and ultimately moved the cause along.[51] As Gilbert and Williamson report, the rift between them seemed to develop quickly:

Gibb said of Switzer, "Then there was another woman (Switzer) who had gotten an 'illegal' number. I guess Jock was angry, and then the marathon really closed down. By the time I got to the finish line, I didn't know what was going on. She was an hour behind me, and I had no idea that there was all this turmoil going on. At the finish line, they weren't as friendly as they were the year before, and I wondered why."[52]

Clearly, Gibb was not into the organization of the sport as much as she was in love with the sport. And yet, while they disagree, what holds them together in this narrative is that in the end, both women were leaders in drawing attention to the inequalities for aspiring women distance runners. The objective of advancing women's rights in distance running was attained through the efforts of Gibb and Switzer and many others who had determination and perseverance to run even when they were told they could not, and this holds true in spite of any lingering discord between them.

A CONTINUING STRUGGLE

Roberta Gibb and Kathrine Switzer will forever remain integral figures in the fight for equality and justice in women's sport. Those two women literally chose to run past prejudice and exclusion in their fight to be included in a sport they loved. And after their brave, determined stands, it became just a bit easier for other talented athletic women, including the likes of Joan Benoit and Mary Decker Slaney, to be able to concentrate more on their passion for competition and less on fighting the obstacles that Gibb and Switzer helped tear down.

In 1979 Benoit, as heralded a figure as exists in women's running, won the women's division of the Boston Marathon followed by her acclaimed gold medal in the marathon—the first women's marathon in the modern era—in the 1984 Olympic Games in Los Angeles. Perhaps not so ironically, Switzer served as the color commentator for the ABC-TV network, which was covering the games the day when Benoit, who would be named one of the ten all-time women's champions by *Running Times Magazine*, won the gold.[53]

Mary Decker Slaney, a contemporary of Benoit's, became the only athlete, male or female, to hold every American record from the 800-meter run to the 10,000-meter run. She qualified for four Olympic teams and competed in her last Olympics in 1996 at the age of thirty-seven.[54]

In the early twenty-first century, a new generation of female distance runners—including Shalane Flanagan and Deana Kaston, coming on the heels of Ann Trason and Lynn Jennings in the 1990s—is profiting from the trailblazers who established women's distance running as an accepted and even heralded sport. But while the acceptance of female athletes has become a reality, there continues to be slow progress toward accepting that being athletic and strong can equate to being female. This is the same battle, though much less overt, that Gibb and Switzer fought in the late 1960s.

The struggle is an ongoing process for women, as well as all the others who have had to fight for equal rights. The age-old adage of "you throw like a girl" or "you cry like a girl" is still heard and is hardly questioned in sports. If, however, this were replaced with an indication that someone threw a certain way based upon race or ethnicity, there would be outrage.

Why, then, are sexist slurs still present and widely used without question? There are of course lingering indications that females, due to their physical nature, lack the power and strength necessary for sport. Physiologically, to compare a female athlete to a male athlete is like comparing a heavyweight fighter to a featherweight fighter. They are both powerful and strong, but must be respected and admired for the training, tenacity, and commitment that each end of the spectrum brings to such endeavors. Moreover, what it means to be both feminine and strong remains a concept that continues to provide social, political, and certainly cultural confusion when placed under the microscope of traditional gender norms. The empowerment of female athletes challenges such expectations of femininity headlong and pierces holes in the veil that continues to value the female as strictly complementary to man rather than his equal. And such is the lesson of the female runners of today and yesterday who elbowed their way into the athletic scene with determination, perseverance, and a demand to be taken seriously as both people as well as athletes.

NOTES

1. Kathrine Switzer, *A Biography*, February 8, 2010, http://www.kathrineswitzer.com/bio.shtml (November 11, 2010).

2. Malcolm Gladwell, *The Tipping Point* (New York: Back Bay Books, 2002).

3. Jim Hodges, "You've Come 26.2 Miles, Baby," *Los Angeles Times*, April 16, 1995, http://articleslatimes.com1995-04-16/sports retrieved April 27, 2011.

4. E. J. Tisdell, "Feminism and Adult Learning: Power, Pedagogy and Practice," in *An Update on Adult Learning Theory*, ed. Sharan B. Merriam (San Francisco: Jossey-Bass Publishers, 1993), 102.

5. M. F. Belenky, B. M. Clinchy, N. R. Goldberger, and J. M. Tarule, *Women's Ways of Knowing: The Development of Self, Voice and Mind* (New York: Basic Books, Inc., 1986). See also M. B. Nelson, *The Stronger Women Get, the More Men Love Football* (New York: Harcourt, Brace & Company, 1994).

6. Roberta Gibb, *Good Girls Don't Run*, January 1, 2004, http://sports.jrank.org/pages/1626/Gibb-Bobbi-Good-Girls-Don-t-Run.html retrieved (November 17, 2004).

7. Shanti Sosienski, *Women Who Run* (Emeryville, CA: Seal Press, 2006), 4.

8. Gibb, *Good Girls Don't Run*.

9. Ibid.

10. Ibid.

11. Ibid.

12. Tom Derderian, *Boston Marathon: The History of the World's Premier Running Event* (Champaign, IL: Human Kinetics Publishers, 1996).

13. Anita DeFrantz, "The Changing Role of Women in the Olympic Games," *Olympic Review* XXVI, no. 15 (June–July 1997): 18–20. Quote on page 19. (Editors' note: Tunis's column unleashed a floodgate of apprehension as the specter of exhausted women ran headlong into the perception that child-rearing could one day take a backseat to this sort of liberation, which is what most scholars point to as having been the impact of Tunis's ill-fated and horribly misleading remarks.)

14. Roberta Gibb, *A Run of One's Own*, June 24, 2011, http://ww.runningpast.com/ gibb_story.htm (September 19, 2010).

15. M. A. Landers and G. A. Fine, "Learning Life's Lessons in Tee Ball: The Reinforcement of Gender and Status in Kindergarten Sport," *Sociology of Sport Journal* 13 (1996): 92.

16. Gibb, *A Run of One's Own*.

17. Charlie Lovett, *Olympic Marathon*, n.d., http://www.marthonguide.com/history/ olympicmarathons/chapter25.cfm (September 14, 2010).

18. Gibb, *Good Girls Don't Run*.

19. Ibid.

20. Gibb, *A Run of One's Own*.

21. Ibid.

22. Ibid.

23. Jim Hodges, "You've Come 26.2 Miles, Baby," *Los Angeles Times*, April 16, 1995, http://articles.latimes.com/1995-04-16/sports/sp-55388 retrieved (November 11, 2010).

24. "Early Morning Run," review of *Marathon Woman: Running the Race to Revolutionize Women's Sports*, November 10, 2010, http://earlymorningrun.blogspot .com/2010/11/book-review-marathon-woman.html (November 18, 2010).

25. Ibid.

26. Katherine Hobson, "Kathrine Switzer: Run, Women, Run," *U.S. News and World Report*, April 8, 2007, http://www.usnews.com/usnews/news/articlelsl/070408/16qa.htm (April 25, 2011).

27. Switzer, *A Biography*.

28. Lin Molloy, review of *Marathon Woman: Running the Race to Revolutionize Women's Sports*, April 10, 2007, http://www.coolrunning.com/cgi-bin/moxiebin/bm_tools .cgi?print=6050;s=6_1;site=1 (September 17, 2010).

29. Ibid.

30. Switzer, *A Biography*.

31. Ibid. Note: Switzer's more recent book, *Marathon Woman*, was released in February 2007. The subtitle, consistent with the struggle for access in sports for all women, is *Running the Race to Revolutionize Women's Sports* (New York: Da Capo, 2007).

32. Ibid.

33. Gwilym Brown, "A Game Girl in a Man's Game," *Sports Illustrated*, May 2, 1966, www.SIVAULT.com (November 10, 2010).

34. Lovett, *Olympic Marathon*.

35. Ibid.

36. Brown, "A Game Girl."

37. Ibid.

38. Boston Marathon Race Summaries, November 1, 2010, http://www.boston marathon.org/BostonMarathon/RaceSummaries.asp?myears=14 (November 15, 2010).

39. Ibid.

40. Quotes found in both David Powell, "How Manhandling of Switzer Opened the Door for Women," *The Times*, April 10, 2007, http://www.timesonline.co.uk/tol/sport/ more (November 15, 2010), and Hodges, "You've Come 26.2 Miles, Baby."

41. Kathrine Switzer, *Marathon Woman: Running the Race to Revolutionize Women's Sports* (New York: Da Capo, 2007). See also Robert Sullivan, *100 Photographs That Changed the World* (New York: Time, Inc., 2003).

42. Ibid.

43. History/Road Runners Club of America, September 1, 2011, http://www.rrca.org/abouthistory/ (September 15, 2010).

44. Ibid.

45. Mina Samuels, "Run Like a Girl," June 17, 2011, http://www.minasamuel.comrun likeagirl.htm (June 30, 2011).

46. Matt Carpenter, "1959 Pikes Peak Marathon," August 7, 1959, http://www.skyrunner .com (April 27, 2011).

47. Bill Gilbert and Nancy Williamson, "Women Are Getting a Raw Deal," *Sports Illustrated*, May 28, 1973, 95.

48. Carol Gilligan, *In a Different Voice: Psychological Theory and Women's Development* (Cambridge: Harvard University Press, 1982).

49. Elizabeth R. Hayes, "A New Look at Women's Learning," in *A New Update on Adult Learning Theory*, ed. Sharan B. Merriam (San Francisco: Jossey-Bass, 2001), 35–43, 36.

50. Ibid., 36.

51. Gilbert and Williamson, "Raw Deal," 95.

52. Ibid.

53. Brian Metzler, "Rare Air, Common Ground," *Running Times Magazine*, September 2010, 12.

54. Tim Layden, "Paralysis by Urinalysis," *Sports Illustrated*, May 26, 1997, http://www .usatf.org/news/view (November 16, 2010).

GO MAMA! BRANDED BY BEAUTY

How Danica Patrick Swooned Her Way into Sponsorship

—LISA R. NEILSON

INTRODUCTION

The photos featured in the April 2003 issue of the popular British male magazine, *FHM*, are typical of their kind: young, attractive broad, scantily clad, poses suggestively for the camera with a seductive look in her eyes. The twenty-year-old in the pictures, though, is not so typical. At the time of the photo shoot, the young woman was neither a top fashion model nor an aspiring actress; she was neither in the more blatantly self-conscious entertainment business, thinking of herself solely as an athlete, nor on a quest to become another playmate of Hugh Hefner.[1] Her name is Danica Patrick, and at the time, she was a race car driver looking for a ride.

Patrick's decision to partake in the photo shoot requested by *FHM* editor Scott Gramling undoubtedly became her best career decision to date. Not only was it the jumpstart she was seeking to enter the world of IndyCar racing (the IRL); it was also the beginning of a marketing strategy that has branded Patrick into a household name. Today, she is considered one of the most influential athletes in the world, and her marketing power currently ranks with that of LeBron James and Peyton Manning. This chapter explores how Patrick's choice to be branded by beauty has been the driving force in keeping her on the racetrack while opening the doors of auto racing to a new generation of female drivers.

THE RIDE'S THE THING

Auto racing differs from other sports in that in order to participate, an athlete needs more than just talent and skills and a lucky sighting by a scout with a keen eye. A driver's prowess is only one part of a winning formula. Sponsors are necessary to pour big sums of money into providing a driver with the best possible equipment. To put it bluntly, it is the best and most powerful equipment that in the end wins races. If a driver lacks a supportive sponsor to pay for things like tires, engines, and mechanics, he or she is forced to drop out of the circuit regardless of ability. Hours of training and decent finishes, as well as popularity, can mean nothing.

Historically, women drivers have especially faced incredible difficulty in landing corporate sponsors. Indy pioneer Janet Guthrie is one such example. In 1977, Guthrie was the first woman to compete at the Indy 500 and had to overcome disdainful treatment from fans, media, and fellow drivers who believed that professional auto racing was no place for women. Guthrie claims that corporations discriminated against her as well in failing to provide sponsorship. Similarly as with the general public, they believed that women lacked the strength and endurance to compete in the sport. In the eyes of prospective sponsors, this meant that not only were women unlikely to be successful, but also that they were a danger to everyone on the track. These fears kept sponsors away.[2]

Despite Guthrie's impressive career finishes on the road racing circuit in which she finished as high as fifth in Indy events and sixth in NASCAR competitions, she was forced to give up the sport in 1983 because no company was willing to support her. Female drivers who followed in Guthrie's footsteps faced similar obstacles—that is, until Danica Patrick entered the picture.

ON THE STARTING LINE

Initially, Patrick gave little thought to the *FHM* photo spread. In 2002, she had just joined a successful racing team co-owned by former Indy 500 champion Bobby Rahal after failing a three-year attempt at an English circuit featuring young, ambitious drivers. Whereas Patrick had been labeled a teenage racing prodigy in the Midwest, her performances in Europe were disappointing. After returning to the States, she was already looking for a career comeback at age twenty.

When the magazine approached Rahal about using Patrick in the photo shoot, he encouraged Patrick to say yes (Rahal was always interested in publicity that might drum up sponsors), and she agreed.[3] The feature was titled "The Hottest Thing on Wheels since Roller Girl," and hot it was! Photographer George Holz captured Patrick's attractive features: her long raven hair, her petite and athletic figure, and her sensual stare. He photographed Patrick wearing a red bikini in one shot, a red leather bustier with black leather string panties in another, and black leather hot pants in a third. All five shots presented Patrick in sexually suggestive positions while sitting in or leaning against a bright yellow '57 Chevy. *FHM* readers loved the feature, and Patrick's first pinup photos soon went viral.

It wasn't until 2005, though, that the feature really started to work for Patrick. She graduated to the IndyCar circuit after racing two seasons for Rahal in the Atlantic Championship series. As Patrick prepared for the Indianapolis 500 in May 2005 with the Rahal Letterman Racing team, her popularity soared. The media and fans got wind of the *FHM* pinup pictures while websites carrying them crashed.

Patrick was bombarded with interview opportunities the week of the race. The young driver finished an impressive fourth and landed on the cover of *Sports Illustrated* while few writers even mentioned—or remembered—winner Dan Wheldon in their coverage. The race reportedly attracted more viewers than it had in years; television ratings rose 60 percent from the prior season.[4] Many attributed this sudden peak of interest in Indy racing to the presence of a new, competent female American driver who had successfully crossed into a male-dominated sporting terrain. From that moment on, this new Indy icon would become known to more than just racing fans.

FEMMING UP!

Grabbing the momentum of the Indy success and attention, Patrick decided to market herself aggressively. While she consistently focused on being a skilled open wheel driver—not a skilled *female* open wheel driver—in her interviews with the media, she had no qualms about using her good looks and sensuality in her advertising campaign. Patrick had never planned on being an auto racing pinup girl, but when the fans liked what they saw in the *FHM* photos, she recognized a strategy and made it her own. What eventually became known as the "Danica brand," as she calls it, though, wasn't enough by itself to keep her on the racetrack; she knew she would need the backing of a lucrative and loyal sponsor.

In May 2005, that's exactly what Patrick got. Her accomplishment at the 2005 Indianapolis 500 and her *FHM* pinup photos caught the attention of Bob Parsons, founder and C.E.O. of the world's largest Internet-domain registrar, godaddy.com. Parsons liked the image Patrick projected: feisty, edgy, and a little bit naughty yet wholesome and all-American, too. He considered her to be an ideal spokesperson for his web hosting company, known for its racy marketing. Parsons agreed in 2006 to become Patrick's primary sponsor as she signed with the Andretti Green Racing team, driving the No. 7 neon green Dallara Honda. Finally, Patrick had scored what prior female racing pioneers had not: a secure ride. No longer would she have to worry about finding sponsorship money. At Parsons's request, Patrick subsequently joined the Go Daddy Girl lineup and immediately played a prominent role in the company's often sexually suggestive commercials. And she continues to be one of five Go Daddy Girls featured on the company's website and in its annual Super Bowl ads that have, at times, been banned from the network due to inappropriate content. Patrick is as much associated with godaddy.com as she is with motorsports. She is as much a sexy entrepreneur as she is a skilled race car driver, and it is unlikely that she could be one without the other.

How does Patrick feel about using her body—her exposed body, that is— to stay in the competition? In reference to the *FHM* photographs, Patrick says, "It helped me get the ride. The bottom line is, it takes money to go racing. If there's money there, and it puts me in a really good car, then I can go show what I can do."[5] She knows that women like Guthrie and the 1992 Indy Rookie of the Year, Lynn St. James, both had the talent to drive competitively but lacked the financial resources to contend with the front-runners. Patrick may have found herself in a similar situation if Parsons had not taken an interest in what he saw as a highly marketable image.

And yet, Patrick is unapologetic for using her sex appeal and baring her skin in order to promote herself. In "Drivers to divas: advertising images of women in motorsport," Patrick notes that in regards to her image based on sex appeal, ". . . I'm going to use it to my full advantage, just like anybody else would who has a niche."[6] If she had decided against it, she may have risked elimination from the sport, like Guthrie and other female drivers.

Patrick's decision to market herself through her looks is criticized by many, both inside and outside of the sport. At the Indianapolis 500 qualifiers in 2010, one veteran driver stated, "If she wasn't pretty, nobody would write about her."[7] Some drivers in the field feel Patrick needs to win more in order to give the "splash" some substance. Headlining as much as she does belongs to a top runner, doesn't it? But here one wonders if Patrick is being held to a higher standard than her male counterparts. While she may not win every race she enters, she consistently races competitively, often finishing in the top twenty. Her best Indy 500 finish came in 2009 when she placed third—the highest finish for a woman in the event's history—and she took the 2008 Indy Japan 300, making her the first woman to win an Indy race. In regards to her 2010 crossover into NASCAR, legendary NASCAR driver Darrell Waltrip writes, "[Her performance] impressed me that she wasn't just out there because she could be. She was out there because she is good. She was tenacious. She didn't quit . . . She came up from the back of the pack and got a great finish."[8] In contrast, the amount of press male drivers on the same level as Patrick receive—whether they win or not—is hardly questioned; many *never* score a big win, but because their ad campaign is a fraction of Patrick's, their results are not as highly scrutinized, and the criticism against them is much less.

Regardless of whether one sees Patrick's marketing scheme as positive or negative, it certainly has changed the way women in motorsports have been promoted. In contrast to Patrick's steamy photos, the few Texaco Oil advertisements from the late 1970s in which Guthrie appeared featured her in full racing gear and emphasized her athleticism and expertise in auto racing. They mirrored advertisements of her male racing cohorts and showed no skin or sex appeal. Guthrie was recognized as a driver first; her gender was downplayed. And yet, by 1980, the oil company pulled its funding, and Guthrie's racing career ended with no other support in sight. Similarly, ads featuring St. James, who competed in the eighties and early nineties, were also identical to those portraying male drivers of the time. No provocativeness tinged the pictures of St. James at any time, nor did her femininity. In fact, St. James was adamant about how her sponsors presented her, demanding tasteful images that highlighted her racing expertise.[9] St. James retired from the sport in 2001.

When Sarah Fisher came along in 1999, a shift developed in the promotion of female drivers. Fisher was only nineteen when she appeared on the racing scene; within two years she became the first female to drive an entire IndyCar season and won the Most Popular Driver award in that series for three consecutive years, as noted on her website. Although Fisher marketed herself similarly to the previous ladies, emphasizing her athleticism and skill in most of her ads, her Tag Heuer spot was different. She was still captured in her racing gear, but her face revealed an alluring, sensual expression.[10] When compared to today's standards, it was tame. Fisher didn't bare any skin, but it was the first time that sexuality coupled with the presentation of female race car drivers. Interestingly, Fisher is still very much in the sport as the first woman with full ownership of her own team.

SEXUALITY AT ANOTHER LEVEL

Patrick, of course, has taken Fisher's self-exposure to the next level, but she is hardly the first—or only—female in professional sports to do so. Women in the tennis world have notoriously marketed themselves in sexually suggestive ways. Russian tennis pro Maria Sharapova appeared in the *Sports Illustrated* swimsuit issue (2006) in a six-page bikini photo spread; that same year,

Maxim magazine ranked her the world's hottest athlete for the fourth consecutive time. In 2008, Ashley Harkleroad from the Women's Tennis Association appeared as the cover girl for the August 2008 issue of *Playboy*, the first professional female tennis player to pose nude for the magazine. Included on the list of *Playboy* cover girls from other sports are Olympic figure skater Katarina Witt (1988), volleyball's Gaby Reece (2001), and Olympic swimmer Amanda Beard (2007).

Even golf has its pinup girls: Australian-born Jan Stephenson asked the LPGA tour in the mid-1980s to embrace her marketing plan that included Stephenson posing nude in a bathtub with nothing but golf balls surrounding her, while glamour gal Natalie Gulbis was deemed too hot for the USGA with her 2005 spicy wall calendar.[11] Winter Olympians are in on it, too: shots featuring those attractive female skiers and snowboarders from the 2010 winter games in their teeny bikinis—not winter racing gear, as one might expect—can be downloaded from numerous websites. Regardless of their sport, many accomplished female athletes are exposing their bodies in publicity spots in order to get noticed off the playing field. Patrick is no exception.

Combining achievement with savvy PR is a smart marketing tool for any athlete. While athletes typically earn gobs of money during their playing careers, the paychecks they are accustomed to seeing stop upon retirement. As a result, many athletes seek to supplement their earnings both during and after their careers through product endorsements. Today's increased media coverage has produced greater visibility and name recognition of sports stars that for many can result in self-branding. From the athlete's point of view, becoming highly marketable is naturally desirable, as it puts more money in his or her bank account. The athlete's team and the respective sport in general can also benefit.

Derek Jeter offers a credible example of this phenomenon. The New York Yankees shortstop has endorsed numerous products during his continued successful MLB career, including Gillette razors, Gatorade, and the Ford Edge. The companies behind these products hope Jeter's charm, likability, and even physical appearance prompt consumers to purchase what is being advertised and build a loyalty to those products. Hence, the companies' profits increase. The New York Yankees, in turn, benefit from the marketing scheme in that more fans might decide to support the team because of Jeter's exposure. Indeed, as the fans start to identify with him from the frequent media spots and magazine ads, creating a desire to follow his career, *his* team then becomes *their* team. These fans might buy tickets to a ballgame, subscribe to MLB TV, and outfit the entire family in overpriced team jerseys and fitted baseball caps. Both the team and the league experience an increase in their revenue stream. It's a win-win situation for all parties involved. What athlete wouldn't want to become branded?

Patrick's self-branding has catapulted her beyond the land of gas and grease. *Forbes* estimated her net worth to be $12 million in 2010, with almost half of that earned through endorsements. Her fan base extends well beyond followers of auto racing, and she is proof that branding oneself successfully takes more than skill and success in the sport, as authors Frank Veltri and Steve Long report in the *Cyber-Journal of Sport Marketing*. In discussing what companies consider when choosing athletes to pitch their products, Veltri and Long state, "Marketability also depends on many intangible factors . . . [that] include the consumer's perception of the athlete's level of skill and success in his/her sport and individual characteristics, such as image, charisma, physical appearance, and personality."[12] Indeed, athletes like Patrick who score well in these areas and who then establish a proven track record in serving as a spokesperson may have numerous companies vying for their representation.

Two rating systems that companies use to measure a sports celebrity's potential are the Sports Q rating, used strictly for athletes, and the Davie Brown Index (DBI), used for athletes and other celebrities, and the more well-known of the two. The DBI measures the appeal, relevance, and charisma of an individual, as well as his or her influence on consumers' buying behavior. The DBI surveys consumers four times per year, so an individual's rating may fluctuate. It is safe to assume that an athlete who consistently scores high is pulling in steep sums from endorsements.

Patrick has been reported ranking as high as eighth on the DBI among female athletes (her 2010 NASCAR debut may have pushed her further up the list), and Peter Boyer of *The New Yorker* states that the Danica brand is now a multimillion dollar business. Compared to other racers on the DBI, Patrick recently tied for third with seven-time NASCAR Winston Cup champion Richard Petty, just behind Jeff Gordon and Dale Earnhardt, Jr., and stands as the lone female driver on the index.[13]

The question for a female athlete like Patrick, then, becomes whether posing provocatively for the camera can raise her marketability, moving her up the DBI and increasing her revenue stream. The answer to that is both a resounding yes and possibly even a no, at least in some instances. As evidenced, being provocative can raise a female athlete's opportunities for product endorsement, which in turn increases her supplemental income. Sharapova and Serena Williams, for example, lead female athletes in endorsements with Sharapova raking in an estimated $22 million per year, while Williams can boast of an estimated $14 million.[14] Williams, like Sharapova, has often been captured in revealing tennis outfits; she posed for the 2009 *Body Issue of ESPN The Magazine,* an annual publication featuring athletes who bare it all. These ladies are considered to be as prosperous *off* the court as they are gifted *on* the court.

And yet, while splashy marketing may be profitable for the individual female athlete, does it increase fan base—and, therefore, the revenue stream—for the athlete's sport, or women's sports as a whole? Some believe no, and fear that it may even trivialize women's sports in some regards. Sportswriter Aditi Kinkhabwala comments: "Sexy pictures don't make people more likely to read about women's sports, they don't make anyone more likely to attend a women's sporting event, and they sure don't drive any season-ticket sales."[15] Kinkhabwala emphasizes the lack of positive results from the sexy marketing of female athletes. In her article "Sex Sells? Not So Fast," she includes research from Professor Mary Jo Kane, director of the Tucker Center for Research of Girls and Women in Sport at the University of Minnesota. Kane's research shows that most men viewing the images (most obviously the target audience) enjoy the hot shots, but none feel compelled to actually go watch the women compete or tune in on television, and many even dismiss some of the women's athleticism. There is not an improved understanding of the game or the competition, Kane's studies show, nor any further appreciation of the female athletes themselves.[16] The women's teams and women's sports in general, then, gain nothing from the sexy marketing of its female athletes; such marketing solely benefits the individual female athlete—except in Patrick's case.

Patrick *has* increased both attendance at auto racing competitions *and* television ratings and attracted new fans to the sport. Some even credit her for saving the IRL, and most recently, for pumping up support for NASCAR. With all the media and fan fuss surrounding her at her 2010 NASCAR debut, some writers joked about NASCAR changing its name to DANICAR.[17] One wonders why her situation differs from other female athletes who fail to draw new fans to their sporting events. Is it because professional auto racing has become its own beast, so to speak? Unlike other sports, where men and women compete in separate leagues, auto racing simulates real life, pitting driver against driver, regardless of sex, on a level playing field under one roof. Fans can root for any driver or team they wish at one sporting event. If a new female driver enters the scene, fans do not have to spend additional money or time at another venue in order to follow her. It may be as simple as that.

Additionally, though, Patrick's beauty queen looks have certainly captured the attention of the average warm-blooded male racing fan. Never before has a race car driver looked so attractive *off* the track! Contrary to Professor Kane's findings, Patrick's femininity and sex appeal seem to lure many of her male fans to the grandstands, especially since almost half of them are under the age of thirty. And yet Patrick's persona *on* the track—sans bikini and donning an unattractive, desexing fireproof driving suit—speaks of a confidence and power reminiscent of women like Cleopatra who conquered the world's most influential men while ostensibly looking good in doing so! Patrick's overly firm handshake and her run-you-down-with-femininity attitude may be what some of these male fans are unconsciously latching on to. Theirs is a fantasy in which they experience the ride of their lives, mixing desire and power, not just a pretty face. Patrick, then, becomes an interloper in the male world of racing—a seductive, authoritative, charismatic gate-crasher difficult to refuse or, at the very least, difficult to avoid.

WHAT ABOUT THE BOYS?

Male athletic charisma has been promoted in advertising ever since Jets quarterback Joe Namath allowed then-unknown Farah Fawcett to "cream his face" with Noxzema skin cream on national television in 1973. Broadway Joe, as he was called, created a playboy image with his early 1970s "racy" series of ads for Noxzema and other products like Brut cologne ("If you're not going to go all the way, why go at all?" questions Namath), and Beautymist pantyhose, which featured Namath wearing a pair. While some considered the marketing tasteless, it generated a new presentation of athletes as more than just talented and fit competitors. They were now openly recognized as sexy and attractive beings, too.

Today, it has become customary to see images of bare muscular legs, washboard abs, and shapely arms of fit athlete stars—male *and* female—plastered in magazines and flashed across television screens, selling everything from sports drinks to cable network services to automobiles. But the majority of promotions that are categorized as racy—even as soft porn, at times—feature female athletes. Male athletes may certainly be viewed as sexy, but more often than not they are fully clothed, revealing little to no skin. For example, a recent Gillette razor ad stars Derek Jeter with Tiger Woods and Roger Federer, all neatly dressed in black suits, looking distinguished and professional. The Miami Heat's Dwayne Wade sports a simple long-sleeve white polo shirt as he gabs about his "favorite five" for T-Mobile. And a spot for Glacéau Vitamin

Water pits the all-American third baseman for the New York Mets, David Wright, against Mike "The Situation" Sorrentino, a star from the seedy reality television show *Jersey Shore*. As one might guess, "The Situation" (as he has nicknamed himself) proudly bares his chiseled chest as the two men train together, but Wright only goes as far as displaying his large and decidedly athletic biceps.

Certainly, some risqué ads of male athletes do exist. Pro soccer star David Beckham's seductive pose in his skimpy Armani skivvies leaves little to the imagination. But in a 2007 study published in the *Journal of Current Issues and Research in Advertising*, researchers found that male athletes were depicted as reserved and modest in more than 60 percent of the ads in which they appeared. In contrast, 71 percent of the ads featuring female athletes were classified as suggestive, and 10 percent as partially nude.[18] One wonders, then, if female athletes are more willing to accentuate their sex appeal, or if they feel required to do so in order to gain popularity and increase their paycheck.

One of the most popular male athletes who pulls in an exorbitant amount of money from endorsement contracts is Colts quarterback Peyton Manning, and his ads are anything but suggestive. Manning, labeled by some as the people's quarterback, is as apple pie as they come. Wesley Morris, in his article "Mr. Popularity," describes how through the years Peyton's "averageness and coolness" have won over Americans' hearts. "It's not hard to understand why advertisers and consumers have fallen for Manning," writes Morris. "He's made himself adorable, a dorky suburban dad who's more of a football fan than an NFL star." He is seen and thought of as accessible and relatable, and as an average guy—not a sultry Adonis whom viewers want to undress. This "affable, goofy everyman" has soared to success in the advertising world and currently ranks as one of the most likable athletes in America without a trace of splashy, suggestive marketing.[19]

In contrast, Patrick's projected image fails to reflect that traditional, iconic attitude Manning pitches and that America seems to love. She's a pretty face and a hot body and is not afraid to flaunt either. In this way, she is a throwback to Namath, luring fans with sex appeal and charisma.

At the same time, what also makes her untraditional is the fact that she is a competitor in a male-dominated sport. While more women than ever work behind the scenes in the marketing and technical jobs of professional motorsports, the number of women behind the wheel remains considerably lower than the number of male drivers. Patrick has proven that she belongs on the track with her competitive performances and can easily be classified as the best female driver in Indy racing today.

In the latter respect, Patrick is more like Manning in that they are both highly successful in their sport. Interestingly, it seems that Patrick's marketing has made her into a combination of the images the two male superstars project—she is both Namath *and* Manning, both sultry female driver *and* number one female athlete in her sport. This combination has allowed her to become a crowd pleaser as well as a marketer's dream, while also allowing her to remain focused on her racing endeavors, not a feat all female athlete "pinup girls" have been able to accomplish.

THE COST OF SEX APPEAL

As Women's Tennis Association's Anna Kournikova discovered, sometimes becoming a hot commodity in the endorsement world can be costly. Once ranked No. 8 in women's singles at age nineteen in 2000, Kournikova was "never one to be shy about her body, parlayed her success on the court into revealing magazine covers and lucrative endorsement contracts."[20] She brought in an estimated $10 million annually off the court, but her performance on the court suffered for reasons that have yet to be fully fleshed out, and by 2003, only three years later, she had slipped to No. 305 in the world. To this day, Kournikova is known as the female tennis player who "made bank" off her looks without having actually accomplished anything noteworthy on the court.[21]

So far, Patrick has been careful not to make the same mistake. Her role as a Go Daddy Girl and her endorsement of products like Secret deodorant, Tissot watches, and Peak antifreeze may occupy some of her time, but Patrick remains dedicated to her training and her competitions. Her recent foray into NASCAR presents an entirely new set of goals for her, and her dream of some day winning the Indy 500 still sits on her "To Do List." Simply put, she has a lot of work ahead of her on the race track to keep her busy.

Many worry, though, about the type of role model Patrick presents. Her feats on the track are certainly notable, making her *the* most accomplished woman in motorsports history. That should be enough to inspire young girls to enter the sport. But some fear her marketing campaign perpetuates the unrelenting objectification of women, especially in advertising. The "sex sells" mantra has been clearly proven by Patrick, some suggest. They wonder about the real reason for her popularity. Is her name recognition beyond motorsports due more to her driving skills or the visuals she presents in her off-the-track photo shoots?

After her appearance in the popular *Sports Illustrated* 2008 and 2009 swimsuit issues, it is not farfetched to say that Patrick might easily be mistaken for a Victoria's Secret model instead of an Indy or NASCAR athlete. When more blog entries surfaced about how hot Patrick looked in the barely-there black bikini versus her third-place finish at the 2009 Indy 500 (the best of any woman to date), the root of her fame certainly invited further scrutiny. The Women's Sports Foundation (WSF), for example, remains skeptical of the notion of female athletes being portrayed as sex symbols, as some say Patrick is promoted. In the article "Mixed Media: Images of Female Athletes," posted on its website, the WSF discusses how many current images of highly accomplished women athletes fail to focus on their sport or their great feats, and instead accentuate their sexiness and allure, and eroticize their bodies. This in turn, the Foundation believes, "trivializes and marginalizes women in sports."[22]

Another voice in opposition to the objectification of women is pioneer racer Guthrie, who has outspokenly disagreed with Patrick's capitalization of her good looks. Guthrie applauds the young driver for her accolades on the track and is delighted to witness women finally competing on even terms with men, and why wouldn't she? She certainly knows all too well that finding sponsorships remains the largest obstacle for women in racing, but she renounces the practice of marketing provocative photos to get recognized. As she proclaims in *USA Today*: "Danica's appearance in that girlie magazine established a persona that a number of women drivers weren't happy to see but was very clearly successful for her. You might call it old-fashioned, but most of us wanted to be judged on the basis of what we accomplished than how we looked."[23] Clearly, a generational divide stands between Patrick and Guthrie. Guthrie entered the sport in the midseventies at age thirty-nine while Patrick began her career at the young age of twenty-three. To be sure, when Guthrie came onto the racing scene, women were not even allowed in the pits at many racetracks. Women were slowly gaining more rights as citizens, but existing hostile attitudes were slow to change, especially in the world of sports. Guthrie was smart and competitive and simply wanted to make it as a professional race car driver. With the country in the midst of the shake-up brought about by the women's movement, Guthrie's efforts to make strides in the sport solely through her abilities and accomplishments rather than her sexuality were certainly more reasonable if not admirable. Guthrie as a pioneering figure had to prove that she was just as good as the men. Anything else could have easily been dismissed as a spectacle not unlike, for instance, the Indianapolis Clowns trotting out Toni Stone in 1953 to generate interest during those waning days in Negro League baseball.

Some young female drivers of today share Guthrie's view. They recognize Patrick as an agent of change in the sport, but they question the cost of this change. Twenty-two-year-old Alli Owens, a wannabe NASCAR driver, fears that all of America, including potential sponsors, now see women in motorsports as sex symbols as a result of Patrick's marketing campaign. She claims that this can create funding issues for female racers who choose not to expose themselves as sexual objects in their marketing campaigns, something the young driver experienced first-hand when she was dropped after refusing to give possible sponsors the "bikini-ready look" they wanted. Not knowing where to turn for sponsorship, Owens decided to raise money herself from fan donations and small companies through her own PayPal account on her website.[24] She successfully raised thirty-five thousand dollars, enough to get her to a qualifying race for the Camping World Truck series opener at Daytona International Speedway on February 18, 2011. Owens failed to qualify, however, and, according to her website, is still looking for potential sponsors in order to keep her career afloat.

Other racers facing similar obstacles include Shawna Robinson and Chrissy Wallace. Unwilling to use their sexuality in advertising as Patrick does, these women eventually found themselves out of the racing circuit due to a similar lack of sponsorship and its resulting lack of funding.[25] One might think, then, that the "Danica method" is the only route to take in order for women in motorsports to gain sponsorship. It is certainly a looming precedent.

But a larger audience sees Patrick's path as positive. Many in the sport consider both her popularity and her accomplishments as a means of paving the way for younger female drivers. She is proof that women can win *and* obtain sponsors. Those interested in forging an independent racing career watch her closely. In contrast to Guthrie, for example, her fellow racing pioneer Lynn St. James contends that Patrick's presence is empowering to girls, and she has little patience for those who criticize Patrick for using her looks to acquire funding. Male drivers, notes St. James, do it all the time without ridicule.[26] Says St. James: "She's taking the whole gender to a different level, and the whole sport to a different level, too."[27]

AN ONGOING DEBATE

Since Patrick entered the picture, more girls are participating in competitive racing, including go-karts, quarter-midget, and drag racing, and more young daughters are attending professional racing events with their fathers than ever before.[28] Young female racers like Simona de Silvestro, named the 2010 Indianapolis 500 Rookie of the Year, recognize and appreciate Patrick's accomplishments. Says de Silvestro, "I think why in Indy cars there are so many women is because Danica did a good job . . . I think she opened the door for us."[29]

Accomplished athletes in the sport, as well, welcome the interest Patrick has brought to racing. According to four-time Sprint Cup champion Jeff Gordon, "[Danicamania is] bringing attention to the whole sport. That's nothing but a good thing."[30] Kevin Harvick, a veteran American stock car racer, agrees: "She's very good for our sport and I think everybody understands that she's going to be good for our sport."[31] Although at times "Danicamania" has turned some competitions into media frenzies that pose quite a nuisance, the sparked interest in Patrick has resulted in record television ratings and increased race attendance which naturally benefit other racers.

Patrick clearly owes her opportunities in motorsports in part to Guthrie, who struggled to break the gender barrier in what was once an all-male world. In the process of trying to make it as a professional race car driver, Guthrie faced intense hostility and discrimination. Unlike Guthrie, however, Patrick has grown up in a very different world where women today have access to sports, professions, and endorsement contracts that were mere fantasies in Guthrie's day. Social values and morals have changed, as well. In this "look at me generation," where individuals post their relationship status on public social networking sites, share questionable photographs online with strangers, and drop more "F-bombs" than those dropped on Dresden in Vonnegut's *Slaughterhouse Five*, tolerance for sexy publicity stunts has increased dramatically. Standards for what is thought to be "risqué" or "sensual" are no longer the same as forty years ago. Athletes' marketing campaigns have adopted these changes, leaving Patrick's various campaigns to serve merely as more examples of such shifts.

In an effort to become memorable and noticed, Patrick ran with the popularity of her *FHM* photo shoots, picking up primary sponsor godaddy.com along the way. This propelled her into the spotlight of the IRL, and with it came success on the track. With her No. 7 mobile billboard, her splashy persona, and her more recent jump to NASCAR, Patrick appears to be sticking around. Her attractiveness and her sex appeal, coupled with her expertise, have given Patrick the ride for which she was looking while transforming the contemporary and certainly more popular world of motorsports. As a result, new generations of young female drivers seem even more poised than ever to start revving their engines accordingly.

NOTES

1. These images can be viewed on http://danica-patrick.tripod.com/danicapatrick_htm_01/.

2. Anonymous, "Women Crank Up Indianapolis 500," *Northern Advocate*, May 28, 2010, http://search.proquest.com/docview/347078159?accountid=28549 (June 13, 2010).

3. Peter J. Boyer, "Changing Lanes," *The New Yorker*, May 31, 2010, http://www.proquest.com.online.library.marist.edu/ (June 13, 2010).

4. Ibid.

5. Ibid.

6. Sally R. Ross, Lynn L. Ridinger, and Jacquelyn Cuneen, "Drivers to Divas: Advertising Images of Women in Motorsport," *International Journal of Sports Marketing & Sponsorship* 10, no. 3 (April 2009): 204–214; *Academic Search Elite*, EBSCOhost (June 14, 2010).

7. Robin Miller, "Fans Turn on Danica at Indianapolis," Foxsports.com, May 28, 2010, http://msn.foxsports.com/motor/story/Danica-Patrick-becomes-public-enemy-at-Indianapolis (July 1, 2010).

8. Darrell Waltrip, "Danica, I Am a Believer," Foxsports.com, February 11, 2010, http://msn.foxsports.com/nascar/story/Waltrip-I-believe-in-Danica-020810 (July 1, 2010).

9. Ross et al., "Drivers to Divas," 208. These images can be viewed on http://lynstjames.com/.

10. Ibid., 209. This image can be viewed on http://pressdog.typepad.com/dogblog/2008/04/fishers-sponsor.html.

11. Brent Kelley, "Too Hot for the USGA," About.com, July 30, 2004, http://golf.about.com/b/2004/07/30/too-hot-for-the-usga.htm (July 2, 2010).

12. Frank R. Veltri and Steve A. Long, "A New Image: Female Athlete-Endorser," *The Cyber-Journal of Sport Marketing*, no. 2 (1998), http://www.cjsm.com/Vol2/veltrilong24.htm (June 15, 2010).

13. David Newton, "Patrick Signs with JR Motorsports," ESPN.com, December 8, 2009, http://sports.espn.go.com/rpm/nascar/nationwide/news/story?id=4725025 (June 25, 2010).

14. Alyssa Roenigk, "For Sale by Owner," ESPN.com, October 7, 2009, http://sports.espn.go.com/espn/news/story?id=4540728 (September 20, 2010).

15. Aditi Kinkhabwala, "Sex Sells? Not So Fast. Women's Sports Needs Substance, Not Pretty Pictures," SI.com, May 10, 2007, http://sportsillustrated.cnn.com/2007/writers/aditi_kinkhabwala/05/09/better.half/index.html (August 1, 2010).

16. Ibid.

17. David Newton, "Danica-Mania a Boost for NASCAR, Too," ESPN.com, February 10, 2010, http://sports.espn.go.com/rpm/nascar/cup/columns/story?columnist=newton_david&id=4903760 (September 9, 2010).

18. Stacy Landreth Grau, Georgina Roselli, and Charles R. Taylor, "Where's Tamika Catchings? A Content Analysis of Female Athlete Endorsers in Magazine Advertisements," *Journal of Current Issues & Research in Advertising* 29, no. 1 (Spring 2007): 55–65; *Communication & Mass Media Complete*, EBSCOhost (July 22, 2010).

19. Wesley Morris, "Mr. Popularity," Boston.com, October 14, 2007, http://www.boston.com/news/globe/ideas/articles/2007/10/14/mr_popularity/ (September 20, 2010).

20. Roenigk, "For Sale by Owner."

21. Ibid.

22. Women's Sports Foundation, "Mixed Media: Images of Female Athletes," Women's Sports Foundation.com, n.d., http://www.womenssportsfoundation.org/Content/Articles/ Issues/Media-and-Publicity/M/Mixed-Media-Images-of-Female-Athletes.aspx. (October 9, 2010).

23. Nate Ryan, "For Patrick, the Question Has Become: Can She Win?," *USA Today*, n.d., *Academic Search Elite*, EBSCO*host* (June 13, 2010).

24. Ashley McCubbin, "Danica Patrick and her Fellow Females: Looking at the Female Race Car Driver," Bleacherreport.com, April 5, 2011, http://bleacherreport.com/ articles/655277-danica-patrick-and-her-fellow-females-looking-at-the-female-racecar -driver (May 4, 2011).

25. Ibid.

26. Ryan, "For Patrick, the Question Has Become: Can She Win?"

27. Christine Brennan, "Generation of Girls Gets New Mentor," *USA Today*, n.d., *Academic Search Elite*, EBSCO*host* (June 13, 2010).

28. Ibid.

29. Anthony Andro, "Fast Females No Longer a Novelty in IndyCar Series," McClatchy-Tribune News Service, June 5, 2010, http://www.proquest.com.online.library .marist.edu/ (June 22, 2010).

30. Newton, "Patrick Signs with JR Motorsports."

31. Rea White, "Drivers Excited about Danica's Arrival," Foxsports.com, March 17, 2010, http://msn.foxsports.com/nascar/story/nascar-drivers-are-excited-about-racing -with-danica-patrick (July 1, 2010).

Afterword
The Goddess Dethroned

—JACK LULE

INTRODUCTION

Agricultural societies, quite naturally, placed a high value on fertility. The very lives of the people depended upon the ability of the earth to give and sustain life. These societies came to worship one god above all—a mother goddess who would bequeath and assure fertility. In early Greece, for example, the mother goddess was Gaia, or Earth. Sumerians gave supreme tribute to their mother goddess, Ninhursag. We see remnants of these gods in our own references to Mother Earth.

In time, however, agricultural life was subjugated to the dominion of kingdoms and empires. Invasion, imperialism, war, and domination transformed social life. New, often more fierce, male gods arose to replace goddesses. Fertility, formerly controlled by the goddesses, now was ruled by male gods. Fertility indeed was to be understood not as the sphere of women, but as the potency of the male god mating with the goddess. The goddess now had power in relation to the male. She had value as a sexual object. She had become wife. Concubine. Consort.

Gerda Lerner, in *The Creation of Patriarchy*, assiduously chronicles the historical development of patriarchy and the subjugation of women.[1] The process, she points out, almost always includes the dethroning of fertility goddesses and their replacement by dominant male gods. In her study of Western society, for example, Lerner finds that, in Greece, Gaia eventually gave way to numerous lesser goddesses, such as Athena, Aphrodite, Artemis, and Persephone. Zeus came to be seen as the Father of Gods. Hebrew monotheism likewise repudiated fertility goddesses with its stress on God the Father. Outside the realm of religious life, Aristotelian philosophy complemented this transition with its view of women as physically inferior and incomplete in relation to men. Women not only had been removed from power; they were subordinated as the "weaker sex." Lerner concludes:

> It is with the creation of these two metaphorical constructs, which
> are built into the very foundations of the symbol system of Western

civilization, that the subordination of women comes to be seen as "natu-ral," hence it becomes invisible. It is this which finally establishes patriar-chy firmly as an actuality and as an ideology.[2]

MYTH TODAY

Gods and goddesses may seem far removed from the stories of Babe Didrik-son, Marion Jones, Billie Jean King, Danica Patrick, and other women ath-letes. However, as I have argued throughout this splendid series of books, myth often proves to be an exemplary vehicle for thinking through the inter-sections of sport and society. Myths are told to capture and, at times, enforce the values and beliefs of a society. As we read of the literal trials and tribula-tions of women athletes, as we view their struggles not only against athletic opponents, but against gender roles, social norms, ideology, patriarchy, and power, we realize we are not only in the realm of the sports story. We are in the realm of myth.

We first must arrive at an understanding of myth today. For many people, myth is a dead term. It refers only to ancient Greek and Roman tales, for-ever frozen in time. Others see myth more broadly across cultures and eras, but still see myth as fantastic tales and beliefs, most often held by primitive peoples. Still others believe that myth simply refers to a false belief, a contrast with "reality."

However, other scholars have recognized something essential and endur-ing in the stories of myth. The historian of religion Mircea Eliade, cited earlier in this book, argued that "certain aspects and functions of mythical thought are constituents of the human being."[3] He wrote: "It seems unlikely that any society could completely dispense with myths, for, of what is essen-tial in mythical behavior—the exemplary pattern, the repetition, the break with profane duration and integration into primordial time—the first two at least are consubstantial with every human condition."[4]

Psychologist Carl Jung too saw myth as essential. "Has mankind ever really got away from myths?" asked Jung. "One could almost say that if all the world's traditions were cut off at a single blow, the whole of mythology and the whole history of religion would start all over again with the next genera-tion."[5] Joseph Campbell, author of numerous books on mythology, goes so far as to say, "No human society has yet been found in which such mythological motifs have not been rehearsed in liturgies; interpreted by seers, poets, theo-logians, or philosophers; presented in art; magnified in song; and ecstatically experienced in life-empowering visions."[6]

Every society, it seems, needs stories that confront the human condition. Modern societies, though, sometimes believe the very fact of modernity leaves myth behind. They believe myth is for ancient or primitive societies. They believe they have no need of heroes, villains, exemplary figures, or portrayals of good and evil. It's a wonderful story: modern humans have replaced the primitive cultural beliefs of the past with scientific knowledge, technological advances, and objective reports of the real world. It is of course the very stuff of myth.

"MYTH TODAY"

French writer and philosopher Roland Barthes recognized how modern myths mask and disguise their purpose and influence today. He saw great danger in the process. His book *Mythologies*, composed in the 1950s, analyzes how modern myths lie beneath vehicles as varied as professional wrestling, advertisements, and novels. Barthes explains the volume's origins: "The starting point of these reflections was usually a feeling of impatience at the sight of the naturalness with which newspapers, art and common sense constantly dress up a reality which, even though it is one we live in, is undoubtedly determined by history."[7] Capitalism, consumerism, political structure, gender roles, attitudes toward art, and myriad other facets of social life have been *put into place*—determined by history—but are made to seem *natural*. They "go without saying."[8]

How does this occur? For Barthes, myth is the means. In a now-classic section, "Myth Today," Barthes argues that myth is the set of stories a society tells itself that attempts to make particular ideologies seem natural and beyond question. He says, "Myth is depoliticized speech. One must naturally understand political in its deeper meaning, as describing the whole of human relations in their real, social structure, in their power of making the world."[9] It is a lovely line: myth has the "power of making the world."

Barthes emphasizes though the studied *naturalness* of myth. "Myth does not deny things," he says. "On the contrary, its function is to talk about them; simply it purifies them, it makes them innocent, it gives them a natural and eternal justification, it gives them a clarity which is not that of an explanation but that of a statement of fact." He continues:

In passing from history to nature, myth acts economically: it abolishes the complexity of human acts, it gives them the simplicity of essences, it does away with all dialectics, with any going back beyond what is immediately visible, it organizes a world which is without contradictions because it is without depth, a world wide open and wallowing in the evident, it establishes a blissful clarity: things appear to mean something by themselves.[10]

MODERN MISOGYNY: IT GOES WITHOUT SAYING

What does all this mythologizing and French philosophizing have to do with the subjects of this book—women, reputation, and sports? In fact, the great challenges facing women athletes are the *myths* surrounding and girding women athletes. They are myths of male superiority and female subordination. Barthes helps us see that these myths of misogyny and sexism, however, are now seldom explicit or overt. Instead, they go *without saying*. Yet they implicitly structure athletic organizations, opportunities, regulations, roles, responsibilities, media coverage, and audience expectations.

In doing so, the myths also offer, without argument or explanation, another related, blissfully clear, firmly entrenched ideology: women athletes do have value—as sexual spectacles and prurient objects of fantasy and desire. The ideology is given a clarity, as Barthes said, which is not explanation, but a statement of fact. From uniforms to team names to magazine covers to television broadcasts to advertisements, women athletes are offered as sexual, rather than athletic, beings. To the extent that women athletes succeed, they do so under these circumstances, under titles and terms not of their choosing.

The invidious, insidious nature of myth today can be seen in contrast to times past. In previous decades, sexism and misogyny were still proudly displayed. Laws, rules, headlines, and broadcasts made plain the sexualized nature of the female athlete and the overt, taken-for-granted assumption of women as the weaker sex. In such contexts, Roberta Gibb was forbidden to run in the Boston Marathon. Kathrine Switzer was attacked by marathon officials when she attempted to compete. Women sports were invisible on television and magazines. Billie Jean King won acclaim for beating a fifty-five-year-old man—not for her illustrious career.

These were *not* myths, in Barthes's use of the term, but legalized, institutionalized degradation and discrimination. The patent and blatant injustice of the discrimination, particularly in the context of the 1960s, led to protest and challenge. Laws were dismantled. Rules were changed. Title IX was passed. The Boston Marathon *welcomed* women. Sexism and misogyny, of course, did not disappear. The ferocity of patriarchy simply left the world of dialectic and debate, regulation and reform, for myth.

The dynamic has been similar in the fight against race discrimination. The dramatic and emphatic institutionalized racism and segregation of the 1950s have been replaced by what sociologists call "modern racism." An elusive phenomenon of abstraction, disavowal, and symbolic expression, modern racism denies its very existence. "Racism, as defined by modern racists, is consistent only with the tenets and practices of old fashioned racism," such as open support for segregation and acts of explicit discrimination, says social psychologist John B. McConahay. "Thus, those endorsing the ideology of modern racism do not define their own beliefs and attitudes as racist."[11] One hallmark of modern racism is that explicitly racist rhetoric often is absent while muted racist beliefs are proffered in shadows and shades of expression.[12]

In a similar way, perhaps we can speak of a *modern misogyny* in which adherents can renounce the active sexual discrimination of the past while holding to beliefs shot through with patriarchy. Women have been freed of legal and societal restraints against their participation in sports, the myth goes, and the results are plain. Women athletes are pale imitations of their male counterparts. Their value all along has been as venues for sexual spectacle.

The beliefs are never spoken, never argued, but appear continually with blissful clarity in Danica Patrick advertisements, television programming decisions on professional women sports, *Sports Illustrated*'s swimsuit issue, funding decisions for high school athletics, NCAA regulations, locker room locations, salaries of coaches, and countless ways that, in Barthes's terms, go without saying.

Lerner uses language that is strikingly similar to Barthes's in *The Creation of Patriarchy*. She states: "[W]e should note the way in which inequality among men and women was built not only into the language, thought, and philosophy of Western civilization, but the way in which gender itself became a metaphor defining power relations in such a way as to mystify them and render them invisible."[13] It is the mystification and invisibility of patriarchy, gender stereotyping, and misogyny that is of most interest here. The ceiling is glass for a reason. It is not supposed to be seen. Or, rather, it is to be seen through, as if it was not there.

FIGHTING THE MYTH: "YOU'VE COME A LONG WAY, BABY"

Much of the power of the preceding chapters comes from the efforts of women to wrest control of their own story. Babe Didrikson attempted to manage the mythologizing of her life. The All-American Girls Professional Baseball League (AAGPBL) tried to negotiate cultural conceptions of women, patriotism, and sports. Roberta Gibb ran in nurse's shoes since there were no running shoes for women. Billie Jean King confronted blatant misogyny and helped drive it underground. Danica Patrick used sexual spectacle for her own purposes in hopes of transforming auto racing for drivers and audiences. It is humbling to think of the struggles faced by these women as they met challenges not only on the playing fields, but in their individual sports, and in society at large.

"You've come a long way, baby" was a 1960s advertising slogan heralding the introduction of a new cigarette made specifically for women, Virginia Slims. The slogan of course was supposed to celebrate and co-opt the advances made by women in that era. Virginia Slims went on to sponsor the Women's Tennis Association championship and still produces cigarettes for women. The multiple ironies of the language and the message, in the context of this volume, are bitter.

The irony is even greater in the long view of time, *longue durée*. In the Greek pantheon of gods descended from Gaia, one deity was designated the ruler of the hunt. Depicted almost always with bow and arrow, amidst wild animals and hunting dogs, the deity was feared and revered by fellow deities as well as the common people. And when the Gigantes—the Giants—attacked Olympos, home of the gods, the deity fought fearlessly and slew the giant Aigaion with arrows.

The deity, of course, was Artemis—a goddess, a woman. Would modern society install a woman to lead the hunt? Have we come very far at all . . . , baby?

NOTES

1. Gerda Lerner, *The Creation of Patriarchy* (New York: Oxford University Press, 1986).

2. Ibid., 10.

3. Mircea Eliade, *Myth and Reality* (New York: Harper & Row, 1963), 183–84.

4. Mircea Eliade, *Myths, Dreams and Mysteries* (New York: Harper & Brothers, 1960), 31–32.

5. Carl G. Jung, *Symbols of Transformation* (Princeton, NJ: Princeton University Press, 1976), 25.

6. Joseph Campbell, "The Historical Development of Mythology," in *Myth and Mythmaking*, ed. Henry Murray (New York: George Braziller, 1960), 1–2.

7. Roland Barthes, *Mythologies* (London: Paladin, 1972), 11.

8. Ibid., 143.

9. Ibid.

10. Ibid.

11. John B. McConahay, "Modern Racism, Ambivalence, and the Modern Racism Scale," in *Prejudice, Discrimination and Racism*, eds. John F. Dovidio and Samuel L. Gaertner (Orlando, FL: Academic Press, 1986), 92.

12. David O. Sears, "Symbolic Racism," in *Eliminating Racism*, eds. Phyllis A. Katz and Dalmas A. Taylor (New York: Plenum Press, 1988), 57.

13. Lerner, *The Creation of Patriarchy*, 211.

Contributors

Dr. Lisa Doris Alexander is Assistant Professor of Africana Studies at Wayne State University in Detroit. She received her Ph.D. in American Culture Studies from Bowling Green State University. Her research deals with issues of race, class, gender, and sexual identity in professional sports and popular culture. She is the author of the book *When Baseball Isn't White, Straight and Male: The Media and Difference in the National Pastime* (McFarland). Her work has appeared in *Fame to Infamy: Race, Sport, and the Fall from Grace* (University Press of Mississippi), *NINE: A Journal of Baseball History & Culture*, and *Black Ball: A Journal of the Negro Leagues*.

Dr. Kathleen A. Bishop received her Ph.D. from New York University where she is a member of the Faculty of Arts and Sciences. She has edited two books, *The Canterbury Tales Revisited: 21st Century Interpretations* and *Standing in the Shadow of the Master? Chaucerian Influences and Interpretations*, and has published articles on the works of Geoffrey Chaucer. Dr. Bishop has presented her research at conferences in the United States and Europe. Formerly, she spent over ten years as an editor at McGraw-Hill, and she served two terms as first vice president of ACT-UAW (the NYU/New School faculty union).

Dr. Angela J. Hattery is a sociologist and serves as the Associate Director of the Women and Gender Studies Center at George Mason University. Her research focuses on social stratification, gender, family, and race. She is the author of numerous articles, book chapters, and books, including *Social Dynamics of Family Violence* (2012, Westview Press), *Prisoner Reentry and Social Capital* (2010), *Interracial Intimacies* (2009), *Interracial Relationships* (2009), *Intimate Partner Violence* (2008), *African American Families* (2007), and *Women, Work, and Family* (2001).

Dr. Jack Lule is a Professor and Chair of the Department of Journalism and Director of Global Studies at Lehigh University. His research interests include globalization and media, international communication, and cultural and critical studies of news. He is the author of *Globalization and Media: Global Village of Babel* (Rowman & Littlefield) and the award-winning *Daily News,*

Eternal Stories: The Mythological Role of Journalism (Guilford Press). Called "a landmark book in the sociology of news," the book argues that ancient myths can be found daily in the language of the news. He is also the author of more than fifty scholarly articles and book chapters, is a frequent contributor to numerous newspapers and periodicals, and has served as a commentator about the news on National Public Radio, BBC, and other media outlets. He is a member of the editorial board of *Journalism and Mass Communication Quarterly* and *Critical Studies in Media Communication*.

Lisa R. Neilson is a teaching associate in the English and Writing Department at Marist College in Poughkeepsie, New York. She has taught at Marist since 2001. Prior to that, she showcased her writing talents as a sports columnist for the Journal Register's *Sunday Freeman* for seven years, where her work appeared in more than four hundred publications. Her research focuses on early baseball in the Hudson Valley as well as a wide range of aspects of American baseball. She has presented her research at the National Baseball Hall of Fame Symposium on Baseball and American Culture. She teaches Composition, Introduction to Literature, and the History of Baseball at Marist.

Dr. Roberta J. Newman teaches in the Foundation Studies program at New York University, where she teaches a course on baseball. She is the author and coauthor of numerous articles on sports and is the coauthor of a book-length study of the economic ramifications of desegregated Major League Baseball on the African-American business community.

Elizabeth V. O'Connell is a Ph.D. candidate in history at the State University of New York at Stony Brook, studying U.S. popular culture and gender identity during the early years of the Cold War. Her dissertation, *Gods of the Diamond, Heroes of the Republic: Major League Baseball and American Manhood, 1945–1963*, analyzes the construction of a hegemonic masculine image among major league ballplayers across a variety of media. She has developed a survey class in American popular culture history, as well as electives studying the Walt Disney Company and its relationship to American society and a thematic course, Popular Culture and the American Child.

Dr. David C. Ogden is Professor of Communications at the University of Nebraska at Omaha where he has taught since 2001. His research focuses on cultural trends in baseball, specifically the history of the relationship between African Americans and baseball. He has presented his research at the National Baseball Hall of Fame Symposium on Baseball and American Culture, the *NINE* Spring Training Conference on Baseball and Culture, and Indiana State University's Conference on Baseball in Culture and Literature. He is coeditor and contributor to *Reconstructing Fame: Sport, Race, and Evolving Reputations* (University Press of Mississippi) and *Fame to Infamy: Race, Sport, and the Fall from Grace* (University Press of Mississippi) and has published in *NINE: A Journal of Baseball History & Culture, The Journal of Leisure Research,* and *The Journal of Black Studies.*

Dr. Martha Reid is Professor of English at Moravian College in Bethlehem, Pennsylvania. Dr. Reid joined the English Department faculty on a full-time basis in 1999 after serving Moravian for nineteen years in various administrative positions, including Vice President for Academic Affairs and Dean of the College. She regularly teaches courses in twentieth-century literature, the British novel, and early modern English drama, and she loves Shakespeare and murder mysteries.

Dr. C. Oren Renick, JD, MPH, ThM, FACHE, is Professor of Health Administration at Texas State University in San Marcos, Texas, and Director and Principal Investigator of the Texas Long Term Care Institute. He is also Adjunct Professor of Population Health at the Medical College of Wisconsin and is a frequent contributor to professional journals and presenter at professional conferences. His major scholarly interests are civil rights, service-learning and civic engagement, health care law and ethics, managed health care delivery systems, and baseball and American culture. He is Executive Editor of the book on intergenerational service-learning entitled *The Ties That Bind.*

Dr. Joel Nathan Rosen is Associate Professor of Sociology at Moravian College in Bethlehem, Pennsylvania, where he coordinates the Africana Studies program and serves as founding codirector of the college's Center for the Study of Media in Culture (*CoSMiC*). Dr. Rosen's research focuses primarily on the relationship between human activity and stratification as informed by cultural idioms such as music and sport. He is the author of *The Erosion of the American Sporting Ethos: Shifting Attitudes Toward Competition* (McFarland) and *From New Lanark to Mound Bayou: Owenism in the Mississippi Delta* (Carolina Academic Press). He is also the coeditor of *Reconstructing Fame: Race, Sport, and Evolving Reputations* and *Fame to Infamy: Race, Sport, and the Fall from Grace* (University Press of Mississippi). Additionally, he has authored or coauthored several book chapters and has been published in such varied peer-reviewed journals as *Theory in Action, Criminal Justice Policy Review, The Sociology of Sport Journal, The Journal of Mundane Behavior, NINE: A Journal of Baseball History & Culture, The Journal of Sport History,* and *Media History Monographs.*

Dr. Yvonne D. Sims is Assistant Professor of English at South Carolina State University in the Department of English and Modern Languages. Her research focuses on the intersections of race, gender, and class in popular culture with particular emphasis on film studies. She is the author of several book chapters, peer-reviewed articles, and the book *Women of Blaxploitation: How the Black Action Heroine Changed American Popular Culture* (McFarland Publishers, 2006). Currently, Sims has two articles under review: "J'ai Deux amour: Josephine Baker and the Duality of Identity in the United States and Paris, France" and "Blacula and Blade: Tortured Souls/Cultural Outsiders in Vampire Film Narratives." She is also working on a manuscript tentatively titled *A Star Is Born: Josephine Baker and the Construction of Stardom.*

Dr. Earl Smith is Professor of Sociology and the Rubin Distinguished Professor of American Ethnic Studies at Wake Forest University. He is the Director of the Wake Forest University American Ethnic Studies Program. Dr. Smith was Chairperson of the Department of Sociology, Wake Forest University, from 1997 to 2005. During the 2008–2009 academic year he was the Arnold A. Sio Distinguished Professor of Diversity and Community at Colgate University. Prior to his appointment at Wake Forest University, he was the Dean, Division of Social Science, at Pacific Lutheran University (PLU) in Tacoma, Washington. He also served as Chairperson of the Department of Sociology at PLU. Dr. Smith has numerous books, articles, and book chapters in the area of professions, social stratification, family, and urban sociology, and has published extensively in the area of the sociology of sport. His most recent sport books are *Race, Sport and the American Dream* (2009) and *Sociology of Sport and Social Theory* (2010).

Lea Robin Velez, LMSW, is Program Director for Back on My Feet, a program in Dallas, Texas, that promotes self-sufficiency through running for those experiencing homelessness. She also has taught in the Social Work Department at the University of Texas at Arlington since 2007. She is a personal trainer and coach for several individuals in the Dallas area who are preparing for a long distance run and has also authored an anger management curriculum for middle school students in San Antonio, Texas.

Kimberly Young is a social studies teacher at Weston High School in Weston, Massachusetts. She received a BA in history from Boston College in 2004 and an MA in Gender and Cultural Studies from Simmons College in 2010. Her chapter grows out of her undergraduate Scholar of the College research project which received the John McCarthy, S.J. Award in History. She has presented at the National Baseball Hall of Fame Symposium on Baseball and American Culture and the National Council of Social Studies. She has also participated in professional development programs in China, Ghana, Mexico, Peru, Uganda, Korea, South Africa, India, and Turkey.

Index